Peter Boylston

John Charáxes

A Tale of the Civil War in America

Peter Boylston

John Charáxes
A Tale of the Civil War in America

ISBN/EAN: 9783337137359

Printed in Europe, USA, Canada, Australia, Japan

Cover: Foto ©ninafisch / pixelio.de

More available books at **www.hansebooks.com**

John Charáxes:

A TALE OF THE CIVIL WAR IN AMERICA.

BY

PETER BOYLSTON.

PHILADELPHIA:
J. B. LIPPINCOTT COMPANY.
1889.

PREFATORY NOTE.

BY THE AUTHOR'S LITERARY EXECUTOR.

PETER BOYLSTON, who says that he has walked the streets of Boston for more than sixty years, left this book to be published by his literary executor, who gives the following account of him.

Greentown, where Peter Boylston says he was born, is an imaginary place, of course, but it resembles the birthplace of one of his ancestors. He was descended from Thomas Boylston, an early English settler in Massachusetts, of whom it may be inferred, from old records, that he was a gay young man in London, and that his habits were not formed on the puritanical model. We read that, not being a member of the Church, he was never admitted a freeman. His friends in England had not full confidence in his prudence and discretion, and they employed an agent to purchase an estate for him in America. In 1650 he brought a suit against one Thomas Pratt for withholding money sent him by his uncle in England. But on the testimony of John Sawin, who swore that in 1648 the uncle told him that he had assigned his house and lands in New England in trust for young Boylston, the latter was non-suited. This roystering Tom Boylston, said not to have been an exemplary husband or Christian, had a daughter Sarah, who married Captain Thomas Smith, a butcher of Charlestown, and a son Thomas, born January 26, 1644. Thomas became a "chirurgeon" of Muddy River, Brookline. This Dr. Thomas Boylston, of Muddy River, had twelve children, the eldest of whom was Edward, a tailor in Boston; next came Richard, a "cordwainer" of Charlestown; then Abigail, who married Ebenezer Brooks, of Medford; and fourth, Peter, who became a shopkeeper in Brookline. The rest of them need not be enumerated; they are all gone into utter darkness long ago. But Peter Boylston, shopkeeper, who died in 1743, was the grandfather of Peter Boylston, author of this story.

John Boylston, the father of Peter Boylston, the author of this tale, died young, leaving a widow and this son Peter, the only child they ever had. Peter, the author, died in the year 1881; and his confidential friend and literary executor, who has edited the work, made over the MSS. to the present publishers.

Peter Boylston was a remarkable man. He had fine abilities and was a good deal of a scholar; but in the last fifteen or twenty years of his life he lived very much in the past. He was exceedingly fond of talking of certain persons, whom he said he had known before the civil war, and he told many interesting anecdotes about them. Whatever they were to others, to him they were all so many real persons; he lived so constantly in a state of recollections, or seeming recollections, of them,—he talked about them so much to his wife, who was very nearly of his own age, and who died at about the same time,—that one could not question the sincerity of his belief in their existence. In fact, the writer of this note has heard him describe these persons so vividly, and has so often heard Mrs. Boylston echo and confirm what her husband said, that he could not doubt that these two old people were perfectly convinced they were speaking of persons whom they had known and known intimately. When the editor came to examine the MSS. he was persuaded that he ought to give to the world the whole story just as it was written, and as one of which it can be said, *si non é vero, é ben trovato.* For himself, he feels bound to accept it as *vero*, not only from internal evidence, but from having, after Mr. Boylston's death, become acquainted with the two youngest individuals in the story, although he never saw any of the others. There are some characters in the book who are well known historically, and there is a great deal of accurate local knowledge in regard to the places where the scene is laid and the persons who flourished there at the times referred to.

Boston, February, 1889.

CONTENTS.

JOHN CHARÁXES:

A TALE OF THE CIVIL WAR IN AMERICA.

CHAPTER I.

A NEW ENGLAND VILLAGE.

IT is uncertain whether this book will have a hero and a heroine or neither. This will be left to be determined by that portion of the public who may patronize the work, whether they get it from the circulating libraries or are led to purchase it outright by the favorable notices which I anticipate for it, but which I shall take no steps to secure. The newspaper critics are now the sole autocrats in literature, and they are known to be beyond the blandishments of authors and publishers. As this is my first and only production, it cannot be heralded as a new story by So-and-so, under whose name there stands in his or her publisher's catalogue a long list of books with extraordinary titles, said to be filled with thrilling scenes and the most wonderfully-drawn characters. A new magazine was started recently, in the prospectus of which it was announced that contributions would be accepted on their merits and not on the celebrity of the writers. On the same principle I expect this book to make its way. At the same time, I presume that my name will very soon be placed on the list of one hundred American authors whom everybody ought to read.

I have not been very solicitous about the title of my work. I have chosen one for the sake of brevity. It will do as well as another for the purpose of identification. I have had no trouble in regard to the names of

the characters; for, as they are persons whom I knew,
I have not had the embarrassment which Sir Walter
Scott felt when, in writing one of his immortal fictions,
he repeated Falstaff's wish expressed to Prince Hal:
"Would that thou and I knew where a commodity of
good names could be had." I have called my friends,
with whose lives this story is concerned, by their right
names. A few persons, who may be said to be historical, are brought upon the scene by the names which
belong to them; but they are not the principal person-
ages in the *dramatis personæ*. Such of them as are not
distinctly named the reader can easily recognize. In
other cases, I give express notice that the characters
are not portraits. If any one undertakes to construct
what is called a "key" to the characters in this book,
I can tell him beforehand that it will be far from complete and will be quite inaccurate.

And now, without further preface or introduction, I
will let my pen run freely, feeling no embarrassment or
restraint of any kind.

It was in the year 183– that a young lawyer began
what promised to be a brilliant career in that renowned
New England city which before and since that time
has been called the Athens of America,—for what
special reason I never knew. I knew a great deal
about that notable town and its people in the period at
which this story begins, and I know a great deal about
them now, for I have walked their streets for more than
sixty years. I am not about to suggest anything for
or against the claim of Boston's resemblance to Athens.
I could, if I were so inclined, trace some parallel, or
show that there is none at all. But this would be an
unprofitable digression, because my readers and I are
more concerned with the local peculiarities which have
to do with the first part of these memoirs than they
have with the supposed pre-eminence of the chief town
in New England over other places in America. At all
times in its history Boston has been a remarkable
place: at the time when these memoirs begin it was
not less so, but it was then, as it had always been, a
provincial city; it had not begun to wear the aspect

of a metropolis, as it does now to some extent, in relation to one of the most striking and energetic communities in the world, the New England States. Our story will not tarry throughout in the characteristic precincts and moral and intellectual atmosphere of Boston, for "westward the course of empire takes its way." But the lives of two of the persons in this book were powerfully affected by what occurred to them in that place in the year 183–, when it seemed for a short time to those who knew them that their destinies were indissolubly interwoven and that the remorseless scissors could not sever such ties.

Henry Brewster was the only son of a Congregational minister in a country town about twenty miles from Boston. Dr. Brewster—he received the degree of D.D. from his *alma mater*, old Harvard, when Henry was ten years of age—belonged to that order of clergymen who, under the ecclesiastical system of Massachusetts,—as it had been moulded by a chief justice of her highest legal tribunal, very much according to his own notions of the statutes and the customary law,—held their positions by a tenure that, with other special features, made the system bear a considerable resemblance to an established church. The minister was settled for life by a contract between him and the legal body called "the parish," which embraced all the inhabitants of the township. There was a stipulated salary; there was generally a parsonage and some land, usually called the "ministerial lot," on which the minister could pasture his horse and cow, or he could take the rents and profits in any other way. If the salary was small it was sure, for there was a tax on property for the support of public worship, and there was no public worship but that in the parish meeting-house until schisms and divisions came in later, and Baptists, Methodists, and such like began to go off from orthodoxy and to hold services in halls or to build meeting-houses of their own. At length people who thus dissented from the faith, and kept away from the meeting-place of their fathers, grew restive under a tax for the support of a public worship that they would not attend; and this forced an alteration of the State Constitution in 1820, and an establishment of the religious bodies on a basis of perfect religious freedom. But until this change took place the old ministers remained in their respective parishes, with all their legal rights and their personal dignity. And when the change came the old clergymen remained undisturbed until they died. Even when the Unitarian schism came about, attended by a strenuous theology controversy, the congregations, for the most part, waited until the death of the old minister occurred and a new one was settled before they changed their religious sentiments.

In his own parish the minister was called ".the Parson," and out of it he was called "Parson Brewster" or "Parson Brooks," as the case might be. He dressed in black, with a white neck-cloth, knee-breeches, black silk or worsted stockings, with silver or plated buckles in his shoes; but although he sometimes wore a queue, he rarely wore hair-powder, although some of his most dignified and wealthy parishioners did. In the pulpit he wore the black Geneva gown,—of silk, if his parishioners could afford to give him a silk one, if not, it was of some black woollen stuff,—and over this, in winter, was used a long dark-blue cloth cloak, which he sometimes kept on during the service, as the meeting-house was but feebly warmed by its iron stoves, notwithstanding the long sticks of wood which the sexton put in endwise at an early hour in the morning and with which he again replenished the iron box just before he went to ring "the first bell." We used to carry foot-stoves to meeting, consisting of a square tin box with small round holes in the top, surrounded by a skeleton frame of wood. In these little portable stoves we brought hot ashes and live coals from our kitchen fires. Our mothers and grandmothers carried in their big fur muffs—no such dainty little rolls as a modern lady wears on one wrist, but a muff of much ampler dimensions—a hot brick, wrapped in brown paper; and when the little hands of the children became too numb to be borne without crying, these bricks were a great comfort in the long sermons. But it was in sum-

mer, when the lower sashes of the windows, with their
small panes, were held up by a notched wooden button,
and the stray wasp or bumble-bee came humming in
out of the sun, and the music of the hymn floated out
and away almost to an echo from the hill a quarter of
a mile in the rear, where the bobolink was warbling
his notes "in liquid sweetness long drawn out," which
mingled with the voices of the young men and women
in "the singers' seats," who were bawling to the accompaniment of a bass-viol, a clarionet, or a flute,—it
was at that season that Sunday morning was the time
for tender memories, and religious thoughts, and en-
joyments that we never had on other days, our best
clothes forming no small part of the satisfaction.   The
poorest of us were clean and decently clad on that day,
whatever might have been the garb of man or woman,
boy or girl, on the other days of the week.   Many a
young maiden wore a ribbon reserved for this meeting
with her swain, whose new straw hat was sported at
no other time, and whose well-brushed coat, although
made by a tailoress, was as good a specimen of the prevailing fashion as could be seen in our village.   We
young people used to come upon the meeting-house
green—I cannot write church—at the ringing of the
first bell, curious to see who intended marriage and
with whom, of which it was the business of the town
clerk to inform us.   This custom needs some explanation.   The law required the "banns" to be published by
a written notice posted for three successive Sundays at
the meeting-house door.   The notice read,—

"William Livermore, of ——, and Hannah Jerusha
Aldrich, of ——, intend marriage.
"I—— S——, *Town Clerk.*"

There would be in the month of June from one to
five of these notices tacked up at the side of the door
which led up the broad aisle.   The announcement was
called "breaking the windows;" and when we had
learned what we had known perfectly well for two,
three, or four years, according as William and Hannah had been "keeping company" for one or the other

period, and had seen the pair walk up and read their own notice without a visible sign of expectation of what windows were to be smashed that morning, as if the town clerk had taken it upon him to do the breaking of his own motion,—you may depend upon it he did not do it without his proper fee of twenty-five cents,—we strolled off into the graveyard behind the meeting-house.

But before I conduct you thither I must tell you about the courtships. They began often in youth, and they lasted until the parties were able to marry. Very likely the old parson had baptized them when they were babies, had taught them in the Sunday-school; and by whom should they be married, if not by him? Their intercourse had been perfectly free from the time when they were children, and rarely was there any unfortunate result of this freedom between the sexes. By the time they were married they knew each other as they needed to know, and the love that thus grew up and thus lasted was a love that would stand every trial. There were no divorces, because there was no hap-hazard marrying, as there is now among all classes. A wedding was a great affair, not for numerous and costly presents, not for paragraphs in newspapers and descriptions of the bride's dress and of what this bridesmaid wore and what another wore, not for the vulgar publicity that is now given to that event in people's lives which should not be paraded before the public, but it was a great affair to the simple people of a simple society. The marriage took place in the home of the bride, always in the evening. I never saw a marriage in a church until I entered what is called the world. There was no wedding-tour and no heathenish custom of flinging rice from an old shoe after the bride's carriage. She did not leave her father's house in a carriage of any sort, but she and her bridegroom walked quietly to their new abode. After a few days there were two gatherings at their own house,—one of their married, the other of their unmarried, friends. At these parties there was always wedding-cake, made at home, but as well frosted as if it came

from a confectioner's; there were different games; but
there was no kissing of the bride by anybody. After
these two receptions were over the pair took their
places among the married folks, and perhaps Hannah
Jerusha began to use her needle on certain small arti-
cles that might be wanted by a little stranger by and
by. Such was a wedding that I have seen many and
many a time among my own kindred; but I shall never
see another, as there are a great many other things
that these old eyes will never see again. Oh, days of
innocence and peace, where are you? And who am I,
an old man who sits here scribbling about times and
persons that his future readers will perhaps care nothing about?

But let us go into the graveyard. There we roamed
until the ringing of the second bell was ended and the
first strokes of the succeeding "toll" admonished us to
be in our pews,—there we roamed in the sun among the
graves, some of which were more than a century old,
wherein "the rude forefathers of the hamlet slept,"
interspersed among which were the fresh mounds
heaped upon the last resting-places of those who had
been buried recently. Sometimes there would be a
broad perpendicular head-stone of heavy blue slate, or
a massive horizontal slab of a dark-brown stone, supported on low pillars of the same material firmly set in
the ground. On these, respectively, was inscribed the
name of "Mehitable, consort of Leonard Bacon, Esq.,"
or "wife" of the more humble yeoman who had never
been justice of the peace, captain or lieutenant in the
artillery company, and on the more ambitious monument you might read the name of the Esq., or the dea-
con, or the militia officer, the head of the family lying
beneath, and the names of the children, with dates of
birth and death. On these stones there were rude
sculptures of an angel's head and a pair of wings; and
in the home of the living descendants there would be a
fac-simile of the gravestone worked in floss-silk on a
piece of canvas, with the figure of an angel under a
weeping-willow, in an impossible yellow gown, with
large white, folded wings at her back, and leaning with

2

an uncovered arm on the monument, while her blue eyes looked up to heaven. This heirloom, framed and glazed, was at once a sacred memento of the dead and a cherished proof of the handiwork of Aunt So-and-so, alongside of whose "sampler," worked when she began this art in her school days with the letters of the alphabet and scraps of poetry, this monumental portraiture of the family burial-place hung for generations, as long as there were any descendants left in the old homestead.

There were also many tombs in our graveyard, and sometimes one of these would be standing open, to receive a new-comer, and we looked in with awe upon the mouldering old wooden coffins piled one upon another, and on the brick pavement of the vault we saw the little boxes in which the infants had ended their little lives. Over the arched green mound that rose above these receptacles there stood, perhaps, a white marble shaft, which informed the passers-by that this was the family tomb of ——, Esq., erected by him in the year of our Lord, 17—.

If in all this there was a great deal to sadden young hearts and plant in them dark thoughts about the mysteries of death, there was some salutary influence upon those whose natures could be touched to the finer issues. There was rarely any levity among us about such things. Endless were our talks about the dead whom we remembered or could not remember, their intermarriages and their descendants. There was no scandal to be rehearsed about any of them, for

> " Along the cool sequestered vale of life
> They kept the noiseless tenor of their way;"

and if they had no great virtues to be commemorated, they had committed no very flagrant sins to be visited upon their children. We did not plant flowers about the graves, nor was the turf remarkably well kept. There were some lilac-bushes and a few wild roses along the stone wall that separated the graveyard from the hay-field on the side towards the hill; and although " that yew-tree's shade" was not there, or any " babbling brook," a gigantic elm that stood in one corner spread its branches far and wide. The wild bees sucked the red and white clover-blossoms on the other side of the wall, and in the hottest part of the summer there might be a hornet's nest in a break in the wall, of which we were wary enough, as your hornet, when he goes for you, comes at your head straight as a bullet. I have already put the bobolink on one of the bushes, with his capacious throat and his black and red plumage. But he did not have the landscape to himself. The blackbird was there, and the robin, various other families of the thrush tribe, the yellowbird, who is or was the New England canary, and that marvellous "fire-hang-bird" ("fiery-hanging-bird" shortened) in his scarlet and gold uniform, who hung his nest on the lowest end of a pending bough, high up in the air, where it swung to and fro in the breeze. Him we never shot, from some superstition that ill luck would befall any one who killed him. All of the feathered songsters were safe, of course, from "the fowler's eye" on the day of rest, and even on other days we pursued none of them that I have mentioned excepting the robins; but these we peppered as soon as the Fourth of July released us from the penalty of a statute that protected the young birds until they were grown. We made it a point to have a pot-pie on the Fourth, even if the traditional four-and-twenty blackbirds had not been bagged, for the robins were better, and we did not care to have our pie baked, although the blackbirds, according to the nursery canon, ought to be. I will mention but one other variety of the feathered tribes,—the wild pigeon. A dozen or so of these, in their dark-blue coats, would sometimes swoop down among the tops of the elms, and, if it happened to be a week-day, you may be sure that some of them dropped. If I chose to go on through the swallows and the martens,—for the latter we always provided a box on a high pole in our yards, that was an exact model of the meeting-house, with spire and belfry and every door and window represented,—if, I say, I were to complete the catalogue of our birds, I could make

as good a list as charming old White, of Selborne, has
given us of the birds of his neighborhood. But I have
other things to do; and before we go into meeting
I will say that when, in after-years, I saw an English
country church-yard,—and I visited one in Warwick-
shire where my own yeoman ancestors lie, and which
was said to be just like Gray's Stoke-Pogis,—I had
long before learned. to feel the beauty and pathos of
the Elegy. It was in the reading-book in our public
schools, as was a great deal else from the "wells of
English pure and undefiled;" for American literature
had not then furnished substitutes for the prose and
poetry of Old England,—has it yet furnished good
ones? I must say that I would no more put into the
hands of a child any specimens of our own literature,
and expect him or her to acquire a good English style
without studying the masters of the language who
preceded us all, than I would let the pupil derive his
intellectual nourishment solely from British writers of
the present day.

But here I am, off in another digression, and my
readers are not yet inside the house of worship, the
regular, typical New England meeting-house in a rural
parish, of which I know not if there is extant a single
perfect specimen. The Old South in Boston, although
in somewhat the same style,—style? I hear you ask,
contemptuously,—is so surrounded with other buildings
and encroached upon by streets, that it will not help
you to see our meeting-house, on its wide green at one
end of the village, and no other structure very near it
but the long wooden shed under which we put our
horses and vehicles, and the gun-house farther off,
in which the artillery company kept their brass six
pounders.

Perhaps you go to church in some sumptuous house
of God, where you pay a heavy pew-tax, and listen to
a ritual, and prefer it to be intoned, and the rector
preaches in his surplice, and there is a choir of boys
and men, and a great organ and a high-salaried organ-
ist, and the chanting is superb. Perhaps you are a
ritualist of the ritualists, and you like to have flowers

and candles on the altar, and are used to see the clergy assume different postures at different places within the chancel. I make no question that you are very devout, and the æsthetic in religion is a very good thing; and the English Prayer-Book is a magnificent legacy from the past to the present and the future. Perhaps you are a Roman Catholic, and to you the services of your Church have a meaning, in all their minutiæ, that I never could understand; so I will not ask you to look in upon a Puritan congregation in the days of my child-hood. But if you are a Presbyterian, or a Baptist, or a Methodist, albeit you may worship in a very costly church, seeing that you and your fellow-parishioners are rich people, who like to do your religion handsomely, although you do not depart in doctrine and service from the established ideas of your denomination, per-haps you will take a little interest in a public worship that preserved the Puritan repugnance to any approach to Rome or Westminster in outward observances, while the Creed was stiffened with many a belief that is now very much modified, if not entirely rejected. One thing, however, you will please to understand, be you what you may: that to me the various avenues that are opened to human souls, along which they can have access to their Maker, each walking as best suits him, not only afford a very interesting study, but are proofs of the wonderful adaptation of Christianity to human nature. In this aspect—do not start—they seem to me equally valuable.

My readers must figure to themselves a rectangular wooden building, of pretty massive frame, with two rows of windows one over another on the longest sides, and a steep gable roof. At one end is a square tower of the same strong timber as the main building, with a belfry surmounted by a tall spire, on the top of which turns the invariable "rooster," who faces the wind in a very spirited manner and turns with the slightest vari-ation of the current. The bell was one of considerable size and good tone. It needed to be, as the parish ex-tended on two sides four or five miles from the meeting-house. We used to tell large stories about the performances of that old bell when it was rung with the full swing of its ponderous tongue at an alarm of fire. For tolling, there was a smaller piece of iron with a round knob on one end, hinged on a fulcrum, and operated by a separate rope. It gave its strokes upon the under side of the bell as it hung motionless upon the beam that formed the axis for the wheel. There was a clock in the tower, just under the belfry, with a dial on each of two sides, that could be seen from afar, and notwithstanding the swaying and creaking of the timbers produced by the heavy swing of the bell, the great gilt iron hands on the dial kept on their appointed round undisturbed, and the time of day or night was always what that clock said it was, no matter what chronometer or other time-piece might assert it to be. In the room below the belfry, where the sexton was tolling the bell, there was a pane of glass inserted in the wall of the main building, through which he could see when the minister was ascending the pulpit stair. As the reverend person set his foot on the lower step, the last stroke was sounded and the congregation were in their pews.

These pews were none of your long narrow modern slips, but good square structures, with wooden seats all around, which turned upon hinges. Some were cushioned and some were not; and whether bare or covered, when the occupants stood up during prayer—kneeling was never practised—the seats were turned up for standing room, and when the prayer was ended they came down with some clatter. You know the Congregational form,—the short prayer, then a hymn, then reading of the Bible, then the long prayer, then another hymn, then the sermon, and last the doxology and the benediction. Perhaps you do not know a custom of very ancient observance, although it is not, I believe, wholly gone out. Before the long prayer the minister read the "notes," "put up" by those who had suffered bereavements in the preceding week. They ran thus: "J—— W—— asks the prayers of the congregation that the death of his wife may be sanctified to him and his children for their spiritual and everlasting good." And then how fervently and with what adaptation to each case, first, the widower, then the children, then the relatives, and lastly the congregation, did the parson "notice" all!

Dr. Brewster's sermons would perhaps not have interested you. There was not much more of doctrine and controversy than was needful to keep his flock faithful to the old beliefs, although he was a learned man, and well deserved his D.D. But his was what used to be called practical preaching; rebuking sin, setting forth the beauty of holiness, the efficacy of repentance, the promises and denunciations of the gospel. It was not without fruit, inasmuch as he kept the greater part of his people quite perceptibly free from the vice of intemperance, which was then the prevailing sin of New England, and had been for a long time. They were not exposed to many other vices or backslidings. I have sat under a great variety of preaching, and have been a worshipper in many different forms of public religious observances; but no cathedral service, Protestant or Romish, no deep-tongued organ, no ritual, however perfect, ever touches my old heart even now as did the simple, bare, unadorned—perhaps you will say irreverent—Congregational form, under which were first aroused what religious feelings I possess.

But I must tell something of the other life of the dear old birthplace of my friend Henry Brewster and myself, for we were boys of about the same age. The principal occupation of the inhabitants of Greentown was to cultivate the soil on which they were born and which they had for the most part inherited. The life of farmers and their families in that part of Massachusetts in the early part of this century was a hard one. The soil was never what it is in other regions, but the "stubborn glebe" would yield a subsistence, and to energy, thrift, and the other rural virtues it would yield more, especially to those, and they may be said to have been universally its careful readers, who followed the sage advice of "The Farmer's Almanac, calculated for the Meridian of Boston, but will answer for Other Places,

by Isaiah Thomas, Worcester, Massachusetts." Living
was comparatively cheap, for "the era of good feeling,"
which set in politically in the administration of President Monroe, was preceded and followed, after the
peace of 1815, by a very considerable state of prosperity for the whole country. But agriculture was not
the only employment of the inhabitants of Greentown.
The river Charles wound its devious way through the
township, and at a natural fall at one end of our village
there had been a dam built at a very early period.
This water-power, the oldest in America, turned the
wheels of a grist-mill, a paper-mill, and a small cotton-
factory. In the last were produced the coarser manufactures of cotton goods, which began those great industries now constituting so much of the wealth and
power of New England. Below the dam was an important shad-fishery, belonging by customary law to
the town, and leased annually to a rough set of men
known as "the fishermen," composed of certain families who had followed that pursuit for several generations, making a kind of close corporation, the members of which were rather immoderately addicted to
New England rum, being a good deal exposed, as to
their external surfaces, to the water, and eschewing
its internal use. There was likewise a hat-factory, in
which were made the bell-crowned and narrow-brimmed
beaver hats of the period; and around the great ket-
tles of hot water stood "the hatters," dipping and dipping and beating and beating the felt which was to
be shaped by another set of operatives into the hat-
bodies, and then passed to a third set to receive the
coating of fur, and then to be lined and bound by
women at their homes. Machinery for products of
this kind had not attained a stage of any importance,
so that the number of hands employed was very considerable. The men and boys engaged in these em-
ployments would have been for the most part a rather
wild population if the rule of "the selectmen" had not
been a pretty vigorous one. As it was, the constable,
the justice of the peace, and the general good morals
of the place kept our days and nights in very tolerable

order. Strict care was exercised over the young girls employed in these industries, and I remember but one instance in which anything unfortunate occurred.

We had our fire companies, of course, two of them, the members of which were exempted from militia duties. The engines were worked by hand, by levers called "breaks," and the water was passed in leather buckets into the tub along a line of men and boys. As the buildings were everywhere wooden structures, these fire companies were very important institutions, and to be the "foreman" of one of them was a post of some dignity and responsibility. Once a month there was an inspection and exercise of the whole apparatus, and it was really remarkable that the stream of water from the hose could be thrown so high and with so much force, considering that the machinery was worked by human muscle alone.

But our military organizations were the great attractions for the young people. A good deal of military spirit had come down from the Revolutionary period and through the War of 1812–15. The artillery company was well equipped and well manned; to command it was a high honor; and it was regularly drilled in target-firing, in which I have seen round shot thrown with considerable precision. There was an eccentric captain during my boyhood who took it into his head to plant his battery on the bridge at three o'clock in the morning of a Fourth of July, and to bang away furiously through a whole national salute, marching back and forth between the guns with the blazing "port-fire" in his hand,—that mysterious torch which it was said could not be put out if you thrust it into water. The cartridges consisted of flannel bags, with the powder sewed up tight; and when they were rammed home the priming was effected by piercing the bag through the touch-hole with a tin tube filled with powder, having a small cup on its outer end, supplied with a few grains from a powder-horn after the tube had been driven in. Percussion-caps, you will understand, had not been introduced. The first one I ever saw was on a fowling-piece, when I was about twelve years old.

The bridge exploit of our brave Captain Soper almost shook some of us out of our beds, and it broke a good many windows in the nearest houses. It was thought to be excusable for once on account of the day, but the selectmen ordered that such practice should in future be out of the village.

We had, too, a troop of light horse, well mounted and extremely brave in loading and firing their pistols and handling their swords. This troop was composed in part of men of an adjoining town; and as they generally assembled on the other side of the river, we heard with delight their bugles ring out a march as they descended the hill towards our bridge. They formed the escort of President Monroe's carriage when he passed through our town on his way to Boston upon his well-known tour in New England. They did the same duty when General Lafayette came through, under an arch erected in our square decorated with evergreens and flowers and inscribed with the words "Welcome, welcome, Lafayette."

These were great days: and I must tell you more of the influences under which we boys were born and brought up; for it was here that my friend Harry Brewster, with whose life we are somewhat concerned, received the bent of his character. We had among us a few old soldiers of the Revolution; and there were two officers—one a major, the other a captain—who had served under Washington. The last was at the head-quarters of the great commander at the time of Arnold's treason, and it was his special duty for some time to watch the "Vulture," as she lay in the Hudson below. Both of these old gentlemen had sheaves of Continental money in their houses, not worth a cent. But they were in comfortable circumstances, notwithstanding the scandalous neglect of Congress. The major had a fine family of beautiful daughters, all of whom married most fortunately and went far away into the great world. From these men of the heroic age of our country we learned a great deal that we never forgot; and we learned, too, what those liberties were for which they fought and suffered, and what

that Union was which was afterwards formed under
the Constitution. They were Federalists of the school
of Washington, these old officers of the Revolution;
and their politics were of the national, continental, but
moderate tone that marked the men who founded our
present government. I must not forget, either, to refer
to one occurrence in the boyish life of Harry Brewster
and myself, which left an impression never to be effaced.
We were in the outskirt of the vast audience when
Daniel Webster delivered his first Bunker Hill oration,
at the laying of the corner-stone of the monument that
crowns that famous summit. Our Revolutionary towns-
men were to be present, and Dr. Brewster was asked
to accompany them. He took Harry and myself with
him, little as we were, for he rightly thought that it
would be something to be remembered. We could not
be upon the platform, but the doctor placed us under
the charge of a trusty parishioner of his, who stood
with us upon the slope of the hill, at the edge of the
crowd, where we were near enough to see the grand
figure of the orator and occasionally to hear the roll of
his voice as in some of the more impassioned passages
its clarion tones rang through the assembly in front of
him. We heard him say, "Venerable men! you have
come down to us from a former generation;" and we
saw the old men, bowed with age, and their silvered
heads, rise and stand while he addressed them.

Did we comprehend the full force of what we then
saw and heard? Certainly not, at the time; but there
comes a time when, from such early impressions, the
whole meaning is rounded out in its full proportions.
Whatever else you put into the hands of a youth to
read, if you wish him to have a true conception of the
spirit of our revolutionary epoch, give him that oration
of Webster's as one of his first lessons, and then follow it
with some of the other masterpieces of the same orator.

It was in such associations that Henry Brewster
grew up. His early education was in his father's
house. He became an industrious, thoughtful, and
earnest boy. At Harvard he took a high rank, gradu-
ating with distinguished honor in the year 182-. At

about that time there was a new professorship of law founded in the University. Brewster was one of a remarkable class of young men who formed the first pupils in the revived law school at Cambridge, to which one of the most accomplished jurists in the world gave a new impulse and, for a time, a national renown. The young men who were educated as lawyers in that institution at that period had no superiors in their profession, according to my observation, and it has been a pretty wide one. They have for the most part passed away, after filling admirably various positions on the bench and at the bar. Henry Brewster gave early promise of a fine career.

CHAPTER II.

A RAPID LOVE-AFFAIR.

VERY few of my readers will be able to recall, in that part of Boston to which I am now to lead them, the Pearl Street of fifty-odd years ago,—a short street, extending from Milk Street; a little below the Old South Meeting-House, to Fort Hill. This was one of the trinity of hills whence Boston derived the name Tremont, or the Tri-mountain town. Fort Hill has long since been carted away, leaving only Beacon Hill and Copp's Hill of the three elevations, one at the west and one at the north part of the town. At the time of which I am writing Pearl Street was occupied on both sides by the town residences of wealthy merchants, and in it dwelt, in a square and spacious house of his own erection, Mr. James Bradshaw, a prosperous man, architect of his own fortunes, engaged from early life in the East-India trade, and a large ship-owner in other branches of commerce. He had not been entirely successful in escaping some of the disastrous effects of the late war with England; and there were left on his hands some of those " French Spoliation Claims"

which have become historical on account of the conduct of our government, and which remain unsettled
to this day. Still he had enough property remaining
to enable him to become a rich man before the time
when these memoirs commence. His family consisted,
at that time, of the wife whom he had married in his
youth, three married daughters, and one daughter who
was unmarried. Of that young lady, Isabella Bradshaw, there is a good deal to be told. Without making
a minute description of her, it is enough to say, at
present, that from her childhood she had been a noted
beauty. Her education and character must be learned
from the narrative of her life as it goes on. If I could
but succeed in making her as interesting to my readers
as she always was to me! I shall doubtless incur some
criticism,—perhaps I shall encounter some reproof,—
because I may appear to have yielded too much to
fascinations that I ought to have resisted. But I am
to describe a woman whom I knew and admired, notwithstanding her faults. Of these I shall make no
concealment. I must truly relate what befell her. It
is not for me to make the incidents of her life, either
for punishment or reward.

In the year 183–, Isabel Bradshaw was at the age
of twenty-three. She had never been in love, and in
truth it seemed to be her chief aim in life, as it was
apparently her sole occupation, to make every man
who came within her influence fall in love with her,
and to give him no return. Whether this was from
set purpose or from a careless love of admiration and
sheer thoughtlessness, the mischief that she could do
and did was the same. She never tried her attractions
upon me, however, as she did upon other men. I had
left my heart behind me in my native village before I
knew her, and she was aware of it. I am bound to
chronicle her good qualities as faithfully as her bad
ones, and to relate that she never knowingly interfered
with the peace of any other woman, single or married.
After she knew of my engagement to a very lovely
girl in the country, daughter of a physician in my native place,—she is still spared to me in the serene old

age at which we have both arrived,—Miss Bradshaw
and I became very good friends. She once did me the
honor to say that when I married and brought my
wife to Boston she should make it a point to call upon
her immediately and have the pleasure of her acquaintance. But my marriage did not take place until Isabel had been gone from Boston for some time, and as my
wife did not become acquainted with her until a later
period, I lost the benefit of that finer penetration into
the early character of my beautiful friend which my
wife's female instinct would have given her, if their
acquaintance had begun earlier and had embraced the
years when I was an occasional visitor at Mr. Bradshaw's hospitable mansion. As it was, my wife's
knowledge of Isabel's life from the age of eighteen to
twenty-three had to be taken from me at second hand,
as we talked over its history; but very likely, if her
personal observation had accompanied mine, she would
have suggested solutions of Isabel's conduct which did
not occur to me. Possibly there might have been an
intimacy, in which Isabel would have been led to make
a confidante of my wife, who was a little older, and
who would doubtless have acquired some influence
over this singularly attractive, but to me often unaccountable, creature.

But how shall I describe Isabel Bradshaw's young-
ladyhood? Flirtation is but a feeble word to convey an
idea of her multifarious and simultaneous conquests. A
girl who is accounted a flirt generally has some one
affair on hand at a time, and when she is done with
that she takes up another. Isabel carried on half a
dozen such affairs at one and the same time. The poor
moths would flutter and whirl around the dazzling
light, and one or more, growing desperate and giddy,
would plunge at the flame, and fall with singed and
blasted wings to the ground, never to rise again.
Others would be a little more wary, and would escape
final scorching, but they could not keep away from the
intoxicating charm of that dangerous candle. To drop
the metaphor—it is "something musty"—and to descend to the real human individuals, I must tell you that

year after year, when I visited at the Bradshaws', I
have seen Isabel entertain half a dozen men who were
all desperately in love with her, in the most spirited
manner, making each one believe that in her secret
heart she had a feeling about him that might ripen
into "something to his advantage," but which just now
could not be made more certain to him. At one time
the circle of her admirers consisted of the following,
among other men : there was a middle-aged bachelor,
of good family, with just a very moderate property,
who had mathematical tastes and accomplishments.
He had been a devoted slave of my fair friend, in a
cautious way, ever since she was eighteen. Another
was a merchant of about the same age, who lived with
two maiden sisters; and this gentleman, a most dull
and commonplace person, was an old friend of two of
Isabel's brothers-in-law; and their wives, Isabel's sisters, shared the regard of their husbands for this de-
luded gentleman, who was constantly sending flowers
to the enchantress. Then there was a Frenchman,
who—poor fool—had dreams of cutting out all his
rivals in the favorable regards of "Mees Braidzhowe ;"
and a Spaniard, who sometimes had the honor of being
asked to bring his guitar and to sing a Spanish ballad
to his own accompaniment on that romantic instrument. Isabel rather liked foreigners, and as all fish
came readily to her net, she considered the foreign as
good sport as the native element. There was also a
young Southerner, fiery, jealous, and impulsive, who
became sadly involved in the meshes, and who went
away at last desperate to a degree, and went, I believe,
to the bad. At all events, he asserted, I fear with too
much reason, that Isabel had given him positive encouragement and had then cruelly frowned upon him.
All of these men, oldish and young, with the exception
of the mathematical gentleman and the Southerner,
were in commercial pursuits. Mr. Bradshaw's social
and business position and his habits of hospitality led
him to open his house freely to all who came properly
introduced to him. Besides the regular *habitués* of his
mansion whom I have mentioned, there was always a

crowd of young men around the Bradshaw box at the
theatre and their seats at a concert, paying attentions
to Miss Isabel and bringing her bouquets. In the
family gathering at home there were often present the
married daughters of the house and their husbands, and
always on Sunday evenings.

Isabel's conversational powers were such as would
have adorned a different circle. Her education had
not been neglected in matters purely literary. From
the age of thirteen to seventeen she had attended, as a
day pupil, a school kept by a gentleman in Boston, who
educated the daughters of many wealthy parents for a
long series of years. He was an admirable teacher,
and he had the art of selecting good teachers in
branches which he did not teach himself. Isabel, although not much of a student in anything, did learn a
good deal at this school. She knew something, when
she left it, of the history of her own country and a
little of the history of other countries; was fairly
grounded in geography, and had read or heard read,
some of the masterpieces of English literature. She
spoke French, not with a Parisian accent, but fluently
and correctly. German was not then a part of a young
lady's education. Latin was, and she went creditably
through three or four books of the Æneid. She knew
Italian pretty well. In music she was fairly well
taught. She played on the piano rather better than
most young women of her time, and she sang such
pieces as she chose to learn—they were not many or
difficult—with good expression and apparent feeling.
Since she left school she had read nothing but novels and
some poetry; but that part of her life comprehended
some of Scott's earlier prose fictions, his poetry, and
Byron's.

A girl with fine natural gifts, who had enjoyed this
education, if placed in a different circle, and with a
wise mother's influence to guide her in her intercourse
with the other sex, might have had a different character than I am obliged to describe my friend Isabel's
early character to have been. But her mother never
did anything to guard her youngest daughter against

the abuse of her extraordinary powers of fascinating
the other sex. Her other daughters were sensible and
perfectly correct women, who had never needed the
discipline that Isabel ought to have had, and who had
married well and happily. The conversation in the
Bradshaw circle did not run much into topics that
might have called forth Isabel's natural powers. Between her and her male admirers it was mostly made
up of such materials as form the staple of all flirtation,
with an occasional dash by her into something that
seemed a sentiment towards the particular man at the
moment favored with the *tête-à-tête*, and not overheard
by the rest of the circle. Her brothers-in-law talked
with her father about "freights;" whether they were
"up" or "down;" their wives talked to each other
and their mother about the last new dress or something about their children. The last new book was
seldom discussed, public events still more rarely ; but
the celebrated actors and singers of the time were much
canvassed. Mr. Bradshaw himself, although a man of
sense and information, seldom led the conversation in
his house to any very elevated plane. At his own table
he was a gentle and genial host, fond of giving handsome dinners, and always circulating the choicest
wines. His rise in the world had been entirely due to
his own energies, and he had the confident, resolute,
and practical character that belongs to that class of
Americans who make their way by their brains, exercised in honorable and upright paths. His reputation
and credit as a merchant were A No. 1. He was liked
and respected. As a father of such a girl as Isabel, I
am sorry to say that he did not show his good sense in
the most important part of her life until after Henry
Brewster appeared among them. It was then a question whether Isabel's character was one that was likely
to insure her happiness.

Henry Brewster came to Boston, and was admitted
to the bar in 183–. His father had an old friend and
college classmate in our modern Athens, Mr. Dana by
name. He was a conveyancer, a sound lawyer, and a
favorite adviser of wealthy merchants ; but he had no

forensic gifts, and never appeared personally in court.
Henry had brought from the Cambridge Law School
quite a little reputation as a well-read young man and
a good speaker. The public in the neighborhood of
Harvard then took some notice of such young men;
the fellow who pulled the best oar, or was otherwise
the greatest athlete, being then an unknown character.
Dr. Brewster secured for his son Henry a position as
junior partner with his old friend. Henry's abilities and
industry soon won for him Mr. Dana's entire confidence
and warm regard. It happened that Mr. Bradshaw
was one of this gentleman's steady clients; in fact,
Mr. Dana was Mr. Bradshaw's confidential lawyer, intimately acquainted with his business and most of his
family concerns. After Henry had been for some time
in his office, Mr. Dana one day introduced him to Mr.
Bradshaw and put into his hands an important piece
of business to be attended to for that opulent merchant. Everything was done to Mr. Bradshaw's entire
satisfaction; he became interested in Henry, and, according to his custom, invited him to his house. He
saw that this young man was of a mould superior to
those who were generally to be found in his mansion,
and, although he did not jump to the conclusion that
he might, if he chose, make a son-in-law of the young
lawyer, it did occur to him that Brewster would be
an acquaintance in whom Isabel might find something
better than there then was on her list.

I chanced to be visiting at the Bradshaws' on the
evening when Henry made his first call, so that I can
speak from personal observation of what occurred.
Isabel had been for some time talking with the Spaniard, a little apart from the family circle, as was her
wont. She had a costly fan in her right hand, tipped
with a fringe of delicate white feathers, and she was
trying to make the hidalgo show her how a Spanish
lady, by a simple motion of her fan, signifies to her
adorer that she has a favorable regard for him without
saying a word. This little lesson, quickly given, was
as quickly caught by Isabel, and she was deftly practising it when Henry Brewster entered the drawing-

room. In an instant she signified by a wave of her fan that she expected the Spaniard to vacate the chair by her side, which he did at once. Mr. Bradshaw came forward, shook hands with Henry cordially, then presented him to his wife and married daughters, and last to Isabel. She arose, made him a most gracious courtesy, and invited him to take the vacant chair. This was so far the politeness of a well-bred young lady to a stranger. But it was not long before Miss Isabel gave the new visitor to understand that she had heard of him before. She alluded delicately to her father's satisfaction in what Mr. Brewster had done in the business in which Mr. Bradshaw had made his acquaintance, asked him how he liked Boston, whether he went to many parties, whom he knew, etc., etc. Then she rattled on gayly about the recluse habits which she feared Mr. Brewster was following in the pursuits of his profession; then she spoke seriously of the noble character of that profession, which afforded so many opportunities to redress wrongs, defend the innocent, etc. She had never known many lawyers, she said, but she had always desired to meet with some gentleman in whose pursuits she could sympathize more than she could with the occupations of gentlemen engaged in commerce. This last remark was made in a low tone, so that it was not heard on the other side of the room.

Henry was most agreeably surprised to find this bright and beautiful girl, whom he had never seen before in his life, and of whose existence until that moment he had never heard, speaking as if she felt a personal interest in him, and expressing a hope that they would become well-acquainted. He was at once dazzled by her beauty and flattered by her intimation that she had made a valuable addition to her list of friends. Harry's experience among the gentler sex had been very limited. During his boyhood he had known all the girls in his native village, but he had not become attached to any of them. In his college days he spent his vacations at home, where he saw only those good and simple country maidens and his only sister, who was ten years older than himself, and who,

though a woman of a very lovely character, bore no resemblance to this dashing young lady with whom he
was now talking. When he was in the law school he
did not enter at all into the small and somewhat peculiar society of Cambridge, and since he had been in Mr.
Dana's office his days and nights had been given to
study and work. He may therefore be said to have
been somewhat green in the ways and characters of
women when he first saw Isabella Bradshaw. He
was in temperament a very grave and earnest young
man, but he was not awkward or shy. He was a gentleman in every inch of his body and in every fibre of
his moral nature. His manners gave you the impression that he had seen more of the world than he really
had. In fact, the world that he knew most about was
what was to be found in books and in such affairs of
business as he had then been concerned in.

This first conversation with Isabel was long, and it
seemed to interest her as much as him. I observed
them, for much of what they said was audible enough
and was not intended to be otherwise. They talked on
many subjects, and Harry talked well. Isabel stimu-
lated him and drew him out, and I never saw him so
animated. She was doing her best to excite his admiration, and her best was always something very fine
and successful. Before Harry made his bow and disappeared, at about ten o'clock, I saw plainly that the
conquest was complete. In short, if there ever was
such a thing as love at first sight, I saw a case of it that
evening. What Isabel then thought of him it was not
given to me to know; but I know that she was rarely
mistaken in regard to the impression which she produced upon any man who approached her, and that
when she put forth her power she was perfectly sure
of the effect. Whether she was equally sure to be
careful about the use that she intended to make of it
in this instance, I will not pronounce with confidence.
I doubt if she knew herself, and if she did not know, I
have no right to assume that I did.

I shall not dwell long on the history of this affair.
It was rapid and impetuous on Harry's part, although

he was not without those misgivings all along which
every man who loves suddenly and can love deeply
always feels when he is not yet assured of success.
Isabel, who did not on this occasion allow her feelings
to run away with her any more than she had ever done
on any other of the same sort, found she was getting
some new ones that she had never before experienced.
She made up her mind to accept Harry whenever he
should come to the point, and she saw plainly that
this was not far off. At first, his visits were made in
the evening, when the family were always in the drawing-room; but, after a few weeks, he came in the afternoon, as often as he could get away from his office.
Isabel took care to be generally at home at that time
in the day, and she did not keep him waiting long.
She came down with a frank grace and a winning smile,
and they had many hours such as can come but once
in a lifetime. At last, one summer's evening as the sun
was going down, and they were sitting just inside of
the lace curtain which hung before an open window,
Harry poured out his passion. He told her how he had
loved her from the hour when they first met; how he
had doubted and feared that one so beautiful and lovely,
the daughter of a wealthy father, who could command
the most eligible match that the society of Boston or
of our whole country could offer, would accept the love
of a poor young lawyer just beginning the world; yet
how deep and fervent was the love that he now offered
her, etc., etc. I am a poor hand at these tender passages, but you will understand Harry's feelings, and
can give them expression as well as I can. Isabel
listened very quietly to his impassioned eloquence, and
her better nature was touched. Here was a young
man of a noble character who offered her the greatest
of all gifts, a heart perfectly unsullied, and the devotion
of a life which she might believe would be one that
any woman should be proud to share. All her former
conquests seemed, as they were, poor dross in the com-
parison. Their ages, their tastes, their ideas,—Isabel
rapidly reviewed these things in her mind, and she
honestly thought that they were suited to each other in

c

their tastes and ideas,—would make everything delightful; her father's kindness would make amends for all disparity of fortune. She held out her hand to Harry, and, without a blush or the least sign of agitation, she said, simply, "I accept your love, Mr. Brewster, and will give you mine." It was the first time in her life that she had ever said this to any man.

My old pen is not fit to describe the raptures which followed. I wish it were, for your sake, my dear young readers, for I know that these things are expected, and that in the circulating libraries they affect the number of copies that will be kept on hand; but I must content myself with saying, in general, that the endearments which make the heaven of such moments were abundant and after the universal mode of such performances. But passing over some of the details, there is one thing that I must relate, because it was so pretty and so natural. After an hour or more of this perfect bliss, Harry asked her not to call him Mr. Brewster any more, but to find and become used to his other name. "I will," she said, sweetly; "you shall be Harry when there is no one else by but some member of my family, but when there are other persons to hear me I shall call you Mr. Brewster. You know," she added, with an arch smile, "that I shall have some day to promise to love, honor, and *obey* you, and I think women may as well begin before they are married to show that they look up to their future husbands." Harry protested, of course, that he did not want any looking up from her, but she gently laid her pretty fingers on his lips and said, "Hush, dear; if I do not look up to you I shall become mischievous." How could there be a better beginning?

If I were writing a novel I should have told of all the endearments that followed the compact which made Henry Brewster the accepted lover of Isabella Bradshaw. The novelist can invent anything he pleases, and he is expected to describe, with proper delicacy, every incident which followed the felicitous ending of a courtship in an engagement. The novelist can even look into hearts, and can inform us whether the young

lady loved the young man as much as he loved her. I
can only relate what Harry afterwards told me, and
what I could infer. I presume that there was the
usual tender scene, after the declaration and the acceptance ; but I must leave my readers to imagine it, saying
only that an hour or more elapsed before these two
young people were disturbed. At the end of that time,
Mr. Bradshaw's step was heard in the hall, approaching the door of the drawing-room. Isabel sprang to
her feet and met her father as he opened the door,
whispering to him, "Mr. Brewster is here, sir, and I
believe he has something to say to you."

"I dare say he has. It is time," Mr. Bradshaw said,
with a hearty laugh. He caught his daughter in his
arms, kissed her forehead, and, holding her for an instant longer, he added, with tender seriousness, "Dear
child, I *am rejoiced.*" He then let her run up to her
mother's chamber, entered the drawing-room, and said
gayly to Harry, whose hand he pressed warmly in both
of his own, "My young friend, I can guess what you
have to say to me, and I will spare you a formal
speech. She is yours, and I am delighted to give her
to you. I have watched you two people for some time,
and I am free to say, without any disparagement to
either of my sons-in-law, that I am very happy in
this match. I will do for Isabel just what I have done
for each of her sisters : I will give her a house and
will furnish it. You must do the rest. Now, walk
down to tea, for I hear the servant coming to call us.

Harry, I need not say, was warmly welcomed by the
mother and two of the married daughters, who had
come in to tea. Isabel was calm, and appeared to be
very happy. The whole family were assembled later
in the evening ; the sons-in-law greeted there new
brother very kindly, all visitors were to be told that
they were not at home, and the evening passed away
in almost unspoken contemplation of a new happiness.
As for Harry, when he walked to his lodgings late that
night, I wish you to know that he was experiencing
that exquisite bliss that comes but once in a man's life.
Yes ; but once. Other and subsequent loves may be

safer than the first one; may have more of the solid
elements of happiness. But that triumphant and intoxicating joy never comes a second time.

What does this old gentleman mean? I hear some
captious critic ask,—what does the old goose mean by
bringing out the *dénouement* of a courtship and its successful result at the beginning of his book, instead of
conducting the worthy pair through an involved series
of obstacles and difficulties to the proper reward of
virtue and truth and fidelity at the close of his second
volume? Do you not know, critical reader, that early
love is but the beginning of life, and that life must
have a long sequel of joys and sorrows, good fortune
and bad, which may or may not be of one thread back
to the event which happened twenty, thirty, or forty
years before the last scene of all? Did you never see
the coming on of the dawn, heralded by the first faint
streaks of light, followed by the gorgeous hues which
precede the rising of the great orb, and then the blazing
disk ascends quickly above the horizon, and a new day
is born? And do you not know that from that hour—

"The bridal of the earth and sky"—

to the going down of that day's life there must be many
changes, and the blue vault may be overcast, and the
thunder may roll and torrents may descend, if happily
the resplendent bow of promise and peace shall span
the eastern heavens as the sun breaks through the
western clouds? I have observed the first dawn of an
early love, and its many changing hues, and then its
glorious effulgence of light and hope, and have asked
myself whether the two beings who have thus begun
to live will walk together hand in hand until the evening of their days. Who can tell? Heaven is above
us all.

On the day following the engagement of these two
young people it was duly announced to all their friends
and acquaintances. Mr. Bradshaw spoke of it on 'change
with extreme satisfaction, nodding his head slightly
towards the building where Harry's name had been

borne on a modest sign for about two years, as much
as to say, That young lawyer up there is a man of
great promise, and I consider my daughter as very fortunate in her choice. All the gentlemen to whom he
thus imparted his feeling about this event in his family
congratulated him warmly. Their wives and daughters
at home received the intelligence with a good deal of
surprise. Isabel was regarded by most of her sex
through the whole of Boston society with mixed opinions. Some of the elder ladies, especially those who
had sons, considered her a dangerous girl; some of
the younger ones acknowledged that she was very
beautiful, but they had not always been content with
the influence of her beauty upon their male and unmarried friends. But there was a social duty to be
performed, alike by the old and the young. It was an
established custom, when a new engagement was announced, for everybody to call and congratulate the
lady, and generally these visits were made in the forenoon. There were commonly more ladies than gentlemen at these somewhat formal calls, for the gentlemen were engaged in business at that part of the
day, and they tendered their felicitations more casually
when they chanced to meet the fair *fiancée*. Isabel,
arrayed in a very becoming dress,—her taste in dress
was always exquisite,—received her visitors with a
calm smile, which did not quite suit some of the elder
ladies, who looked for a little more of what they called
" proper feeling." It was rather an ordeal for a young
lady who had never been universally popular with her
own sex in her native city. But Isabel carried it
through the two or three days of the ceremony with
much grace, and whether her feelings were deep or
shallow she did not consider to be a matter that concerned any one else, if she thought of them at all. It
was not so, however, with her visitors. I do not speak
of the present, but at the period when Isabella Bradshaw became so much talked about everybody in Boston society not only knew everything that could be
known about everybody else, but characters, conduct,
past history, and future probabilities were discussed

with a minuteness and fine-spun analysis that were
most remarkable, if not edifying and salutary.   My
readers must therefore expect to hear of some things
which I hope never reached my friend Isabel.

Two middle-aged and married ladies left Mr. Bradshaw's house together.   Mrs. Henshaw's carriage stood
at the door.

"Let me take you home," she said to Mrs. Newcome;
"we will drive 'round the Common, as the day is so
fine."

Mrs. Henshaw had a son, and Mrs. Newcome had a
daughter, both in society.

"Well," said the former lady, after they were seated
in the carriage, "I never expected to see Isabella Bradshaw engaged, for I never believed she could love any
man, and I doubt if she cares more for this young
Brewster than she has for any of the others by whom
she has been so long surrounded.   I am thankful that
my son Albert never fell in love with her."

"I think," replied Mrs. Newcome, "that you do Isabel
injustice.   I have known her since she was a child. She
and my Sarah were at school together, and, although
they have never been intimate, I have always found
that Sarah gave Isabel credit for some good qualities.   I
understand that Mr. Brewster has a great deal of character, and I think that we are all bound to believe it
to be best for Isabel to marry a man to whom she will
have to look up, and who will be able to develop her in
the way that she needs."

Mrs. Henshaw shook her head : "My dear friend, a
girl who has lived for years on the admiration of a miscellaneous crowd of men, for not one of whom did she
ever care a fig, but all of whom she has kept dangling
after her until they have made fools of themselves, will
never be content with the life that she will have to lead
as the wife of a hard-working young lawyer.   Albert,
I am thankful to be able to say, was warned in time.
He has not visited at the Bradshaws' for two years.
He had too much pride to put himself in competition
with any of Miss Bradshaw's admirers."

"Well," answered Mrs. Newcome, "let us hope for

the best. But here we are at my door. Will you come
in ?"

"No, thank you, not now. I am going to call at the
Warners. Good-by !" and she drove on.

The Warners were a family who considered themselves, and were considered, the *crème de la créme* of
Boston society. And here I should like to know if, to
be exclusive; to be able to say, "We do not know them
at all ;" to have inherited, not made, wealth ; to have
had a father or a grandfather who may have sold pins
and needles or retailed molasses, but who somehow in
his later years managed to assume the bearing and to
have the manners and ways of the very highest class,
and to have his children accepted as the *haute noblesse*,
—if all this and a certain indefinable claim, which is
not made up of any real superiority, but comes to be
admitted, do not give a family a right to consider
themselves as higher than their neighbors, what in this
republican land of ours will enable them to stand in
that elevated position? The Warners certainly stood
there.

Mrs. Warner and her daughter Mary were in their
drawing-room when Mrs. Henshaw's card was brought
in, and they received that lady as they commonly received their visitors whom they considered to be very
nearly as good as themselves.

"Have you heard of the new engagement?" asked
Mrs. Henshaw, after the warmth of the weather had
been duly remarked upon.

"What engagement?" inquired Miss Warner.

"Miss Isabella Bradshaw, to a young lawyer of the
name of Brewster. It was announced yesterday."

Miss Warner looked at her mother, as if to ascertain
whether they should admit that they had heard of this
event.

"We do not know them at all," said Mrs. Warner,
"and therefore we have not been in the way of hearing of anything that concerns the Bradshaw family.
I have always understood that Miss Bradshaw is a co-
quette, and that her mother has been in the habit of
allowing her to receive the visits of gentlemen when

she was not herself present, in the evening or during the day."

Miss Mary Warner was a young lady who had never in her life received the visit of a gentleman without the presence of her mother's watchful eye and ear, and she was in a fair way to reach that state in which she would never have to announce to her friends that she expected to change her condition. Yet she was a girl who might have had many advantageous offers, if the men of her acquaintance could have approached her under circumstances which would render love-making a possibility. She was highly educated, was pleasing, and attractive. But she had lived all her life under a system in which Isabella Bradshaw could not have breathed. The only chance that any gentleman had for saying soft things to her was in a quadrille,—round dances were not allowed,—and when the dance was over she was immediately gathered under the maternal wing, to remain there until the next partner came up to receive Mrs. Warner's approving nod. I have seen in the same assemblies some rather less-restricted young lady take the arm of a young gentleman and walk up and down the floor of the ball-room between the dances. But not so Miss Warner.

" I have heard my brother Thomas say," Miss Warner remarked, "that Miss Bradshaw is very beautiful, and I believe I once saw her at a distance. I suppose they are not people of culture. Do you know the gentleman to whom she is engaged, Mrs. Henshaw ?"

" Yes," said Mrs. Henshaw, "and I know all the Bradshaw family, and I have not a very high opinion of Miss Isabella. I have just made the usual call there, and I must say that I never saw any young lady on the very next day but one after her engagement—I understand that it took place only the night before last—show so little of what one would call proper feeling. She was just as calm as if you had called to congratulate her on finding a bracelet that she had lost, or any other trivial occurrence in life. I was really astonished."

" Do you not think," inquired Mrs. Warner, in rather

a stately manner, " that this custom of young ladies receiving the congratulatory visits of all their acquaintances on the announcement that they are engaged to
be married is one that would be better honored in the
breach than in the observance? An engagement is a
very solemn event in a young lady's life, and in all the
best circles that I have known it is so considered. I
am sorry that even some people of culture do not seem
to regard this custom as a questionable one. I know
that it has been long established, but I am sure that
Mary, when she becomes engaged, will be willing to set
a better example. But you say that you know this
Mr. Brewster. What sort of person is he?"

Mrs. Warner, although she moved in a very elevated
sphere, had as much curiosity as most people, and was
often willing to talk about persons who were, as she
considered, much below her in the social scale.

"I have seen young Brewster," said Mrs. Henshaw,
" and I like his manners. I believe that he distinguished
himself at Cambridge. He comes of an excellent family.
You must have heard his father, the late Dr. Brewster, preach; he has sometimes exchanged with your
minister, Dr. Fowler."

"Oh, you mean that Dr. Brewster, of Greentown,
who died some few months since? Yes. He was one
of the pillars of Congregational orthodoxy. Is this
young lawyer his son?"

"He is the only son of Dr. Brewster," replied Mrs.
Henshaw, "and Mr. Henshaw says that he is rising
rapidly in his profession."

"I am sorry," remarked Mrs. Warner, "that he
should not have seen more of our best society before
forming such a connection. But we have not been out
much lately, and have not given many parties. We
should have very willingly admitted into our circle a
son of Dr. Brewster. I wonder that he did not give
his son a letter to my husband when he came to Boston."

"Perhaps," said Mrs. Henshaw, " the young man has
not been much in society, because he is a great student."

"Ah!" said Mrs. Warner, "those are the young men
who are likely to be fascinated by such a girl as Miss

4*

Bradshaw. Mr. Warner told me that Mr. Bradshaw invited Mr. Brewster to visit his daughter about three months ago. I cannot conceive of a father's doing such a thing."

"Perhaps, mamma," said Miss Warner, "Mr. Bradshaw thought that young Brewster would be a good match; he is so well spoken of."

"Very likely, my dear; but neither your father nor I would have given you a new acquaintance in just that way."

Mrs. Henshaw here rose, saying that she hoped they would soon return her visit. Albert Warner was a young man whom Mrs. Henshaw wished to cultivate for the sake of a niece of hers.

I protest that these Boston ladies were rather hard upon my lovely friend Isabel. But perhaps my readers will expect me to explain how it happened that in a pretty compact town of forty thousand inhabitants, in which the families of the wealthy were all about on a par in education, manners, modes of life, and most other things, there should have been circles in which it could be said we do not know them at all, when the *them* lived in the very next street and in just as good a house as the social agnostics who made this mild denial of any acquaintance with persons about whom they talked. You know that in the great cities of the world, London or Paris, for example, where there is a vast society, if you comprehend all who lead about the same lives, there are circles and circles, cliques and coteries, a society which is *the* society *par excellence*, and societies which cannot claim to be the real fashion of the world that is constituted by a great metropolis of a great country. Yet, as I suppose,—you understand that I make a supposition,—people who in those great centres really move in different spheres do not in general talk much about those whom they do not visit. In fact, in the little observation I have had in such places, I have noticed that there is not much scandal talked in any circle about the members of other circles, while there is often enough of it about one's friends and acquaintances. But in such a place as Boston was

fifty years ago exclusiveness was a social phenomenon
that did not depend upon the magnitude of the city.
These things are just as likely to be found in a small
as in a large community, resulting, however, from different causes. They have always reminded me of the
saying of a wise and caustic old gentleman : "Man is
an animal of but few tricks ;" and the observation might
have included the women also, although the wives and
daughters will often exhibit a little wider range in some
of their social performances than the husbands and
fathers. Men who met every day on 'change, and
knew exactly how every other man stood financially,
and who carried home all the gossip of State Street,
did not expect their families to be intimate with the
families of all the other gentlemen whose concerns they
knew all about, and whose note they would have discounted at the bank where they happened to be direc-
tors for any amount whatever without the slightest
question.

But I have wandered away from my early friend,
Harry Brewster. How did it fare with him after his
engagement was announced ? It seems, from what Mrs.
Henshaw mentioned at Mrs. Warner's, that he had lost
his father before he became acquainted with Isabel.
The good old parson died about three months before
his son became a visitor at the Bradshaws'. All who
were natives of Greentown, if they were near enough
to reach the old village, were at his funeral. I was
there to do what I could for Harry and to testify my
love and veneration for the pastor who had baptized
me. The pulpit was draped in black cloth, and after
the funeral sermon had been preached, on the next
Sunday, this was taken down and given as a kind of
melancholy perquisite to the widow. The excellent old
lady did not long survive her husband. Harry was
left with no near relative excepting his sister, Miss
Elizabeth Brewster, whom I have as yet mentioned but
incidentally. We shall meet with her later. A recent
graduate from the Divinity School at Cambridge, who
had adopted the new Unitarian opinions, came and
preached for some weeks as a " candidate." He re-

ceived a "call" at the end of those weeks, and was ordained in the customary Congregational mode. The congregation and " the Church," as the communicants were collectively styled, slid gradually under the new preaching into the growing Unitarian body, as did many of the parishes of Eastern Massachusetts. The creed was reformed, and in the place of Dr. Watt's psalms and hymns, or such other orthodox collection as had been used, Dr. Belknap's new hymn-book was substituted. In some of the parishes a fierce theological controversy waged for a time, but in our Greentown we took mildly to the new faith, without much bickering. The new minister was a scholar, and a man of some tact. If he found it needful to encounter Andover in his sermons, he did not do it in a way to make it necessary for his parishioners to engage in much reading.

Miss Brewster surrendered the parsonage immediately after her mother's death, and accepted a position as teacher in a famous boarding-school for young ladies at Troy, in the State of New York. She was there when her brother became engaged to Isabel Bradshaw, and her duties did not admit of a visit to Boston to make the acquaintance of his future wife. Her father, who, as I have said, was an old-fashioned scholar, had for many years been occupied in making a new translation of the Hebrew Scriptures. He had completed it before he died, and the MSS., with his library, passed into Harry's possession. It was never published ; but I have heard good judges, who had examined parts of it, say that it was a learned book.

And now I have only to relate—it goes almost without saying—that Harry was supremely happy. A new incentive to exertion, the best and noblest that can animate a young man and make ambition something by which money and fame are to be sought for the sake of another's happiness, filled his whole being. Every hour that he could gain from business or study was passed with Isabel. They read together, they walked and drove, the long rapturous hours of bliss that seemed so short when he had to leave her—well, you will understand it all. Isabel seemed to be very happy. Her family were all rejoiced, and all believed that now she was safe. And so it went on for five weeks.

CHAPTER III.

A SUDDEN DISASTER.

WITH all Mr. Bradshaw's kindness and liberality, Harry could not expect to marry very soon. Long engagements may be fortunate or unfortunate, according to circumstances. In the present case there was time enough for the enjoyment of all that lovers can enjoy and for learning all of each other that they can learn before marriage. Harry could not be much with his lady-love during the day: he was necessarily confined to his office. They did manage to be together at times, when they could be alone. In the evenings there was generally company at the house, and Isabel could not absent herself from the drawing-room. Mr. Bradshaw's was almost the only house in Boston where the family received visitors in the evening without ceremony, and a great many men had the *entrée* of that pleasant circle. The married daughters were agreeable, though not extraordinary women. Their husbands were sensible and intelligent men. Mr. Bradshaw himself was exceedingly hospitable, and he had a wide connection with the world. There were not many evenings in the week when the chandelier in their drawing-room was not lighted and when Isabel was not assisted by one or more of her sisters in entertaining visitors. On Sunday evenings, which a lover usually considers as a time when he is entitled to exclusive consideration from his *fiancée*, the whole family were assembled; and although Isabel's engagement was known to everybody, and the men who had fluttered around her so long ought to have accepted the inevitable, they did not seem to have done so. They were there as much as ever, and as much as ever they addressed to Isabel their vapid compliments and silly flatteries.

Mrs. Henshaw may have been a little uncharitable, but there was a general truth in her remark, that when a girl has lived for years on incense offered to her by a miscellaneous crowd of admirers she is not very likely to have deep feelings. Isabel certainly liked to be admired, but it would not be just to say that she lived on incense. It must not be concluded that she was a heartless girl, although it might be a question whether she entirely understood herself. Harry was not of a jealous disposition. Isabel had accepted his love and had promised to give him hers. This was a great thing. She had, so he reflected, been very generous in thus promptly meeting his passionate appeal to her. He must not expect too much,—he must not be selfish,—she could not at once give to him the exclusive devotion that he craved. She must continue to fill in her father's house the position she had so long occupied as its ornament and pride until she became his wife. Still, it was annoying to have things go on very much as before. It provoked him to find that the grimacing Frenchman and the solemn, sentimental Spaniard were always in the way. Even the cautious mathematician and the mercantile friend of Isabel's brothers-in-law, who ought to have known better, did not seem to have left off calculating that this engagement might not end in marriage. Nothing, however, occurred to shake Harry's confidence in Isabel's fidelity. If he compared himself with any of these men, he rejected with scorn the idea that any of them could supplant him.

It may be that the French system of matrimonial alliances as it existed, at least under the *ancien régime,* is better than our practice of leaving girls to themselves. I have read a beautiful revelation of those French manners in some memoirs privately printed by the La Fayette family, in which it is told how the aristocratic and religious Duchesse d'Ayen selected the young marquis to be the husband of her youngest daughter, when they were both very youthful; how the treaty between the two families was conducted and concluded; how the marquis had the first interview with the blushing girl; how he was sometimes allowed to walk with her in the garden of the old hotel in the Faubourg de St. Germain; how delightfully it all turned out, and what a wise, devoted, and heroic wife that girl became.

Perhaps the German system of a formal and somewhat public betrothal is a very good one. American girls of all ages are too often allowed to associate with all sorts of fellows. Even when there has been no laxity of parental watchfulness it is perhaps suddenly found, to the horror of every one, that a daughter, reared with all the benefit of mere mental education, and who is naturally refined, is desperately in love with a coachman. When an engagement, apparently suitable in all respects, has been formed with the parents' consent, it is not always considered a very heinous thing to break it. I am not disposed to say that the freedom allowed to our girls does not, on the whole, lead to as many good marriages as bad ones; but happiness or unhappiness, success or miserable failure, in such connections, depends, when there are living parents, very much upon the way in which they have watched over and formed the characters of their daughters. In justice, however, to those parents who have neglected no duty and have yet had to find that their daughter has set her heart upon a boor, it must be allowed that it is not always possible to prevent such misfortunes.

Titania, entreating Bottom, pours out to him the delusions of her disordered fancy:

> "Come, sit thee down upon this flowery bed,
>   While I thy amiable cheeks do coy,
> And stick musk-roses in thy sleek smooth head,
>   And kiss thy fair large ears, my gentle joy."

And then, when she is touched by the potent herb which removes

> "This hateful imperfection of her eyes,"

comes the shameful confession,—

> "Methought I was enamoured of an ass."

Oh, Shakespeare, great master of all the passions, who gave you your marvellous insight, your delicate satire upon human nature? Your little Titania's folly has been enacted over and over again, and will be to the end of time, if women shall so long be subject to the dotage of their imaginations. How often have I seen a sweet and lovely girl kiss the fair, large ears of some egregious donkey, and, alas! the awakening herb, that came seasonably to the Fairy Queen, has come to the human maiden much too late!

Ladies, you must excuse my moralizing. I am an old man, and perhaps I have rather a propensity to look on the serious side of life. I promise you this shall be my last digression, if you will follow to the end the fortunes of two people who were very dear to me.

Mrs. Bradshaw was a good mother, but she was a weak one. She was born in what we sometimes call humble life. Her parents were poor, but very respectable people; she had a common-school education, and was married young. Her husband's remarkable prosperity gave her the means of acquiring the manners of a lady, and she was a woman of delicate feelings. Wealth and luxury, however, do not always bring every kind of wisdom or very enlarged perceptions. Mr. Bradshaw's success in life made him a model merchant. He was an open-hearted and open-handed man, and he had a certain shrewd knowledge of human nature in general. He did not, however, understand how necessary it is to adapt the training of children to their natural dispositions and qualities. He considered it his duty to afford to all his daughters equal advantages of education, and he left the rest to his wife, who was not sufficiently sensible of the difference between Isabel and her sisters. They had none of her fascinations or her power over the feelings of the other sex from their early youth. They were good, sensible, domestic characters, and they married well and happily. Isabel was a girl who needed restraints which her sisters did not, and her mother had never taught her how to regulate her own heart.

Five weeks passed away, in which Harry had nothing to mar his happiness but the trifling annoyances which he endeavored to disregard, while Isabel was all sweetness and tranquillity. At the end of those weeks it became necessary for him to go away from Boston for some time, to attend to an important matter of business in a distant part of the country. When he parted from Isabel there were, of course, mutual promises of writing every day. Harry, I need not say, did his part towards justifying the worthy post-mistress's observation in the "Antiquary :" " 'A great advantage to the revenue o' the post-office,' said Mrs. Mailsetter, 'these love-letters.'" Isabel wrote three times, and Harry showed me the letters when, in the confidence of our long friendship, it became right to do so. They did not evince a great exuberance of affection. Some women do not at first write good love-letters, and some never do, either before or after marriage. Perhaps it is maidenly reserve that prevents them before marriage from expressing on paper all that they feel; and the letters of a wife to a husband are often taken up with mere domestic details. No shade of doubt crossed Harry's mind while he was absent. He excused to himself Isabel's omissions by the probable demands upon her time.

On his return, late in an afternoon, as soon as he could make a brief report to Mr. Dana that he had successfully accomplished what he went for, he flew to the Bradshaws'. Isabel was at home, but she did not come down until some time after the servant had informed her that Mr. Brewster was in the little parlor. When she entered the room he sprang to meet her and to fold her in his arms. She took two or three steps from the door, and then, without a word of greeting, and with her eyes cast down, she stood motionless as a statue. Harry was frightened. She looked so vacant, as if she did not know him, as if consciousness and recollection had gone out of her. He closed the door, and, taking her by the hand, he led her gently to a sofa, as one would lead a beloved person whose mind had gone astray. He sat at her feet, and, holding both of her hands in his own, tried to look into her eyes. She averted them from his gaze. She did not appear to be ill. She was radiantly beautiful, but oh, how changed!

"Good heavens, Isabel!" he exclaimed, "what is the matter? Why do you not look at me? Why do you not speak to me?"

There was no answer. After a long silence, her hands passively remaining in his, without the slightest return of his fond pressure, he said, "Isabel, have your feelings changed? Strange question for me to have to ask you,—do you love me?"

Her eyes closed,—her lips faltered out, "I do not know."

"You do not know! Did you know whether you loved me when we plighted our hearts to each other and your father gave you to me with his blessing? Did you know whether you loved me when you gave me that parting kiss three weeks ago, and promised to write to me every day? What has happened? Has any malicious tongue been busy with my name? Isabel, this is a solemn moment for both of us. Our lives are this instant turning on your answer to my question,—*do you love me?*"

Mournfully, and with a hollow sound, the same words were repeated, "*I do not know!*"

Harry rushed from the house and shut himself up in his room. He walked the floor through nearly the whole night, trying to find some solution of Isabel's strange conduct. Might it be that she was acting a ruse, and that when she had played it out she would burst upon him with more fondness than she had ever shown? It was a terribly serious piece of pleasantry, if that was the meaning of it. That answer, "I do not know,"—what did it mean? If it had been given when he first declared to her his love, he would have known what it meant. What did it mean now? Did it mean that she wished him to release her from the engagement? Who could tell?

At an early hour in the morning he sent for me. I had known him since we were little boys. I had known Isabel much longer than he had. I had often lamented the kind of life she had led so long, but when she became engaged to Harry, I thought, as 'all her best friends did, that she was now to escape from its ill effects. After listening to what he had to tell me, I was much troubled what to say to him. It was a serious situation for me to have to advise him, for I was not above three years older than he, though I had seen rather more of the world. I soon satisfied myself that it was not jealousy that was tormenting him, for, on my alluding to the continued attentions from other men which Isabel seemed to permit, his lip curled with disdain as he answered, "No, Peter, Isabel is not a fool. You cannot suppose that she—— Bah! let us think of something else." I could think of nothing that would explain the mystery. I could only advise him to seek a conversation with Mrs. Bradshaw and her eldest daughter, Mrs. Perkins, as soon as possible. I knew Mrs. Perkins very well, and I offered to call at her house and request her to be at her mother's that afternoon. She consented, and Harry, as I learned afterwards, had the interview with the two ladies which I suggested. They were both very fond of him, and it was a painful subject. They said they had all noticed a great change in Isabel, but they knew no cause for it. They did not believe that she had given to another what belonged to him,—that was impossible.

"My dear Henry," said Mrs. Perkins, "wait a few days. Something may occur that will reveal the cause for this change in Isabel, if her feelings towards you have changed, or else you will know what you ought to do."

At this point in the conversation Mr. Bradshaw came in. He, too, had noticed that Isabel, when there was no one but the family present, was *distrait*, moody, and irritable. He did not understand it. "She has always been like a ray of sunshine," he said. "I never before knew her to be inconsiderate of the feelings of any one who had a right to her attention. Wait awhile, Henry. This may blow over. Stay to tea, and appear to be as little concerned as you can. Fanny, send for Mr. Per-

kins to come and help us through the evening. Give
orders, my dear, that the drawing-room is not to be
open and that we are not receiving."

Mrs. Bradshaw did as her husband desired. Harry
remained to tea. Mr. Perkins came, and before tea
was announced his wife managed to let him know why
he had been sent for. Isabel was at the tea-table, silent,
listless. She never once looked at Harry. Mr. Perkins
did his best to keep up conversation, trying to make
Harry talk about his journey. Mr. Bradshaw said very
little. Mrs. Bradshaw could scarcely conceal her grief.
Mrs. Perkins's thoughts ran quickly forward to the
consequences of a broken engagement. She was a
woman of high principle, and she foresaw the censure
with which Isabel would be visited if this was to be
the end. But if the engagement was to be broken,
how was the breach to be brought about and how was
it to be made known?

When they rose from the tea-table Harry left the
house without attempting to speak to Isabel. He
excused himself to Mrs. Bradshaw, who was, for the
first time since she had known him, not sorry to have
him say good-night. As he was passing Mrs. Perkins
she held out her hand to him and whispered, "Do
nothing hastily. You know what we feel for you."

You think that I ought to have some explanation of
Isabel's conduct ready to be produced. I am obliged
to tell you that I have none. I never understood it,
and I never heard that any one else knew how to
explain it. I can only say that I have known love to
die; sometimes it has died slowly and lingeringly, sometimes suddenly. Did Isabella Bradshaw's love die, or
did it never live? I would tell if I knew, but I do not.
I know that the little god who shot his arrow into
Henry Brewster's heart seemed for a time to be a very
strong cherub with an immortal life.

Harry had been treated so kindly by the Bradshaw
family, he was so much on the footing of a son, Mr.
Bradshaw was so proud of him, that he could not at
once leave off going to the house. But what was he
to do? He could do nothing but put himself for a few

days longer in Isabel's way, so that she might manifest some desire to explain her conduct. He was every evening at the house for just three days more, but Isabel never spoke to him. What could be the meaning of this? Did she consider that after that answer —" I do not know"—it was for him to release her from their engagement? Did she wish to be released? Who could tell? Her father, according to his resolute character, deeply grieved as he was, seeing that she made no sign of any wish to explain herself to Harry, took matters into his own hands. He told Harry that he considered Isabel's conduct as perfectly incomprehensible, but he did not think that, after what had occurred, the engagement should continue another day. " I part from you," he said, " with great sorrow, but I feel bound to say to you that I do not believe Isabel loves you. I am in need of your pardon for having permitted myself to believe that she did. But I think you will understand how a father should have allowed his hopes for his child to become a belief."

This was almost too much for poor Harry. It added to the bitterness of the dreadful discovery. But had there been a discovery? "The point of honor, sir, is easily solved," he said, with deep emotion ; " I can with propriety be the one to say this engagement is broken ; but is it your opinion that I ought to wait no further developments, that no more time should be allowed for Isabel to assign some reason——" He could not go on. Hope was struggling against pride.

" I must counsel you," said the distressed father, "as I would if you were my son and Isabel were not my daughter. I will not have you degraded, and any young man in your situation may seem degraded if he has to bear such treatment from the woman who has exchanged her vows for his without any explanation or one word of regret. I do not see any prospect that the explanation will come. If you consent, I shall say to Isabel that this engagement is ended, and shall make known that it is so, as far as may be necessary."

Ah, what disaster is there in life that can equal this? To have loved, deeply, passionately ; to have trusted ;

to have had every reason for that trust; to have the cup of happiness dashed suddenly to the ground, and to know no reason why this blank in one's existence has come,—this is a fate that may darken the soul more fearfully than all other calamities. I should, however, fail to give a right idea of my early friend if I did not enable you to see that, while he was a person who would suffer to the point of extreme danger, he was yet a man of sufficient strength not to be utterly ruined. What he had to do was to determine whether he could remain in Boston and be pointed at as the young fellow who had been jilted by a girl of whom rather more than half of society had made very unfavorable prognostications, or whether he should go away. Whether he remained or went, he would be talked about for a long time. He had the sensitiveness that belongs to proud and lofty natures, whose feelings are deep and serious. Since he had become engaged to Isabel his circle of acquaintance had been much increased. There had been some dinner-parties made expressly for them, and in all the houses where he had visited he had been very much liked. He could not endure to be compassionated by people who would mean to be kind, or to be laughed at by people who, if not malicious, would be flippant and careless. He must go away and make for himself such new and less miserable existence as might come to him elsewhere. It would be better, too, for Isabel, if he were where they could not possibly meet. To meet as strangers or common acquaintances was a thought that he could not bear. Harry's resolution was soon taken. But he could not leave Mr. Dana without some explanation, or without closing the part of their joint business in which he had been so useful. When he had mentioned his purpose and asked to have a time fixed for dissolving their connection, Mr. Dana said, " I feel for you most sincerely, but there are as good fish in the sea as ever were caught. Give yourself time, my young friend; the wound that is now so painful will be healed."

I am sure no one will dispute the truth of that famous saying, which is always offered as consolation in sorrows of this kind. No one ever drew, by line or net, from the vast ocean in which disport the innumerable inhabitants of the deep, a single specimen that did not leave millions of its peers in all the qualities and beauties of its most perfect individuals. What is one woman, be she as beautiful and lovely as a woman can be, to the great multitude of those in whom can at least be found that which will take the place of what has been lost? Yet, what young man of Harry Brewster's moral fibre ever suffered, as he now had to suffer, who could, in the midst of his desolation, think of a possible substitute? If there comes a time when there can be a second love, it is not until the whole man is so changed that he scarcely knows his former self, and even then, as I have said, there does not come the same supreme felicity.

Harry convinced his kind friend and partner that it was best for him to go away. He asked and received Mr. Dana's promise not to inquire of him his destination. In fact, he did not know where he should finally find an abiding-place. He meant to seek one in the great West. He could tell Mr. Dana nothing more. It was arranged between them that if Mr. Bradshaw asked any questions, Mr. Dana should be able to say that he knew nothing excepting that Harry had not left his country. There was the same understanding with me. Mr. Dana made all the business arrangements that were necessary. Harry owed no debts that could not be at once discharged, and when he parted from Mr. Dana that gentleman placed in his hands a sum of money that fairly represented his earnings, and which would pay the expenses of his journey and maintain him for some time. He did not see Mr. Bradshaw again before his departure. I was the only one of his friends who saw him take the train on the railroad which then extended no farther than Worcester. The rest of his journey would have to be made to Albany or beyond by stage-coach.

He could not go away without bidding Mrs. Perkins farewell. He was calm, collected, not excited at all, when he told her that he should, in all probability, never see her again.

"Henry," she said, "we have all become attached to you. My heart is almost broken. I shall never forget you, never cease to pray for your welfare. You have had my entire confidence,—my husband's, too."

She stopped, for her tears would not let her go on. She regained her composure after a little while, and then said, "My father told me what he had determined about the engagement, but he did not tell me that you mean to leave Boston. Is this necessary?"

"Yes, Fanny, it is. I have made known my intention to no one but Mr. Dana, Peter Boylston, and yourself. None of you, I hope, will try to learn anything about me. It is best—it is best—it will be better for Isabel that I shall be henceforth unknown."

"Will you not see my mother, Henry?"

"No, I think not. I know how she feels towards me. I am very grateful to her, to you all, but I will not try her maternal heart. She will have much to do for——" He could not go on. He did not mean to break down if he could help it.

Mrs. Perkins followed him to the outer door: "Farewell, farewell, dear Henry; I cannot promise you that I shall not try to learn about you. I shall expect to hear that you have made for yourself a name and a life. A young man of your powers and your character is not going to be destroyed by one sorrow, great as it may be. You have one consolation, at least, for you have nothing to reproach yourself with,—nothing whatever."

A woman's instinct in such cases is much finer than a man's. Mrs. Perkins did not remind Henry that the world is full of lovely girls, or repeat to him any of the wise sayings that are usually quoted in such cases. It soothed his proud heart to have the sympathy of such a woman. But, ah! where was she who ought to have thrown herself at his feet and implored his forgiveness? Had he done right in leaving her without making one more effort to unseal her lips before it should be known that they were forever separated? It was a terrible struggle; I could see it as I watched him in the few last hours before he departed on his unknown way. He sternly put down every doubt, and went, as he had determined to go, without seeing Isabel again. When the gulf had come between them they would meet, if they met at all, as strangers. Did you ever see a husband and wife who had been divorced unexpectedly find themselves in each other's presence? I once knew a gentleman, who was in that situation, accidentally enter a room where his former wife was sitting alone, waiting for a friend. I heard that there was a bow, a formal conversation, an attempt to talk about the weather, the opera, etc., and that, after an effort to endure the strain, the poor lady fell to the floor in a fainting fit. The gentleman had to ring the bell, call for assistance, and explain his presence. It has always seemed to me that the situation of divorced persons, where there has been no serious criminality on either side, is most deplorable.

Do not say that Brewster was too proud—that he was weak—in taking so seriously such a termination of such a happiness. He was a man of deep feelings, tender sensibilities, and a just self-respect. Do not these traits explain it all? Perhaps there ought to be some power—some *Deus ex machina*—to interpose and reconcile all lovers' quarrels. But there are cases where Cupid, who has brought the parties together, seems powerless to prevent a separation. What was the secret cause of Isabel's conduct? I have already said that I do not know,—that she alone could tell, and that she did not choose to do so.

At first, Henry thought of changing his name. But he rejected this plan as unmanly and as disloyal to his dead parents and his living sister. The latter he tried to write to, but he thought it best to visit her at Troy, and to tell her in person his melancholy story. I shall follow him no farther in his wanderings than the interview with her whose love and sympathy seemed to him to be all that now remained to him in the world. But before they meet I must tell you something about Elizabeth Brewster.

At the time of Harry's unfortunate love-affair his sister Elizabeth was at the age of thirty-five. We, who were so much younger, had, from our boyhood or girlhood, always regarded her as one of the most admirable women that ever lived. Whatever Miss Brewster said or did was with good reason accepted as absolutely right in the little world of our native town. I have now lived a long life, and have had much intercourse with superior men and women; but I have never known a woman who was so wise as Elizabeth Brewster and who was at the same time so gentle. In her young days she had profited greatly by her father's scholarship; and when he had pupils, as he often did, her knowledge of Greek and Latin and some of the sciences enabled her to be of great service to him. Boys who were fitted for college at Dr. Brewster's always passed good examinations, and they owed it to his daughter that they did so. Nor were her more strictly feminine accomplishments less remarkable than her learning. It often happens that learned women are not gifted with the power to be useful in household affairs, or do not have taste for them if they have the capacity. Miss Brewster was as good a housekeeper as she could have been if she had never read a line of Homer or Virgil, or explained a problem in Euclid. But there was an occurrence in her life which made her, to all her friends and to many who knew her only by repute, the object of an interest almost amounting to veneration. At the age of twenty she became engaged to be married to a young man of the most extraordinary promise, of whose career the highest hopes and expectations had been formed, and whose early death continued for a full generation to be one of the saddest of the memories that clustered around old Harvard. Among that generation this lady's name was never mentioned without being coupled with that of the brilliant lover whom she had lost. Her life was saddened, but it was not darkened. She lived for others after he who had been taken from her and from the world was no more. In person, Miss Brewster was tall and graceful. She had not been accounted beautiful, in the way that beauty is most often spoken of, but her features were regular and her countenance was one of great sweetness and marked intelligence. This is often the most lasting kind of beauty, and it continued with Elizabeth Brewster to the end of her days.

When Harry had given to his sister an outline of his story, she did not try to console him with the commonplaces usually uttered to young men in such unfortunate circumstances. She knew his nature too well, and she was too correct in her judgments, to imagine that she could do him any good by leading him to think that in the almost infinite chances of life he would meet with some other woman whom he could love. Sympathy, silent sympathy, or that which is not often spoken, and a helping hand, she thought the best medicines for such a malady. The first thing she said to him relieved him on a point about which he had almost feared to ask her.

"I will come to you, dear," she said, "whenever you inform me that you are settled, and we will live together. I can in the mean time arrange to give up my situation here. We two are very much alone in the world, and we must never again be separated. But you will find, Henry, that occupation, occupation as soon as you can get it, is your greatest want, and will be your greatest help. Lose no more time in making a selection of a place of abode than is necessary to make it safely. I do not believe that it is of much consequence whether it is a large or a small community. The thing for you to do is to place yourself where you can at once find work in your profession."

Harry endeavored to talk about Isabel, and he was beginning to ask his sister if she thought he had done right in leaving her, and whether she could see any explanation of such an inconsistency as a whole month or more of devoted love and then the sudden and extraordinary change.

"Having never seen Miss Bradshaw," she answered, "I can form no opinion of the cause or the process of such a change. But, my dear brother, why distress yourself with asking whether you could have done anything to discover what is so mysterious? It is best for you that it should remain a mystery. If you should reach something that appears to you to be an explana-

tion, you would find no comfort in it. Possibly, her
father hit the truth,—that she did not love you. If so,
her fault was that she did not tell you so until it was
too late."

Miss Brewster could not bear to speak more plainly
of the wrong which Isabel had committed. Harry's
love was not yet dead; his sister saw the struggle.

"But, Elizabeth," he said, "she had given me every
proof of her love that a woman could give. Her father
was in error if he meant to say that she never had
loved me. I should as soon doubt my existence. Isabel
never meant to deceive me; I do not believe she deceived herself. She certainly did love me, but she suddenly ceased to feel as she had done, and I am without
any means of knowing why."

"Let it rest so," Miss Brewster said. "You can do
yourself no good by trying to understand it. You can
never marry her. Whether your supposition is correct
or her father's is the right one, you two can never
meet again. There would be nothing to build upon.
But let us talk no more about what is inexplicable.
I will only say that my own experience teaches me that
I can help you. The full fruition of my love in this
life was denied to me by an all-wise God. I look for a
reunion beyond the grave. I can therefore think of
my loss without repining. You have not this consolation; and therefore you should brace yourself for the
duties of life, thinking as little as you can of your loss,
and lay yourself open to everything that my sympathies and services can do for you. They will never be
wanting while I live."

Harry pressed her to his bosom, and gratefully
promised to obey her. The light of a wisdom that
rarely erred, of a sister's love that knows no variance,
and a hope which came from a steady faith that whatever is is best for us, shone from her gentle eyes as she
bade him farewell.

And now he goes forth alone towards the boundless
West, to discover some resting-place, where he can find
both rest and work. I shall not describe his wanderings. In those days it was not so difficult as it would

be now for a man to travel through this great country unobserved and without having his movements reported or traced by any one who wished to look him up. Harry's name must be on hotel registers, it is true; but the newspaper press was not what it is now. In Boston, although this extraordinary termination of his engagement continued to be talked of for a long time, and people wondered what had become of him, the newspapers did not refer to it. Mr. Bradshaw was not waited upon by reporters and plied with impertinent questions about his family affairs. He was informed by me in general terms that Harry had gone to the West, and that he relied on the honor of Mr. Dana and myself to say nothing more on the subject, and not to endeavor to discover his whereabouts. Mr. Bradshaw said that he was glad Harry had not left the country. "Talent," he added, "industry, and character will make their way." So it happened that Harry's wish not to be traced suffered no disappointment; and now we will leave him in that weary search.

"Oh, birds from out the East, oh, birds from out the West,
　Have you found that happy city in all your weary quest?
　Tell me, tell me from earth's wand'ring may the heart find
　　glad surcease?
　Can ye show me as an earnest any olive-branch of peace?
　I am weary of life's travels, its sin and toil and care,
　I am faithless, crushing in my heart so many a fruitless prayer."

And how was it with Isabel? Did she droop, and pine, and mourn, and reflect? Had she no hours of self-accusation, and did she make no efforts to learn what had become of Harry? Did she think of him as a worn and weary wanderer, the light of his life extinguished, his heart yearning for what she had once given him so freely, his voice calling to her in the night, "Isabel, oh, Isabel, why have you done this?" She did not know of the strength that a sister's love had awakened in him. If she thought of him at all, she ought to have pictured to herself his despair and desolation.

I did not see her for a long time after his departure. She could have no means of learning anything about him excepting from me, and I did not choose to have her ask me a question, even if she had the wish or the fortitude to ask it. But I did not cease to think of this strange episode in the life of my early friend, who deserved, if ever a man deserved, all the happiness that for a short time he believed he had found, and that promised to be as enduring as his life. At the end of six months after Harry had left Boston, I called again at the Bradshaws' several times. There now lies before me a letter that I then wrote to the dear girl who in our native village was making up her father's accounts and endeavoring to ascertain which of his patients, at the end of the half-year then expiring, would do by him as they would be done by. He had done a great deal for them, and generally with the best results. I have her answer, too; and I shall make an extract from both letters.

"Although you never saw Miss Isabel Bradshaw, your woman's instinct will perhaps be able to suggest some explanation of her conduct to Harry. I have written to you before full details of his courtship, their engagement, its happiness for both of them through a period of nearly five weeks, and its sudden end. What I told you about her demeanor when Harry returned after an absence of about ten days I had from himself. Now, tell me what you think of the whole affair. Having lately learned that Isabel had resumed her old life, and was again surrounded by admirers, I have been several times at the Bradshaws' in the evening. She avoids any separate conversation with me. She is polite, but does not seem to wish to talk to me. To other men she is rather bitter and sarcastic. I cannot divine what will become of her. She is as beautiful as ever. I believe she does not go out much, but she sees as many gentlemen as she ever did. I wish it were possible to do something for her. She has many excellent qualities, really good traits of character, as well as the gift of great beauty and fine intelligence. She is more of a puzzle to me than ever."

"I am not surprised, my dear Peter, by what you tell me about Miss Bradshaw. But as to understanding such a girl,—one, too, whom I never saw,—I should as soon think, to borrow a phrase from my father's vocabulary, of making a diagnosis of a disorder of a very uncommon kind without seeing the patient. The details of the case that you gave me when it occurred do not help me at all. But I will drop the 'shop' and come to the psychology of this case of your fair friend. The question whether she ever loved Henry Brewster, or how her conduct is to be explained, supposing either that she did or did not love him, makes two problems that no other woman's feminine instinct, as you call it, will be likely to solve. Miss Bradshaw herself could solve both of them if she chose, but it seems she does not choose. I advise you not to speculate about it any more. She will probably make an unfortunate marriage, and be a miserable woman. Her life must be embittered by the memory of what she has lost and what she has done. In regard to your visits there, I am not a bit afraid of your becoming too much interested in her. If it affords you any amusement to see how she goes on, you have my free permission to go there as much as you like. I am afraid that you do not give yourself too much amusement of any kind. But I am quite sure that you can do her no good, or exercise any influence over her fate. I feel very sorry for her, because I trust your judgment that she has good qualities as well as extraordinary attractions. When are you coming to see me? Your new slippers are nearly done, but I am half inclined to make you come for them for yourself, and not to send them."

I had, even at this early period, formed the habit of acting on the advice of the writer of the last extract, and have followed it all my life since, in great and little matters, without finding myself misled. I gave up the idea of doing Isabel any good, but I did not cease to learn everything about her that I could. I am able, therefore, to continue the narrative of her life, and to give a correct account of the marriage that she really did make not long after I received the letter last quoted.

CHAPTER IV.

A SUDDEN MARRIAGE.

ABOUT seven or eight months after Henry Brewster disappeared from Boston there was left one day at Mr. Bradshaw's house a card which bore the name "Lionel Gascoigne, F. O." On the corner was pencilled "Tremont House." A letter of introduction accompanied the card, addressed to Mr. Bradshaw by one of his New York correspondents, informing him that the bearer was an English gentleman who had lately been in Washington on some diplomatic business, and asking for him Mr. Bradshaw's well-known hospitality. The writer of the letter also addressed a note to Mr. Bradshaw by the mail, informing him that Mr. Gascoigne belonged to a very old family, and that his father was an earl. It was understood in New York that he was not the eldest son.

The occasion of this young Englishman's visit to America is easily explained. The British government of that time wished to communicate with their minister in Washington by a special messenger, who could explain orally some things about which they did not wish to leave a record in despatches that might be called for in Parliament. It was an errand that required a person who had been for some time in the Foreign Office, and Gascoigne was selected from among the junior clerks as the one best fitted for the service. After he had completed the business for which he came to Washington he visited some of our principal cities, and was well received in their social circles. He had heard a good deal about the beauty of American women before he left England; and as he was unmarried and had likewise heard something of the liberality of rich American fathers, he very naturally thought it might be a good thing to carry home some American girl on whom paternal liberality would perhaps be exercised.

It must not be inferred, however, that he was a fortune-hunter. He merely thought that if he were to meet and fall in love with some girl who might be disposed to marry him, it would not be a bad thing if her father had money or if she had some in her own right. What he had to offer may be summed up in good looks, after the English type, manners which evinced good breeding of the British stamp, a fair prospect of official promotion, and his very ancient birth. He had not found the object of his search—perhaps it is hardly fair to say that he was engaged in a search—when, after visiting Niagara, he came to Boston, which he had been told was the most English of all the American cities, and which he very properly wished to see.

Mr. Bradshaw, on calling upon this stranger, found a young man of eight-and-twenty or thereabouts, who was what I have sufficiently described, and was probably a good specimen of a class of young Englishmen put into official life through family influence. Bradshaw was not a man who cared about birth; and when, according to his invariable custom, he invited this gentleman to his house, he was not thinking of providing his daughter with a successor to poor Harry. Isabel, it is true, was again at home to all visitors; but her father did not suppose that she would ever marry a foreigner, and he hoped that she would not be in a hurry to marry at all. But he did not know much about his daughter's state of mind, and her mother was still less able to understand it. For my part, I think it would have been well if Isabel had been induced to retire from all society for quite a good period of rest and reflection. She did not understand herself. Many girls do not who have led the kind of life which she had since she was eighteen. She knew too well her power over the feelings of the other sex, but, excepting in the case of Henry Brewster, it had been wasted upon men who were none of them her equals intellectually, and for none of whom did she ever care. But a long series of successive flirtations, or a concurrent series of such affairs, is very apt to make a girl ignorant of herself. When Isabel had so unaccountably made Harry believe that she did not love him, the natural solution of her conduct that would have occurred to most persons would have been that she did not know her own mind. After Harry had gone from her forever, if she could have had a good period of rest from every kind of excitement, she might have met with some man of her own country who was superior to her old admirers, and have married him for reasons different from those which led her to accept Lionel Gascoigne after a short acquaintance, if not for better ones. She was young enough to wait and to make for herself a new and a better life. But she gave herself no interval such as she needed. The brief season of despair which followed her conviction that Harry was lost to her—a despair produced by his evident determination to make it impossible for her to let him know that she was ready to humble herself before him if she could win his forgiveness—was succeeded by speculation on what she had better do and a survey of every man who approached her. She could not bear the reproach of society, although it was a silent reproach, for her conduct to Harry. She lived in constant, although unspoken, reproof from her whole family. There was no one capable of both advising and consoling her. When Gascoigne appeared and she found him amiable and agreeable, and learned that he was highly connected and had a career before him in his own country, and then that he was in love with her, she accepted him,— I own this as my belief, but I own it reluctantly,— because he would take her away from Boston. She was willing to trust her own capacity to find in his love a substitute for the one that she had squandered; and I fear this was all the answer she could make to herself, if she ever asked herself whether she could be such a wife as a well-meaning and really good fellow ought to have who offered to her a great deal of honest affection. She took a fearful risk, for it was possible that she and Henry Brewster might meet somewhere in this wide world, and that she might not be able to control herself.

In this mood, after matters between Lionel and her-

self had been arranged, she sought a conversation with
her father, who she well knew felt deeply the disappointment that she had caused him. She wished to
prepare him for Gascoigne's formal application, by telling him just how she felt. " I know, sir," she began,
" that you were angry with me, perhaps you are still,
—because I did not marry—Henry Brewster." She
hesitated, blushed, and trembled when she pronounced
the name, which she could not do without emotion.
Her father did not speak. After a little while she recovered herself and went on: " All that, my dear sir,.
is now over. We none of us know what has become
of Mr. Brewster. He has taken the most effectual
means to make it impossible for me to seek his forgiveness, if I wished to do so. I have made up my mind
to marry Mr. Gascoigne, and have promised to do so
if you will give your consent when he asks for it."

Her father looked at her, tenderly, mournfully. She
sat perfectly still, as if she expected his assent. At
length, speaking very slowly, he said, " My child, you
are old enough to fix your own lot in life, but have you
considered what it will be to leave your country and
the home of your childhood and go among strangers?
I will not say a word about the past,—I try not to
think of it,—I agree with you that Brewster is lost to
you and to all of us. But do you know that this young
Englishman can place you in a position where you can
be happy,—can give you the comforts that you have
been accustomed to? Do you know the difference between an American and an English husband? Look
at your sisters, and say if it is likely that any foreigner
could have been to either of them what her husband
is and what every American woman expects in a husband. What do you know about English aristocratic
life, supposing that these Gascoignes are the best of
their class? Can any other country on earth be to
you what ours is? Do you expect me to show that I
especially value such a connection ?"

" I know," said Isabel, " hardly anything about English life in any class but what I have read in books, and
perhaps they are not to be trusted. But if I am con-

vinced that Mr. Gascoigne loves me, it must depend on myself whether I can be happy as his wife. I do not see that a woman's lot in life ought to be governed by patriotic feelings."

"Perhaps not," her father replied, "but a difference of manners, of modes of life, of the structure of society,—above all, the domestic relations of husbands and wives,—are things of great consequence to any woman who is asked to leave her own land, and especially to every American woman who has been reared as you have. I make no question that Englishmen of good feelings and good principles are good husbands to English wives. But I have great doubts about their being the best husbands for American women like you."

Mr. Bradshaw must be excused for his intense Americanism. It was the strong point of his character.

"I have already considered," said Isabel, "nearly all that you have suggested, but, of course, your greater knowledge of the world and my duty to so kind and indulgent a father as you have always been to me and to all of us ought to make me very careful in what I do. But I must tell you that I am willing to take my chance in forming this connection. I am confident Mr. Gascoigne does not wish to marry me for the sake of your money, although you are known to be a rich man. He is not mercenary, and I do not expect or wish you to do anything to show that you particularly value such a connection. I can say to you what I could not say to any one else. I believe that I have always been thought to have some good looks. I ought to believe,—and it is not vanity, or, if it is, I cannot help it,— I can believe that his regard for me has been influenced by what he considers my beauty, and other things that he thinks he has found in me. I shall not ask you for money to compensate him for the love that he proffers me, and that I believe he feels. I only wish you to give your consent to my marrying him, if he asks for it."

"I am at least pleased, Isabel, that you do not propose to compensate him in dollars and cents for his love.

But people cannot live in this world without money, as no one knows better than you do. You have always had enough of it. But I will be frank and exact with you. What is his salary in his present position?"

"He has told me that it is three hundred and fifty pounds only, but that he is in the line of promotion."

"Three hundred and fifty pounds is not much of an income for an English gentleman to marry an American wife on, is it?"

"My dear father, I cannot discuss these money matters. Spare me, I beg of you."

"I will, my child. I will give you an income of the same amount as his salary; it shall be paid regularly every quarter, and it shall always be kept equal to his pay, if he rises to the best-paid post in the queen's dominions. James Bradshaw's word is as good as his bond, and I believe he never gave either for what he could not pay. Mr. Gascoigne can come to see me whenever he likes, and I shall say to him just what I have said to you. Your mother will attend to your outfit, and the marriage can take place whenever you choose."

Mr. Bradshaw, in a very characteristic way, brought this conversation to a somewhat abrupt and business-like termination, because he saw that Isabel's mind was made up, and that he must let her shape her own lot, as she said and he hoped that she could do. He had great affection for her, but she had grievously disappointed him. I fear that he did not confess to himself that it was largely his own fault that a child of such gifts had not been better taught how to use the power that they gave her. There are such fathers, and very good ones too; men who think it sufficient to give all their children alike the same advantages, but who do not take proper account of the differences in their characters. His other daughters were not brilliant or fascinating, as Isabel was. They were rather commonplace, good women. They never needed the restraints that she did. They were excellent domestic characters from their girlhood. She was a girl who required a tighter rein.

The marriage took place soon after the engagement, because Gascoigne's leave of absence was about expiring, although it had been extended a month on account of the connection he had formed. Isabel might, some people thought, have required him to go home and return for her. But this was her affair and not the concern of the neighbors.

Mrs. Bradshaw spent a great deal of money on Isabel's trousseau, for which all the arts of dress-making and millinery in Boston and New York were drawn upon. There were rich wedding-presents, but the press did not give a list of them and the names of the donors, as is now the custom. They were married in Old Trinity, the church on Summer Street, which was swept away by the great fire in 1872. The company at the church was not large, because Isabel wished to have a quiet wedding. She was married in a travelling-dress. There was a breakfast at the house, after the English fashion, out of compliment to the bridegroom. He behaved in his most becoming manner, and every one was pleased with him. Mr. Bradshaw, in addition to the arrangements for Isabel's income, presented Gascoigne with a check for two thousand dollars, and put into his daughter's purse a handsome sum in American gold. I was at the breakfast, and, when all the other guests had departed, I had the honor of escorting the bride to the carriage that was to take them to the packet-ship on which they were to embark for England. Isabel took my arm, after she had bidden farewell to her family, and tripped lightly down the steps. Her husband had lingered to say a few last words to her father. At the carriage-door she turned and held out her hand to me. "Thank you," she said, "for all your kindness, for your generous forbearance. I shall not forget you. You have been a true friend, and those I never forget. I hope soon to hear that you have brought from her native home the woman who is to be your wife, and whom I ought to have known. Farewell. Be thankful, as I am, that I am off." At this moment, her maid, a buxom and nice-looking colored woman, who had been her personal attendant since she was a child, came down with her dressing-case and got into another carriage. Gascoigne gave me a hearty hand-shake, sprang to the side of his wife, the footman closed the door with a sharp click, and they were driven away. Years elapsed before I saw Isabel again.

I returned into the house after they were out of sight. The ladies of the family had gone up-stairs, to weep,—the inevitable ending of all weddings for the ladies who remain at home. Mr. Bradshaw heard my step and called to me from the little parlor to come in. "I know," he said, "what you have been thinking of all day. Can you give me any news of him ?"

"I only know, sir," I answered, "that he is settled in a Western town, and that his sister is with him."

"I am thankful," he replied, "that he has found a resting-place. Those Western towns are full of tremendous energies, and men do a great deal there in a short time. In his sister's society he will have the repose and comfort that he needs. Thank God, he has at least that blessing."

I walked to my bachelor lodgings, wondering what would be the fate of the attractive creature who had been married that morning and had gone far away into a life of which she could then know very little. I should have asked her to write to me, but I supposed that I should hear from her family some account of her reception in England, and of the new life on which she had ventured. The arrangements for my own marriage soon afterwards occupied most of my thoughts, but I did not omit to learn everything about Isabel that I could gather from her mother and sisters. She had always been an interesting study to me, and now that she had gone, I thought it highly probable that she would, as my *fiancée* predicted, become a miserable woman, or else that her character might, by some means, be very much changed. She certainly had qualities that great happiness or great adversity might develop into an admirable woman. I never lost my faith in her natural disposition. But what was to be the outcome of the risk that she took ? Whatever was the ground of her confidence in Gascoigne, there must be

many things, as her father had told her, in the situation
in which she would find herself, that would affect her
happiness besides her husband's amiable qualities and
good principles. She was going among strangers.
Who or what they might be she could not know, excepting from what her husband had told her or might
tell her on their voyage. And how could this prepare
her for what she would meet in a world of which she
had only read in books?

CHAPTER V.

A SLAVE AUCTION AND WHAT IT BROUGHT.

I MUST not let the bride and groom go away without
giving some account of Isabel's maid, for the way in
which a South Carolina slave-woman came to be in
the Bradshaw household may interest the reader. She
did not travel northward by the Underground Railroad. That institution did not exist when Dinah, at
the age of twenty, was sold at auction in Charleston;
and if it had been in operation, the girl could not have
been induced to avail herself of it. She was born, as
her parents and grandparents were, on one of the cotton plantations of a wealthy family, the heads of which
had, for generations, male and female, always been
Christian masters and mistresses, who had fulfilled their
duties to their slaves in the most exemplary manner.
Dinah was taken into the capacity of lady's-maid at a
very early age, and was thus one of the house-servants
in town and country. She lost her kind master and
mistress in her twentieth year, and, in consequence of
their deaths and of some complications in the affairs of
their estate, a portion of the negroes had to be sold.
As there was no lady among the connections of the
family who specially needed Dinah, she was included
in a list which an auctioneer in Charleston was authorized by the executors to advertise at public sale. These

servants were not unlikely to be in request, for they were known to some of the best families in the State. At the time when this event occurred—a very unusual one in the history of the Pringle property, but common enough on the breaking up of lesser estates—Mr. and Mrs. Bradshaw happened to be in Charleston. The Boston merchant had come there to attend personally to some business relating to one of his ships. He saw the advertisement describing with some particularity the person and qualities of this negro girl, and he proposed to his wife that he should buy her and take her home with them as a nurse for Isabel, who was then a delicate child, and who had never taken well to her present nurse. Mrs. Bradshaw, who had done the part of a weak mother towards spoiling Isabel, was very willing to have a servant to whom she could intrust her child with a certainty that the little girl would be indulged as she had always been. She cheerfully gave her consent to this purchase, provided she could see and talk to the negress in private. An opportunity to do this was afforded, and the result was that Mr. Bradshaw determined to attend the sale himself and buy the girl, if the price were not run up too high.

On a wooden block which rested upon the sidewalk in front of the auctioneer's store there stood a very comely negro girl, as straight as an arrow, whose figure was almost perfectly symmetrical; her hands were small, as were those of other negro girls who had never worked in the fields, but her feet were broad and flat, of the true type of her race. Save for this peculiarity of her lower extremities, she would have made in all respects an admirable model for a sculptor or painter. Her complexion was very dark, but there was a clear brown tint that took away what might have been the less attractive aspect of a perfectly black skin. Yet there was not a drop of white blood in her veins. She was in every fibre and feature a child of Africa, whose ancestors were of the Congo blood, back to the pair whom a British slave-trader had brought from Africa and landed in Carolina, when it suited the policy of our mother-country to stock the Southern colonies with a plentiful supply of slaves, and when the merchants of Liverpool and Bristol drove openly and avowedly a most profitable slave-trade. The girl had the thick lips and typical nose of her race; the whites of her eyes were in high contrast with the pupils; her teeth were regular, strong, and white; and when her pouting lips parted with a smile, there was a grin that was contagious for every one who looked upon her honest and tender countenance. The expression that comes of cultivated intelligence was not there; but there was a natural intelligence and quickness of perception. She was evidently a creature who would give her life to any one to whom she became attached, and her muscular development indicated great powers of endurance. On her woolly head she wore a cotton handkerchief of bright colors, twisted into a kind of turban. She was clothed in a calico gown. A phrenologist, if one had examined her shapely head, would have said that her "bumps" were well proportioned.

The sale was conducted with entire decency. It was evident enough that the girl was what a horse-dealer would call "sound;" and if, in other cases of the human "cattle" put up for sale, there was some examination allowed, such as would be thought fair in the case of a quadruped, this girl was too well known in the city to make it necessary to expose her to that kind of scrutiny. After the auctioneer had read the advertisement, and added that he now offered a servant who had been bred by a deceased lady who was well known and respected by every inhabitant of the city, the bidding became lively. Several ladies had asked their husbands to buy Dinah, and the agents of these gentlemen were on the ground. Dinah's bright eyes glanced anxiously from one face to another as the different bids were made, on each of which the auctioneer dwelt with his customary repetition of "going," "going." "Not half her value, gentlemen." "You must go a peg higher, sir." "It is a rare chance; going, going; who says ten more?" The girl, however, exhibited and probably felt no distress, for she knew that she must go through this, and she believed "dat de Lord" would send her a kind master or mistress. For this confidence in her fate she could have given no reason, if she had been asked for one, excepting that she had been a good girl, as her old mistress, who was now in heaven, had always said she was. She did not know what was in store for her.

The bidding had mounted to very near eight hundred dollars, when, to the surprise of the whole crowd, the Boston merchant capped it with the amount necessary to make up that sum, and the auctioneer, after trying in vain to extract another bid, knocked the chattel down to " What name, sir ?" " James Bradshaw, of Boston," said that gentleman.

Perhaps the novelty of such a purchase by a stranger and a Northern man—a purchase made in person—rather bewildered the agents who represented citizens of Charleston. But the state of things throughout the Union in regard to slavery was not then such as to give rise to anything more than a little wonder what the purchaser would do with his bargain. Bradshaw stepped into the office of the auctioneer, drew his check on a Charleston bank for the money, and received a regular bill of sale. Dinah was sent to the hotel with a note to Mrs. Bradshaw, and in due time she accompanied her new protectors to their home in Boston. After they arrived there, Mr. Bradshaw made known to Dinah that she was free by the laws of Massachusetts ; but to make his own purposes manifest, he executed proper papers to establish her freedom, and had them filed in a public office. He then made, or tried to make, her comprehend that she would be paid wages, and that one-half of her earnings would be retained to reimburse the money that had been paid for her, and the other half would be regularly paid to herself to do what she pleased with.

Dinah did not much concern herself about these matters. At this period of her life she knew almost nothing of the value of money, and cared less. She did not try to grasp the idea of how long it would be before Mr. Bradshaw would be paid by her labor. She was glad to be a free woman, and she felt thankful

"dat de Lord" had done for her what she supposed he
would. If she looked back to "Ole Carliny" with any
regret, she remembered that she had left no near kindred behind her, for her father and mother had both
died before their master and mistress; she had no
brothers or sisters, and she had never had a lover in
her life.

Dinah was soon installed as nursery-maid to the little
Isabel. To dress her young mistress; to comb and
curl her beautiful tresses; to sing her to sleep with the
plaintive negro melodies of the South; to cook for her
dainty Southern dishes; to take her to walk in the Beacon Street Mall, or go to a shop and buy a new doll, or
get her unlimited ice-cream at a Frenchwoman's con-
fectionery in Cornhill,—in short, to do anything and
everything that could pamper an over-indulged child
became Dinah's sole occupation. Yet somehow she
established a better control over this child than any
one else had ever had. It was through the power of
love, and not of authority; for of authority Dinah
knew nothing. When there was something that she did
not choose to let Isabel do, she generally carried her
point. But it was seldom that she departed from the
course of unbounded indulgence.

Nature had given to Dinah, as it has to many of the
females of her race, a most accurate ear and a low,
sweet voice, as clear as the softest "breathing of a
lute." Her singing was, of course, uncultivated, but
the gift of music was in her, to the utmost perfection
of the natural endowment. If Isabel went to a concert with the rest of the family, Dinah always accompanied them, and in a back seat she drank in the
performance with a quiet but exquisite enjoyment that
sometimes filled her eyes with tears. When the concert was over, she rolled Isabel up in a blanket-shawl,
took the child in her strong arms, and put her in the
carriage; then ran on home, and was at the door to lift
her out with the same tender care. She became a
necessity to Isabel, and the child returned her affection.
It was evident that it would almost require death to
separate them. It is incomprehensible to some of us

how very young white children, of delicate temperaments, will take to black women. Perhaps it is the
irony of nature, sardonically quizzing our Northern
notion of an innate repugnance of our race for theirs.
Perhaps our babies find a peculiar softness and tenderness in the negro skin, as they certainly often do find
a love that never tires and a temper that is never cross,
at least to the white child, if they ever are to their own
offspring.

Dinah was a religious woman, according to her light.
It was not deemed well in the South to educate even
the brightest of the slaves who must remain slaves in
what we mean by education,—reading and writing.
Dinah had never been taught to read, but her former
mistress had been in the habit of reading the Bible to
her and explaining some of the stories in it; she once
made Dinah commit to memory the whole of the Sermon on the Mount, and the girl never forgot a word of
it. To her the beatitudes constituted all there is of religion: was she far wrong about this? She was always
quoting them, translated into her peculiar dialect. Of
doctrine she had not been taught much. She had listened to lessons which her mistress gave her, in which
that good lady explained the fall of Adam; and in the
country, on the plantation, she had heard a gray-haired
Methodist preacher of her own race, who knew a great
deal about the Bible, but knew it at second-hand, as
he had never read a word of it in his life, explain the
manner in which "the ole Sarpint" beguiled "Mudder
Eve." But Dinah's idea of that memorable occurrence
was from her childhood and all through her life very
simple,—namely, that the law of obedience was then
and there given in the Garden of Eden. "Ef," she
used to say, "yeou dun don't do what you air tole, or
ef yeou do suthin' dat God has tole yer not ter, yeou'v
got ter pay for't." If there is a safer belief than this,
I do not know that theologians have discovered it.

The Pringle family, by whom Dinah was "raised,"
were Presbyterians. In the city they attended a fashionable church of that denomination, where many of
the wealthiest families were pew-holders and worship-

pers, as their fathers before them had been. The colored servants of these families sat during the morning service in a gallery appropriated to them, but on Communion Sundays, when the Lord's Supper was celebrated, always at noon, the servants came down into the body of the church, and were seated on benches in the broad aisle, their masters and mistresses, old and young, being in the pews. All were served alike, with the bread and wine, from the same massive silver vessels, and by the same deacons. Master and slave, at the table of their common Lord and Saviour, were equal. It was an impressive recognition of the brotherhood of man. (The writer saw this interesting sight in the city of Charleston more than forty years ago.)

The Bradshaw family were religious people too, after a mild type of old-fashioned Episcopalianism. But neither in their church nor in any other in Boston did Dinah, after she had come there to live, ever see what to her was a familiar spectacle in her younger days, black and white people partaking together of the elements which typify the body and blood of the Redeemer. It is true that there had been no slaves in the Northern city for about a century; but there were a good many free negroes, and they were not often treated in the churches of the wealthy as if they were " men and brethren" at the period when these memoirs begin. At a later period, Dinah found a chapel where an extraordinary man, who was called "Father Taylor," preached to the sailors. In this audience there were both blacks and whites. The pastor had a strong gift of eloquence of a peculiar kind, admirably adapted to reach the wild natures of the roving and changing seamen who came to his Bethel. It was an intellectual treat to highly intellectual people to go and hear Father Taylor, but he never varied his discourse on account of the presence of such persons. He knew very well that from their purses came the greater part of the money that sustained his Bethel and supported his family, but he never flattered man or woman, and he perfectly understood his mission to a class of society for whose religious teaching his natural endowments and long experience had singularly fitted him. Dinah sat under his preaching for many a year, through the period during which I have given an account of the life of her young mistress.

When Isabel had entered society, which she did at seventeen, became surrounded by admirers, and had numerous love-affairs on her hands, Dinah's influence over her in everything that did not relate to her health and bodily comfort was over. In fact, her influence never extended to matters of conduct after Isabel ceased to be a child; and Isabel had had when she became a young lady very little moral training in the regulation of her feelings and the government of her own heart. Some people very early doubted if she had a heart; but whether she had or not, it was certain that her love of admiration and her power of fascinating susceptible young men, and men who were not young, would enable her to do great mischief. When Henry Brewster appeared, and Isabel became engaged to him after she had wrecked the peace of many a good fellow, Dinah, like every one else in the household, was rejoiced. She thought Henry nearly as perfect as Julius Pringle, and he was her beau ideal of a young gentleman. When Henry first began to visit at the Bradshaw residence, his ring at the front door was always a very timid touch. Ah! who of my male readers does not remember the time when, desperately in love, his heart beat violently as he laid his hand upon the bell-pull; how he scarcely made any but the feeblest tinkling in the kitchen; and how, when his ring was answered and the door was opened, he scarcely dared to raise his eyes to the servant's face, and in what a low and conscious tone he asked if Miss Mary or Miss Julia was at home? The servant knew why you had called at some unusual hour as well as you knew it yourself; and he or she, as the case might be, pitied you perhaps most sincerely, for your case had been all talked over below-stairs, and your chances had been set down at zero. Look back upon your own early days, and do not consider poor Henry as the weakest of mortals. He merely went through the inevitable

experience appointed for young men who can become
dazzled by beauty and grace of the very first and most
captivating quality.   At that period in Henry's courtship, when he scarcely dared to hope, and his touch of
the bell was so timid, Dinah was always on the watch
for the feeble little stroke ; her ear was so quick that
she could distinguish Henry's ring in whatever part of
the house. she happened to be, and she was down at
the front door before any other servant had moved a
step, to let him in.   "Yaas, sah," she would say, with a
broad gleam of welcome beaming from her black face,
"Miss Is'bel's up-stairs, and I'll run up and tell her dat
yeou hev called."   At one time this was repeated nearly
every afternoon ; and Dinah was sure to throw open
the door of the drawing-room and ask Henry to walk
in.   When he came in the evening one of the other
servants generally answered the door-bell, and he was
ushered into the family gathering as other visitors
were.   When the catastrophe related in a former chapter came, and Henry Brewster's brief season of intoxicating happiness was ended, and he had gone, none of
them knew whither, Dinah was at first utterly bewildered.   She could not understand it, as no one else
could ; but she said little.   She saw that Isabel was
wretched, and she feared that she would become ill.   In
truth, she was ill, for a few days ; and Dinah, without a
word of inquiry or remonstrance, nursed her and cared
for her as she had always done.   After all hope of learning anything about the lover whom she had driven
away was over, Isabel resumed the mode of life that
she had been leading so long when Henry first crossed
her path.   When she married the Englishman, Dinah,
who thought the match better than for Miss Isabel to
become an "ole mäd," was well content to follow her
mistress's fortunes.   In fact, she could not have thought
of anything else, and the whole family were glad that
it was so.

CHAPTER VI.

A STRANGER LANDS AT NEW YORK.

AT about the time when Henry Brewster left Boston a gentleman landed at New York from one of the lately established English steamers, unaccompanied by any one else, not even a servant. He was apparently about fifty years of age. Of what country he was a native, or from what land he came, save that he embarked at Liverpool, he chose to keep to himself. His physiognomy gave no clue to his origin. He appeared to be in good health and had a clear complexion. His manners had the ease and polish that come of long intercourse with the world. His demeanor was quiet, rather grave, self-poised, and perfectly unobtrusive. A general air of placid indifference to things about him might have been remarked by any one who did not observe that he had a pair of quick gray eyes, which glanced everywhere and took in everything, although it was seemingly a cold and unsympathetic glance. On the voyage he had had but little communication with any of the other "first-class" passengers, whose curiosity concerning him had been carried as far as the limits of good manners would allow, but without any result, for there was something about him that repelled intimacy. He had been too great a traveller to attempt much conversation with the captain of an English steamer. As the vessel neared Sandy Hook, and the captain, at the head of the dinner-table for the last time, ordered the customary bottle of champagne, this gentleman accepted the civility of a glass, and capped the taciturn officer's order by one of his own. As the wine circulated along the table he took it freely, but it did not seem to exhilarate him or to loosen his tongue. When the disembarkation occurred, the general voice of the passengers was much divided about him. Some supposed him to be an Englishman; and he was taken,

f

with just as good reason, which was none at all, for a Frenchman, an Italian, a Russian, a German, a merchant, a nobleman, and so on. The ladies were all agreed that he was a well-bred man, but distant and reserved. What his nationality was, or what his past life had been, was a small mystery, talked of until the general dispersion took place at the landing. It had been observed, however, that he spoke English with entire purity and correctness, but neither in that nor in one or two Continental languages in which he had been heard to say something did his accent indicate whether it was or was not his mother-tongue.

At the Astor House, to which he drove as soon as he could get his baggage through the hands of the customs officers,—more than one of whom acted as if he expected a douceur for granting the landing-permit, but without finding any pretext for a lawful exaction,—our traveller registered his name as "John Charáxes," with the sole addition of the words "last from Liverpool." The prompt, quick manager in the office, who had acquired from long practice a surprising faculty of reading at a glance the proper pretensions of a guest, whirled the book round on the marble counter with a smart twist of his left hand, wrote against the stranger's name the number of the best parlor in the hotel having an adjoining bedroom, tossed the key to "David" or "Patrick," whichever of them answered the sharp order of "Front," and told the brawny Irishman to take the gentleman's baggage and show him the way. He had just sent another guest, of less distinguished appearance, but whose money was perhaps as good as anybody's, to much inferior accommodations.

The surname which now stood on the register of the hotel as the last arrival might imply a Greek origin. But the unmistakable English "John" produced a little confusion in the mind of the reporter who came in soon after to copy the names for the evening paper, as the owner of this association of names apparently did not mean to be known to belong anywhere. Mr. Charáxes dined in his own apartment, so that there was no question about placing him at the *table-d'hôte.*

On the next day after his arrival, during the hours of 'change, our traveller walked down Wall Street, in search of the office of a banker to whom he had a letter of introduction from that banker's correspondent in Geneva. In the rush of men and boys along the side-walk, some hurrying to pay a note, some to make a deposit, some to carry an order to a broker to buy or sell this stock or that,—neither telegraph nor telephone was then in all offices of business,—the stranger was frequently jostled aside, sometimes pushed out of the way, without the slightest apology for the rudeness. This first specimen of American street manners did not strike him pleasantly; nor, when he made such inquiries as he had to make in order to find the place for which he was bound, were the answers so polite as he had met with in other parts of the world under similar circum-stances. But he shrugged his shoulders philosophically and threaded his way until he found himself in the office of the banker to whom he had been accredited. This gentleman, a tall man of some sixty years, with a foreign accent that bespoke him as a native of Switzer-land, after perusing the letter of his correspondent, welcomed the stranger very politely; for the letter, although it gave no indication of the bearer's nation-ality or of his purpose in coming to America, spoke of him as a person of great wealth, entire respectability, and agreeable personal qualities. Before the close of the day there stood on the banker's books to the credit of John Charáxes, Esquire, by effect of the charm re-siding in certain bills of exchange, a large sum of money, —larger than was commonly to be found there to the credit of an individual. If some curiosity was excited in the office, or there was any speculation about a possible agent of some foreign government, or, mayhap, a representative of some new enterprise about to be undertaken in America from the "other side," the clerks and book-keepers kept their surmises to them-selves. It was their business to honor the gentleman's checks when they were presented, and not to inquire what he did with his money. Their chief, however, had other duties to perform. According to his custom,

he asked Mr. Charáxes to name a day when he would
dine with him, saying that he should like to ask some
gentlemen whom he thought a stranger would be pleased
to meet. The invitation was frankly accepted, and at
the appointed time Mr. Charáxes presented himself at
the residence of the banker, a large and well-appointed
house in the lower part of Fifth Avenue, not far from
Washington Square. Among the other guests were
Mr. Washington Irving, Mr. Fenimore Cooper, Mr.
Bryant, and Mr. Fitz-Greene Halleck; one or two of
the eminent lawyers of the time; Bishop Wainwright, of
the Protestant Episcopal Church; and Bishop Hughes,
of the Roman Catholic Diocese. There was a prominent and rather bellicose editor of a daily paper, Mr.
Watson Webb; a distinguished civil engineer, Mr.
Horatio Allen; and there were a few elderly gentlemen who represented the Knickerbocker element of
New York society, together with a fair sprinkling of
the enterprising men of New England birth, long settled in New York in various branches of business.
The whole company, about twenty in number, composed a party that a stranger might well be glad to
meet.

The dinner was elegant and sumptuous, but the *menu*
need not be given. The wines were choice, and were
served in good taste; Madeira being the after-dinner
wine that received the greatest share of attention.
When it came upon the mahogany there was an apparent tendency to make it the subject of a prolonged
conversation. Bishop Wainwright, who took his glass
with the gusto of a connoisseur, asked Mr. Cooper if
he had ever tasted anything finer. That gentleman replied that when he was in the navy he had met with
excellent Madeira in Charleston, but not better than
the wine now on the table. This dreary subject was
continued for some time, but it gave place to another
topic, for just then water was a matter of greater interest among citizens of New York than wine even.

" I do not understand," said a member of the famous
"New England Society," "how this city has managed
to live and grow as it has, with nothing for the popu-

lation to drink but the wretched puddle obtained from
wells sunk in near proximity to cess-pools. Why, Mr.
Van Vechten, did not your ancestors think of the Cro-
ton River ?"

Mr. Van Vechten was a respectable old gentleman of
Dutch descent, and a high officer in the "St. Nicholas
Society."

"We got along very well, sir," he replied, "and until
now, when water is so much wanted for other than
domestic uses, we have suffered no inconvenience; but
there has been a great influx of beer-drinking foreigners
among us, and now we must tax ourselves to get water
for the brewers."

"Mr. Irving," said the New-Englander, "I suppose
you would say that Mr. Van Vechten's ancestors
thought more of their Hollands than of any other bev-
erage ?"

"Perhaps not more," Mr. Irving said, "than your
people thought of the rum that they made and sold so
cheaply. I fancy that the Dutch liquor was rather
more wholesome."

"You must tax yourselves now, Mr. Van Vechten,"
said Mr. Allen, "that you may not have to tax yourselves tenfold more heavily hereafter. Thirty years
hence this city ought to have a population more than
double what it has to-day. If this generation does not
make provision for an abundant supply of pure water,
New York will come to a stand-still."

In this conversation on a local topic, taking place
across one end of the table, the stranger could have no
share. At about midway between the two ends, Mr.
Webb had begun a political talk, in which a great deal
was said about General Jackson, his removal of the
deposits from the bank of the United States, President
Van Buren's financial policy, and sundry other matters
then much agitating the political world. To this, too,
our traveller could only listen, learning, however, a good
deal, as was his wont. But at length Mr. Cooper, who
regarded with great respect what he was accustomed
to call *aplomb*, and who had been much impressed by
that trait in the bearing of the stranger, addressed him

directly: " Mr. Charáxes, I believe you have lately
come from England. Have they yet found an answer
to the question ' Who reads an American book ?' "

A smile passed over the countenance of Charáxes,
and he made a polite inclination of his head towards
Mr. Cooper, as he answered, " I think, sir, that you
and other gentlemen at this table have enabled them
to find an answer, if they wish for one. Your literature certainly does no discredit to your origin, and you
are now as independent of England in your intellectual
products as you have long been in government. The
language, too, has been enriched by the expansion that
it has received in America; and, if I may presume to
judge, the best English is now written on this side of
the Atlantic. Dr. Channing, among your divines, and
Daniel Webster, among your statesmen, have a prose
style of unsurpassed excellence. In poetry, Mr. Bryant
has not been behind any British writer of this century. I do not need to speak of Mr. Irving's writings,
for they are as well thought of in England as they are
in America. I have heard Sir Walter Scott refer to
both Mr. Cooper and Mr. Irving in the strongest terms
of regard."

" You knew Sir Walter, then ?" asked Mr. Irving.

" Yes, I was much in Spain and Portugal during the
Peninsular War, and it happened that when Scott was
writing his ' Vision of Don Roderick,' I was mentioned
to him as a person who could give him local information about some of the scenes that he meant to touch
in that poem. One or two letters passed between us,
but it was not until after your visit to Abbotsford, in
1817, that I was there. I happened to meet Scott in
London in 1815, and he then invited me to spend two
days at Abbotsford whenever it should suit my con-
venience; but it was not convenient for me to go there
until 1819. During my short stay he spoke often of
you, Mr. Irving, and of Mr. Cooper, and Mr. Ticknor,
of Boston. But I think, Mr. Cooper, that Scott did
not make your acquaintance until you met in Paris in
1826 ?"

" Yes," said Mr. Cooper, " he called upon me in Paris,

and I afterwards breakfasted with him at his hotel. I tried to find out from him whether Captain Basil Hall was as much of a seaman as he appeared to be in his writings. But Sir Walter rather evaded the question. Did you know Captain Hall?"

"No, I never saw him; and if I had, as I have never been a seaman, although I have been much at sea, I could not judge of Captain Hall's accomplishments in his profession. He certainly wrote entertaining books."

"Did you ever meet Lord Byron?" asked Mr. Bryant.

"I was at Missolonghi when he died, but I did not know him. His effort to do something for the cause of the Greeks was from a very noble impulse, and I concur in Mr. Moore's belief that, if he had lived, his character would have developed into something worthy of his abilities and that would have atoned for his previous life. But the independence of Greece was then an impossibility. Europe was not ready for it."

At this mention of the affairs of Greece it occurred to several of the gentlemen present that the name of this stranger was distinctly Greek, and more than one was on the point of asking some question that might have led him to give an account of himself. But his manner rendered it doubtful whether such a question would not seem to transcend the limits of politeness. He had been received by the host as a gentleman, but as one having no known nationality, and he had been presented to the company simply as a citizen of the world. This, however, did not preclude all efforts to learn how such a person, of such apparently varied experience and extensive acquaintance with men and things, would view American society. Mr. Cooper, nothing daunted by the presence of the pugnacious Mr. Webb, who was not more pugnacious than himself, tried the stranger on the American press.

"I have had but little occasion," said Mr. Charáxes, "to read American newspapers at any time in my life, excepting for commercial purposes and matters of finance; and having been here now for only a few days, I have really had no opportunity to observe the tone of your press."

("He has been in commerce," Mr. Webb said to himself; "I must find out more about him.")

"Well, sir," said Mr. Cooper, "I must warn you that our liberty of the press is shockingly abused. There is no fairness, no dignity. In literary criticism there is nothing but a shallow audacity and a shameless mendacity. Our law of libel is administered by judges who stand in awe of the newspapers, and our juries are composed of men who can have no sympathy with an injured author. In politics there is nothing but a savage and coarse abuse of the opposite party; no discussion of principles, no proper treatment of public measures or public men."

"You present rather a dark picture, Mr. Cooper," replied Charáxes, "but is there not reason to hope that, as your country expands and the people increase in numbers and intelligence, they will come to be less under the influence of the press and to act more upon their own judgment?"

"Possibly," said Mr. Webb, "Mr. Cooper's feelings are a little tinged by his personal experience with papers that have treated him unfairly. But you will find, sir, literature aside, if you remain long among us, that our government is one that must be administered by a successful party; in politics there can be no success without party discipline, vigorous political warfare, and unsparing criticism of public men. Study our elections, sir, if you care to know what the press has to do in promoting the public welfare according to the convictions of its conductors."

"It may be, Mr. Webb," Charáxes modestly observed, "that there is a great deal in what you say; but it seems to me that there is just now a topic that is rising into great importance in this country, and that ought to be handled without any reference to party objects or party success, and with the utmost circumspection. I learned before I came over that an agitation has been recently begun in some of your Northern States on the subject of slavery in the South. I am quite aware of the constitutional limitations which, in your form of government, prohibit any external interference with the domestic institutions of the separate States. But if this anti-slavery agitation should assume formidable proportions and be carried on from a position outside of your fundamental law, will your Constitution be able to withstand the shock ? If I remain long in America I shall be much interested to observe how you will encounter this trial."

" You need be under no apprehension, sir," said Mr. Webb ; " the abolitionists who have started this crusade are a set of fanatics, whom the people are not disposed to follow. Public opinion is sound on this subject. No one of any sense thinks it necessary to put the arm of the law in motion to restrain them. There may be here and there, in little localities, a few votes to be conciliated by local politicians running for local offices. But the subject will be kept out of our national politics and our national elections."

" It is to be hoped so," said the stranger ; " but fanatics have sometimes done a great deal by the sheer force of their fanaticism when they have appealed to the religious and moral feelings of a free people. If, by chance, this question should become one in your national politics, I do not see how your public men are to evade it. But it is not for me to offer opinions on this subject to such a company as this. I only meant to express what must strike any foreigner who comes among you, the certainty that your Constitution requires one thing, and that another thing may be reached by methods that lie wholly outside of your political institutions and public compacts."

These observations, although made without the slightest warmth, and the uncertainty respecting the stranger's real character and his object in coming to America, led to a momentary suspicion with some of the gentlemen present whether he might not have come with a purpose to take some part on the one side or the other of this delicate subject. But he appeared to be so evidently a mere traveller, taking about as much interest in one topic as in another, that the slight suspicion passed off, more especially as the well-certified wealth of the gentleman seemed to preclude the idea of his being an emissary of any sort, or anything but a highly intelligent and observing man of the world visiting the United States for his own amusement.

Before the company separated, Mr. Irving asked the foreign gentleman if he intended visiting Boston ; and on being informed that such was his purpose, the amiable author of the "Sketch Book" asked him if he would do him the honor to take a letter to Mr. William H. Prescott. This civility was thankfully accepted, and before Mr. Charáxes left New York the letter came for him. Necessarily, it could give no other information than Mr. Irving had learned concerning this stranger, but it spoke of his having been well received in New York, and as a person worthy to be as well received in Boston.

On the evening after that of his arrival in Boston, Mr. Charáxes happened to be passing a hall at the door of which was a placard announcing an anti-slavery meeting. He stepped in and took a seat near the entrance. The small audience was composed of both men and women, the latter predominating. Soon after the stranger entered a young man came forward on the platform to speak to the resolution which was before the meeting. He was apparently about twenty-eight years of age; tall, of a most symmetrical figure, a handsome countenance, and a refined and rather aristocratic bearing. Grace and polish were in every movement and gesture. His voice was rich and perfectly modulated. It was evident that he must have been accustomed to public speaking from a very early age: he was so easy and self-possessed. Nature had done everything for him in externals, and the gift of graceful delivery, cultivated from his boyhood, had made him one of the most finished declaimers that ever trod a public platform. His enunciation was perfectly distinct, and nothing could exceed the grammatical correctness of his rounded sentences. He was evidently a scholar, for his command of language and illustration was quite beyond what is commonly found in the kind of oratory which he affected. When Mr. Charáxes heard this person he was just entering upon his career as an anti-slavery

agitator, which lasted as long as there was any slavery
left in the land. He belonged to an old Boston family
of some distinction, and the circumstances of his birth,
education, and social surroundings singled him out in
the estimation of his new associates as a person who
had embraced the cause of the slave from the noblest
of motives, when he might naturally have disdained or
neglected all such philanthropic movements. He was
educated as a lawyer and had begun to practise that
profession ; but he renounced it, because, when admitted
to the bar, he had been obliged to take an oath to support
the Constitution of the United States. He considered
that a renunciation of his privilege of practising in the
courts absolved him from the obligations of that oath.
On the present occasion the burden of his speech
seemed to be an effort to show that the Federal Constitution was, as the abolitionists universally regarded it,
"a league with death and a covenant with hell." It
was most striking to hear this kind of denunciation
poured forth in the choicest rhetoric, without much excitement of manner, but in words of a certain vitupera-
tive sting. His harangue was addressed to an audience
composed wholly of New-Englanders, whose ancestors,
of not more than two generations back, had made those
public compacts with the people of the Southern States
which to a certain extent recognized and upheld the
slavery existing in those States. For a long time before
this kind of denunciation began the prosperity of New
England, and especially of Massachusetts, had largely
depended on manufactures of cotton, in which a great
deal of wealth was invested ; and it suited the abolitionists to couple the Northern manufacturers of the
great Southern staple as in league with its producers
to perpetuate the bondage of the Southern slaves.
There was neither logic nor sense in this vituperation ;
but logic and sound reasoning were never a characteristic of this orator, either in his youth, his middle
age, or to the close of his life. He was a splendid declamatory rhetorician, whose well-turned periods fascinated people in whom the emotions were stronger
than the reflective faculties. In the speech to which

Mr. Charáxes listened, the orator delighted his audience immensely by speaking of the "lords of the loom and the lords of the lash." The most vociferous applause followed this sally, and it became a favorite phrase of local significance. To the stranger who heard it it opened a coming social division in a community where the owners of great establishments, on which to a certain extent depended the general prosperity, could be assailed as oppressors of the poor African. It was one of those minor causes which led to the local growth of a strong anti-slavery excitement, before anything had occurred to evince a purpose in the South to extend the area of their peculiar institution by special measures. At present the mass of the New England people were not disposed to sympathize in these attacks upon men of wealth, whose capital and energy had done so much for the promotion of the general prosperity and for all the local objects of education and benevolence. But the dragon's teeth were sowing.

Another of this young orator's denunciations was directed against the churches, which he accused not only of lukewarmness in the cause of the slave, but of actual and unchristian complicity with the slaves' oppressors. This was one of his popular topics, treated, as usual, with an abundane of rhetoric and sarcasm. When Charáxes left that meeting he had heard a person who was afterwards a very shining light in the galaxy of the anti-slavery agitators, and who was by far the most effective popular orator among them all. The stranger had also, with his usual acumen, perceived how this agitation, from its small beginnings, was tending to the result which he had delicately foreshadowed at the dinner-table of the New York banker; a result which he had rightly apprehended as popular action outside of the obligations of public compacts and constitutional restraints. It was therefore with still stronger interest and with some further insight into this very important subject that he determined to learn more at his first opportunity. In a few days he found himself in the company of some of the same men whom he had heard the anti-slavery orator denounce.

Dinners, the world over, are the most convenient and agreeable mode of showing attention to strangers, at least of the male sex. They have been no less so in Boston than elsewhere, time out of mind. They are almost invariably the response to letters of introduction when the introducing missive is not confined to business purposes. When Mr. Charáxes visited Boston I had the honor to be among the younger acquaintances of the author of " Ferdinand and Isabella." He lived at that time with his venerable father and mother, in a fine old-fashioned house on Bedford Street, long since demolished. It was mere kindness towards an undistinguished young man—characteristic of Mr. Prescott— for him to invite me to the dinner that he gave to Mr. Charáxes, whom I then saw for the first time, and of whom I knew a great deal in subsequent years. The company was not so large as that at the house of the New York banker, and the dinner, although elegant, was more simple. Judge Prescott, the father of the historian ; Mr. Jared Sparks ; Chief Justice Shaw, of the Supreme Court of Massachusetts ; Mr. Franklin Dexter, a very distinguished lawyer, brother-in-law of Mr. Prescott ; and one or two of the great manufacturers, men of far wider intellectual range than is often to be found in the ranks of commerce and business, composed the party. Mr. Ticknor, Mr. Prescott's most intimate friend, whose " Life of Prescott" is so well known, was at this time in Europe. Mr. Prescott received his guests in his library, where, over the fireplace, were crossed two swords, one worn by his grandfather at Bunker Hill, the other was worn by Captain Linzee, of H. M. sloop-of-war " Falcon," which lay in the river and cannonaded the American redoubt during the battle.

The subject that had been lightly touched at the dinner in New York was then beginning to be very anxiously considered by the class of men in Boston who were represented around Mr. Prescott's table. Prescott himself, although by no means indifferent to the public welfare, was a scholar, and his " Ferdinand and Isabella" had been very recently published. His father was a singularly wise and observing person of the Federal school of politics. He had seen with great concern the beginning of the anti-slavery agitation which had sprung up in New England and was likely to bring about very grave questions respecting the limits of free discussion.

Charáxes was anxious to hear this gentleman's views on so important a topic, and an opportunity soon offered.

"You seem, sir, to have observed," said the elder Mr. Prescott, "that the persons who have precipitated this inflammatory topic are determined to pay no heed to the civil obligations imposed by our fundamental law. This is exciting a disapprobation of their proceedings, their methods and writings, which breaks out occasionally in popular violence against their persons and presses, so that there is really arising a question of the limits of free discussion. These so-called 'abolitionists' assume the attitude of martyrs to a principle and to the rights of free speech. Their doctrine, when carried out, dissolves the bonds of society and uproots the foundations of civil obedience."

"This is plain enough, Judge Prescott," said the stranger. "But does your law afford no means of checking a kind of discussion and action that borders upon revolution and may end in it? I should not think of suggesting that under some governments on the continent of Europe such means would readily be found; nor should I point you to what was done in England when the doctrines of the French Revolution were threatening that government. But you have a well-defined Constitution and a government that does not lack strength within its appropriate sphere. Have you made up your minds that this thing must go on?"

"Perhaps," said Judge Prescott, "the chief justice will answer your question. We are all accustomed to rely on his views, when they do not involve his judicial functions; and when they do, we know that the oracle of the law has spoken."

"You will appreciate the difficulty, sir," said the chief justice, "when you come to learn more of our institutions. It might appear, at first, that when a written Constitution has established a Union of States, otherwise independent of each other, and has made certain public compacts between them, there ought to be some power to restrain popular action that is in direct violation of these compacts. But then you must recollect that our existence as an independent people was obtained by a revolution, which could not have been accomplished without the utmost freedom of discussion in all its forms. Moreover, after our national Constitution was adopted the national legislature was expressly forbidden to make any laws abridging the freedom of speech or of the press. This was done immediately, by an amendment of the Constitution in the mode provided by itself. So that we are a people among whom it is very difficult to find any but moral limits to the rights of free discussion, and of those individuals must judge for themselves."

"As a general statement, Mr. Chief Justice," said Charáxes, "I can understand this view of your institutions. But how is it in regard to such attacks as I have heard and read upon the institutions themselves? Is there no way of restraining those who teach that your national Constitution embraces public compacts that ought to be instantly repudiated because they were grossly immoral in their inception and have ever since violated the duties which men owe to God and to their fellows?"

"Some of us," replied the chief justice, "have anxiously considered the question which you put, and, without speaking for others, I will give you the conclusions which I have myself reached. Our complex form of government is perhaps well known to you in its general outline. So much of recognition as has been given by our national Constitution to the slavery that exists in our Southern States involves a right to enumerate the slaves in a certain ratio in the population on which is based the representation of those States in the lower house of Congress, and in a stipulation that fugitives from servitude escaping into a State where such servitude does not exist shall be returned. But then you must observe that in these respects, as in others, the Constitution is subject to change, by a process of amendment; and the persons who are now beginning this agitation may say that a conviction of the sin of slavery must precede any efforts to amend the fundamental law or to get rid of the public compacts?"

"Yes," said Charáxes, "they may say this; but, as far as I can learn, they are not agitating to bring about amendments of the Constitution. They wish to break up the Union. They insist that the wrong and the sin of slavery are so glaring and gross that there must be immediate emancipation, regardless of the mode in which it is brought about, or else that your Northern States must separate from the Southern. If the blacks have sufficient intelligence to understand what is maintained here at the North in their behalf, why does not all this tend directly to invite insurrection? And if this is its tendency, must you fold your hands and let it go on, when it is a plain violation of the public compacts which you made with the people of the slaveholding States?"

"Certainly, sir," answered the chief justice, "it is a violation of the spirit of the Constitution, and the danger is that the people of the South will regard it as a violation of the letter, and will demand the adoption of measures to check it. But such measures must be for the consideration of the national government. Our State governments can do nothing to restrain the license of free speech or free printing, unless the abuse of the freedom comes within the law of libel."

"I am very glad to understand this matter as you have explained it," said Charáxes; "but it seems to me that I have heard attacks upon some of you gentlemen, not by name but by pretty plain designation, which include some of you in the imputation of direct complicity in the sin of slavery. This is all absurd enough, and you must excuse my alluding to it. But what is to be the social effect of this in such a community as yours?"

One of the gentlemen thus appealed to, a calm but very intelligent person, replied, "I suppose the only effect will be that we cannot open our houses to persons who thus assail us. We have devoted our means and our energies to what we believe to be the best interests of our community, and we give employment to a great many people. We cannot close our establishments because the material that we work up is produced by the labor of slaves, over whose emancipation we have no control."

"This is plain enough," said Charáxes, "but among the slave-holders themselves what has been done of late years in regard to emancipation? The world is approaching a condition in which the economical and the moral aspect of slavery will be something very different from what it has been."

"Something was about to be done," replied the gentleman who had now joined in the conversation, "and it was of great importance. It may be worth your while to read a debate which took place in the Legislature of Virginia in the year 1832, just before the anti-slavery agitation began at the North. The slave-holders of that State were on the eve of passing measures to colonize the free negroes, and they contemplated other measures looking to the emancipation of the slaves. Nowhere have the evils of slavery been more forcibly and plainly discussed than they were in that debate. But before there could be any action there suddenly came intelligence of the formation of anti-slavery societies in three of the free States, and the establishment of a press that openly advocated a dissolution of the Union because the national Constitution gave a certain sanction and security to slavery in the Southern States. As a matter of course, this checked all tendency in the South to consider the expediency or the practicability of getting rid of slavery, and brought about a tendency to extend its area and strengthen the political power of the slave-holding States. The real impetus to a further increase of the number of slave States for political reasons, that is, in order to defend slavery as an institution, dates from that period, and it is now impossible to foresee how far this impetus will go. Previous to this the cultivation of cotton and a few other staples formed the principal motive for carrying slave-labor into other regions. But the desire to secure more political power in the Union,

E   g   9

as a means of resisting the aggressions of the anti-slavery agitators, is now added to the producing and economic objects of the planting interests."

"This is very unfortunate," said Charáxes, "and, as you say, it must be impossible to foresee where it will end. One thing, however, seems clear to me; but I speak with deference to the better judgment of you gentlemen, who know a great deal more about this matter than any foreigner can. But it strikes me that this may be the course of things: If no means can be found for putting a stop to this unwarrantable interference, and I think I see the difficulties in the way of that, what between the political interests and the supposed or real pecuniary interests of the South, and the resistance of the North, this subject, which should be kept out of party action, will be forced into the political field. The result will be a crisis in which there may come about finally a sectional division in your national elections. What that might end in no human prophecy it seems to me can foretell. Your Northern statesmen, in maintaining their personal standing at home, will be much embarrassed; the Southern statesmen will be much less so, because they will have a united people behind them. But I crave your pardon, gentlemen, for suggesting that your country is in some peril. I trust most sincerely that the people and public men of your whole Union will find some way to avoid it. Your republic is almost the last refuge of liberty, and your country is a magnificent one. As well as I can understand your history, I do not think that the founders of your government acted unwisely or inconsistently in making a Union of slave and free States, for they were compelled to do so by imperative necessities. It is, I believe, true that your national Constitution could not have been made without what are called the slavery compromises. Whether it can be preserved, now that its provisions are assailed in the way that has been entered upon, is the question of this day."

"Our hope is," said the elder Mr. Prescott, "that the great mass of the people of all parts of our country will continue to regard the agitators as guides whom they ought not to follow. But we cannot tell what may be the influence of their persistency and their inflammatory appeals."

"I should think," answered Charáxes, "that much would depend upon the power of your principal statesmen in the North to hold the people to sober and conservative action. If these agitators once become sufficiently strong to compel or induce political men to seek for popular local favor through any of the aspects in which slavery may present itself, great mischief will inevitably ensue."

At this time, although I had lived in Boston for several years, I had not had many opportunities for listening to the conversation of such men as those who were at Mr. Prescott's dinner. I was then an assistant editor of a daily paper; having charge of the literary department, I became known to Mr. Prescott and to Mr. Ticknor, both of whom were exceedingly kind to young men in any way connected with literature. I had a little reputation as a scholar, which helped me to know persons who might otherwise not have noticed me. I regretted very much Mr. Ticknor's absence from Boston at this time, for I wished to accompany Mr. Charáxes on a visit to that gentleman's remarkable library, more especially that he might see the portrait of Sir Walter Scott, that hung for so many years over the fireplace in that beautiful room; and my acquaintance with Mr. Ticknor would have justified my calling with this stranger. But his house was then occupied by a gentleman to whom I was not known, and to whom Mr. Charáxes did not bring letters.

I was so much impressed by the conversation which I heard at Mr. Prescott's that I made a note of its most important parts and put it away. I had not looked at it until I began to write these memoirs of my friends. The conversation at the New York banker's table was written out and sent to me by a friend of mine, a New England gentleman, who heard it, and this, too, I laid away at the time.

On the day after Mr. Prescott's dinner I called upon Mr. Charáxes at the Tremont House, and he described to me the anti-slavery meeting at which he was a spectator on the evening following his arrival in Boston. He said that he heard a young orator there who seemed to have remarkable gifts, which he thought would probably not be as well used as they ought to be. He told me that he expected to make an extensive tour through the United States, and I gave him some information which he was kind enough to say would be useful to him. He did not know how long he should remain in this country. He had come merely for amusement and observation. If he found a pleasant place of residence, he might remain, but probably not in the South, for he did not think the Southern climate would suit him, and he did not care to settle in a slave-holding State, although he should certainly learn all that a traveller could of the state of society in that region. He left Boston on the following day. At this time I did not know where Henry Brewster was. If I had I should have written and asked my friend to make the acquaintance of this interesting stranger, in case he should have an opportunity.

CHAPTER VII.

ISABEL AT GASCOIGNE HOUSE.

MARMADUKE, fourteenth Earl Gascoigne and Viscount Runnymede, of Gascoigne Manor, County Hauts, was a nobleman of very ancient lineage. His second title was supposed to imply that his remote ancestor of King John's reign took a conspicuous part in the doings of the barons when *Magna Charta* was extorted from that monarch. But if this were really the fact, the Gascoigne of that period was the only one of the family who ever did anything of much importance. The present earl had succeeded to an estate which his grandfather left in almost irretrievable embarrassment, by reason of his having squandered a great deal of

money on the turf, besides gambling against the same
set who won incredible sums from Charles James Fox
when that celebrated statesman was a mere boy. But
this Gascoigne, who frequented White's in Fox's time,
had no rich father ready, like the first Lord Holland,
to pay his son's gambling debts and bid him go again
and do likewise. The father of the present earl had
never been able to rescue the family property from the
incumbrances with which the card-playing and horse-
racing grandsire had loaded it. All that he could accomplish—and he could not always do it—was to keep
down the interest; and more than once considerable
farms passed into the hands of other owners. The
estate was still a large one, however, when Lord Marmaduke succeeded to the property and the title, but
the rents were equal to very little more than the interest on the debts with which the land was charged.
The tenants were of that class of British farmers who
never knew any more about farming than their fathers
knew. They were forever contending with their land-
lords for a reduction of rents, not knowing how a
higher rent may be made advantageous to both tenant
and landlord, by improving the methods of cultivation.
Scarcely a rent-day came round that did not end in a
most unsatisfactory state of feeling on both sides. Still,
very few of the tenants gave up their holdings when
their leases fell in ; and if they had done so, there were
no other farmers ready to step in and take their places,
because the estate was so much embarrassed that bar-
gains advantageous to both parties could not be made.
This impoverished but very noble family, who seemed
destined to live on in a way most unbecoming to their
rank, were as proud as Lucifer, but their pride was unaccompanied by the kind of energy that might have
lifted them out of this fallen condition.

Earl Marmaduke had three sons and three daughters.
The eldest son, heir-apparent to a dilapidated property
and a mouldy title, christened Reginald and called by
courtesy Lord Runnymede, had lived at home ever
since he left Cambridge, where he took no honors and
had very few associates. Feeling deeply the poverty

9*

of his house, and seeing that if the family estate were ever to be rescued from its present condition in his time it must be done by him, he devoted himself to the work. His father, having no capacity for business of any kind, allowed him to dismiss the steward, who, although an honest man, had never done them the least good, and to take the active management of the property into his own hands. The young lord soon persuaded himself that a course of severe economy in the family expenditures was necessary to the accomplishment of the great end; the indispensable precursor to the more distant object of a better rent-roll. To save money, therefore, became the study and occupation of his life. He reduced the household to the lowest scale consistent with decent living; and it was not without difficulty that he could get the old servants to remain on lower wages and put up with fare considerably poorer than they had been accustomed to, or procure others to take their places. But at the period when our dear Isabel came among them, from a land flowing with milk and honey and from a house where there was always some profusion, this ancient British family had been for several years settled in a life closely bordering on parsimony, under the comptrollership of the young lord. He was now about thirty-five; and if he ever thought of marrying he knew that he must marry an heiress. He had never yet had a chance to do anything so lucky.

The second son was in the Church, and he held the family living; but he, too, had not married. He lived in the rectory, with an old lady who kept his house for him. The living was worth but little more than three hundred pounds; and if the Rev. Herbert Gascoigne should ever marry, he also must get something with his wife, for no assistance beyond the living could come from his family.

The third son, our friend Lionel, the cleverest of the family, who was supposed to have made such a good matrimonial speculation on his trip to America, had obtained a clerkship in the Foreign Office by the only piece of luck that had befallen the family in many years. His father seldom attended the House of Lords. He had no house in London, and when he did go to Town he went alone, lived in lodgings, and stayed as short a time as he could. He was rarely kept in Town very long, because he did not often go up excepting to give his vote upon some important measure. He voted with the ministry of the day, when there was anything to be gained by it; and when he could not find that this was the case he absented himself from the divisions. Anything more disreputable in a peer of ancient descent could not well be conceived; but this poor old nobleman's abilities were not equal to the possession of anything that could be distinguished by the name of opinions. Having no stock of that commodity, he had to regulate his votes as one of the hereditary legislators by other considerations. It happened that when Lionel was eighteen years old, and was getting at home such an education as his brother the clergyman, who was a very fair scholar, could help him to obtain, the ministry suddenly found that every vote in the Upper House which they could command was necessary to prevent the throwing out of a measure which they had with much difficulty carried through the Commons. This occurred in the reign of King William IV. I mention the period because the subsequent reign has seldom been marked by transactions of the kind I am going to describe. Lord Gascoigne was written to, and asked to come to Town. He came, and went into lodgings, as usual. A private secretary waited upon and sounded him. He had no convictions or views whatever about the measure, but he had the sagacity to see that the government were in want of votes. He talked in his dull way about the question, and finally said that he had a son for whom he desired an appointment in the Foreign Office. Promises were exchanged, of the vote on the one side and the appointment on the other. When the private secretary reported the bargain to his chief, that minister said that it was rather an expensive one, but it was ratified. Lionel became entitled to write F. O. on his card, and his salary was two hundred pounds for the few first years. He was promoted shortly before he came to America, and his salary was raised to three hundred and fifty pounds. His expenses on that trip were allowed.

But the ladies of the House of Gascoigne now demand our notice. The countess, their mother, had been dead for many years. The eldest daughter, Lady Blanche, was a year or two younger than her eldest brother, and she was a good deal like him in mind and character. She shared with him in the effort to keep down the family expenses; and as she was the female head of the house, he had in her a valuable ally in the battle of life. The family were all low church—very low—and strictly evangelical. Lady Blanche, aside from her household duties, was devoted to missions and mission work, especially to that branch of missionary effort which is more concerned with evangelizing the heathen of distant and foreign lands than with the spiritual wants and moral destitution of people nearer home. She had a small income of her own,—very small, I fancy,—and spending as little of it on herself as a gentle-woman could and appear respectably dressed,—she was a conscientious woman,—she distributed the residue, according to her best judgment, among the missions of her branch of the Church in the remotest parts of the earth. She very seldom went to Town, but when she did she stayed with a friend, the wife of the Rev. Septimus Giles, rector of one of the churches in the city. These two ladies always went together to the missionary meetings in Exeter Hall, where "From Greenland's icy mountains" was sung with great fervor, and the subscriptions of the Hon. Lady Blanche Gascoigne, as well as those of other persons, were duly reported in the printed accounts of the collections. At the time when our lovely and fascinating Isabel came to pass the last week of her waning honeymoon at Gascoigne House, Lady Blanche had been for some months taking in a periodical, then newly established in London, which had opened to her the enormity of slavery as it existed in America. This publication was at that time co-operating with the new sect or faction known in America as "the Abolitionists." Lady

Blanche had thus afforded to her a new field of thought, in the sin which the American slave-holders were committing every day of their lives. Her ideas of the geography, history, institutions, and social condition of "the States" were, to be sure, rather mixed; but she made up in zeal and strength of conviction what she lacked in knowledge.

Lady Maud came next in age to her clerical brother, —that is, she was about thirty. She had had an attachment in her youth, but just what became of it, excepting that she did not marry, I did not learn, when, years later, I conversed with Isabel about her husband's family. I gathered, however, that Lady Maud at one time wrote verses,—poetry Mrs. Lionel Gascoigne did not call it. She had printed some of her effusions in the county paper before Isabel's visit, and the latter saw some of them in an album in which her sister-in-law had preserved them. She said they were very sentimental. *Au reste*, Lady Maud was useful to her eldest sister in making fancy-work, to be sold for the missions to the heathen.

Lady Clare was just a year younger than Lionel, being twenty-seven. Perhaps I am rather exact about the ages of these ladies; and it may occur to my readers that there is a rule of politeness on such points, when the ages of ladies are not essential to anything of importance. But we are not in the same society in which these ladies moved; and besides, they have all passed away a good while ago. I will only add that Lady Clare was the most intelligent and good-natured of the sisters, and that, if it had not been for the narrowness of their lives, and if Lady Clare had ever had half the advantages that Isabel Bradshaw enjoyed, she would have been an agreeable woman. She was better-looking, too, than her sisters, who were very plain.

Into this dismal family Isabel was to be introduced as the American wife of the youngest son, and among them she was to pass Christmas-week. Lionel had not told his wife much about his family. She knew that they belonged by birth to the older aristocracy, that

they had a large estate, and so on; but she knew
nothing about their poverty, their characters, or their
mode of life. She had read all of Mr. Irving's works
that were then current, and she probably anticipated
seeing something like the Christmas at Bracebridge
Hall. Ah! Geoffrey Crayon, how you did idealize that
charming picture! No matter; you had a right to
work it up as you did, and if you never saw it in real
life, who shall complain? I shall not. I shall only say
that if Isabel expected to meet a Squire Bracebridge in
her father-in-law, she was wofully disappointed, poor
young lady, as she was in the *tout ensemble* of the
house and its inmates. I was once on the point of
asking her, when all this was over and she was a rich,
middle-aged, and still very handsome woman, dwelling
in the great land of her birth, what her expectations
were in regard to the family into which she married.
But she had met with many delusions and disappoint-
ments, most of them of her own causing; and as I
knew something of this one, I forbore making the
special inquiry that was on my lips. Before she goes
down to the first dinner at Gascoigne House, I will just
express the hope that my young country-women of
the present day will not be discouraged from marrying
into aristocratic English families by the fate of Isabella
Bradshaw. Our young ladies do better now, I am told,
in these marriages, doubtless because of their superior
moral and intellectual qualities. I cannot allow, however, that any of them surpass my friend Isabel in
beauty, whatever may be their personal charms or
their loveliness of character. I must give one other
caution: for I would not have our young ladies suppose
that all or most of the aristocracy of good Queen
Victoria's realms are like the Gascoignes. I have no
doubt that many an American girl who has cast her
lot upon the other side of the Atlantic has found in such
high connections all that she anticipated and not more
than she deserved. I, for one, hope that such marriages
will be multiplied.

But something must now be said of the expectations
of the Gascoigne family concerning Isabel. None of

them came to Town to meet her on her arrival, probably because it was not convenient to spend money for
the journey. Lady Blanche wrote a rather frigid note,
to say that they would all be happy to see Mrs. Lionel
Gascoigne in the country, and to have her and her husband pass Christmas-week with them. The whole
family, with the exception of Lady Clare, thought that
Lionel ought to have obtained a handsome settlement
from the rich Boston merchant, in consideration of his
ancient birth. They were very much disappointed
when they heard that Mr. Bradshaw had given his
daughter nothing but an income exactly equal to her
husband's salary. They did not imagine that Mr.
Bradshaw's money could benefit their family estate in
any direct way; but Lionel was a rising man; he might
some day be an ambassador, or, at least, a secretary of
legation, and it would be convenient for his sisters if
his wife had a good fortune. They had heard that
Isabel was a great beauty, but they did not consider
that her beauty made amends for the want of such a
settlement as would have been obtained from a rich
British brewer or shipping merchant who had a handsome daughter to exchange for an alliance with a
family as old as the Conquest. To do Lionel justice,
although he came to America with almost a fixed purpose to carry home a rich wife, he had fallen in love
with Isabel very sincerely, as what young man would
not? When it came to the point of settling the conditions on which he was to obtain her, he had the sense
to discover that it would not do for him to say much
about the money part of the arrangement. He was in
profound ignorance of the reasons which led Mr. Bradshaw to be less liberal with Isabel than he might have
been under other circumstances. As Isabel was content with what her father gave her, Lionel rested satisfied; not without counting, however, on his future
promotion in the diplomatic service as an occasion
when his father-in-law would be likely to come down
with a handsome sum, in addition to a quarterly allowance. He found, however, that on his and Isabel's
joint income they could, with great prudence, live com-

fortably in London, which was all that Isabel now
seemed to care for. Lionel would have to give up some
of his bachelor habits, but his love for his wife made
this quite easy. They took lodgings in a well-furnished
house on Clarence Terrace, that looked upon the Green
Park, and their table was supplied by the respectable
lady, widow of a country curate, who let the apartment.
Isabel had a pretty drawing-room and a chamber, on
one side of which there was a small dressing-room for
Lionel, and on the other a bit of a bedroom for the
colored woman whom Isabel brought with her from her
father's house. There was another room on the next
floor above that could be had, if wanted. They reached
London late in the month of November, and in about a
week came the invitation to Gascoigne House. When
the time arrived, Lionel and Isabel went down in a
post-chaise, there being then no railways into Hamp-
shire. Dinah was sent down by the mail-coach with
the "luggage," as they call it in England.

Isabel and her husband arrived at Gascoigne House
late in the afternoon. The family were all in the drawing-room when she entered the hall. The earl, who
was a stiff old man, came forward, and offering his arm,
after he had imprinted a formal salute upon her forehead, led her into the family circle. Lady Blanche was
not much more cordial in her reception of the stranger.
Lady Maud followed the example of her eldest sister,
as she always did. Lady Clare alone kissed her new
sister-in-law in something like an affectionate way. The
young lord and the clergyman, when they were presented, merely bowed. There was no one else in the
room. Isabel, who supposed, as a matter of course,
that there were other guests in the house, thought that
she must lose no time in dressing for dinner, and asked
if her maid had arrived. When told that Dinah was
already in her room, she said she would like to go up
at once. Lady Clare accompanied her through the hall
and to her chamber, and then left her. There was but
one feeble lamp that hung over the great staircase,
and the house to Isabel, who was accustomed at home
to an abundance of light and warmth, seemed chill and

gloomy. Dinah had already laid out the dress which she
supposed her mistress would choose to wear, and on the
dressing-table had placed her case of jewelry. There
was a small fire in the grate, and a couple of wax
candles (not yet lighted) on high silver candlesticks
on the mantel over the fireplace.

When Isabel descended to the drawing-room, leaning
on the arm of her husband, who came out of a dress-
ing-closet where Dinah had laid out his evening clothes,
she was arrayed in a very elegant and becoming silk
dress; her laces, according to the fashion of the time,
were rich and fine, and she wore a set of diamonds that
could not have been matched in that old house for generations. There was no thought of any display in this,
and nothing to which she had not been accustomed all
her life. Her beautiful hair was arranged in the ringlets then in fashion, and when she entered the drawing-
room she ought to have met with a reception to which
a woman who was so lovely and whose manners were
so graceful was fairly entitled. But the family did not
seem to appreciate the acquisition they had made.
Isabel did not know that there was not a single guest
in the house besides her husband and herself until dinner
was announced. Her father-in-law took her into the
dining-parlor and placed her at his right hand. Lionel
gave his arm to his eldest sister.

I shall probably fail in the description of that first
dinner. It was as unlike the first or any other dinner
at Bracebridge Hall as can be conceived. There was a
great deal of family silver, but the dishes were upon
the most moderate scale in number and quality. Isabel thought that a glass of champagne, or some other
"ladies' wine," would be pleasant after her cold journey,
but none came. The beverages were beer and port.
The conversation was as meagre as the viands. A few
dull questions were asked about her voyage, about her
lodgings, what she had seen in London, etc. As she had
seen little but a dense, yellow, cold fog, which made her
long for the glorious sunshine of her native land, that
brings us the Indian summer at the season "when the
people of England hang and drown themselves," as

Addison tells us, she had not much to relate. Lady
Blanche gave the signal for the ladies to leave the table
soon after the cloth was removed, and they went into
the drawing-room, Lionel opening the door for them.
The gentlemen remained, with a decanter of port.

There was a little more light in the drawing-room
than there was before dinner, but not enough to overcome the gloom produced by the dark old furniture and
hangings, or to light up the few pictures on the walls.
Isabel drew her cashmere shawl around her shoulders
—Dinah had been thoughtful enough to bring it down
to the drawing-room while they were at dinner—and
took a seat on the sofa nearest the fire, by the side of
Lady Blanche. There was a pretty striking contrast
between the dress of the fair American and that of the
other ladies. Lady Blanche did not compliment her
sister-in-law on her dress, but she was immensely surprised by her jewels.

"Your diamonds are very beautiful," she said; "I
presume they were a wedding-gift from your father?"

"They were a gift from my father," Isabel answered,
very simply, "but not a wedding-gift. I have worn
them since I was eighteen."

"Indeed! do young unmarried ladies in America
wear diamonds?"

"Young unmarried ladies in America," Isabel answered, with a little smile, "wear anything that their
fathers or brothers give them, or their lovers, if they
happen to be engaged."

"That is very singular. I suppose you have a large
society in Boston?"

"Not what you would call large; but perhaps we
are not very different from the rest of the civilized
world, unless it may be in what some of our young
ladies do. We have some families in which there is
quite an English strictness."

"Do you have philanthropic and benevolent societies
in which your ladies take part?"

"Oh, yes; there is a great deal of that in our different churches, and ladies are constantly working for the
poor in Boston."

" What do they do for the Southern slaves? I have
understood that there are a few noble women in Boston
who are making great efforts to spread a conviction of
the sin of slavery. Do you know Mrs. Camman?"

" I do not know her, but I have heard about her. I
have heard my father say that the spirit in which the
abolitionists have begun this crusade against the people
of the South, because they happen to own slaves whom
they cannot immediately set free, is likely to do a great
deal of mischief."

" But why can they not emancipate them, and do it
now? Why should such a terrible sin be suffered to
exist another day?"

" I cannot make a political argument, Lady Blanche,
but I do not suppose that the blacks in our Southern
States suffer such great misery that strangers are called
upon to interfere. If I may judge from the woman who
has been with me since I was a child, and from what
she has told me,—she was born a slave,—the negroes
of the South must be a very happy people; more so, I
presume, than thousands in your manufacturing towns
and mining districts."

" She was born a slave!" Lady Blanche exclaimed,
clasping her hands together and looking shocked.

" Yes, my father bought her in Charleston, brought
her to Boston, and made her free."

" Was not that giving a sanction to the sin of slavery?
Did not Mr. Bradshaw give the weight of his example
to the dreadful idea that there can be property in
human beings?"

" My father did not so consider it, and I fancy that it
did not matter much to Dinah whose sin was sanctioned,
so long as she obtained her freedom in an honest way."

" What do you mean by an honest way? Can there
be any honesty in the traffic in human flesh?"

" I will tell you, dear Lady Blanche, what my
father considered honest. He bought the girl in
Charleston, and paid her full value to her owners. He
brought her to his house in Boston, made her a free
woman, and made her understand that she was free.
She has always had good wages and perfect liberty to

go and come as she pleased. She has repaid my father long ago for the money which he gave for her, and she now serves me for love as well as wages. You can have no idea of the affectionate attachment of the colored people to white people who treat them kindly."

"It would be better for their race if they could be made to see the terrible wrong that has been done to them."

"I have not studied these things very deeply," said Isabel, "perhaps you have. But that wrong, I have always understood, was done to their ancestors by your ancestors. The present generations of masters and slaves, I have heard my father say, are bound together by very complicated ties."

"Those ties must be broken. Your Northern States ought to insist on immediate emancipation or a separation from the Southern States."

Isabel had concluded by this time that she had heard quite enough on the serious side of this subject, and so, by way of affording a little merriment, she said she could repeat an anecdote about Mrs. Camman, which was thought in Boston to be quite amusing.

"Oh, tell us," said Lady Clare; "it is so interesting to hear about things in America."

"You have perhaps heard," said Isabel, "of the abolition riots in Boston. At one of the anti-slavery meetings, which a good-natured crowd of people who disapproved of the sayings and doings of the abolitionists undertook to disperse, the mayor came upon the ground to protect the persons of those who had made themselves obnoxious to public sentiment. He was a most gentlemanlike man, of exceedingly courteous manners, especially to ladies. Mrs. Camman came out of the meeting very indignant and excited, and stepping up to the mayor, she said, 'Mr. Barton, I am ready to die in this cause!' Mr. Barton lifted his hat, made her a low bow, and replied, 'Madam, I have not the least objection to your dying, but you will oblige me very much if you will go home and die!'"

Lady Blanche did not think the story amusing. The mayor, she supposed, was one of those Northern men

who "truckled to the South." Finding that her lis-
teners did not see the fun of the story, Isabel relapsed
into silence. Perhaps she remembered telling her
father that she was willing to take her chances. But
she probably thought that to be preached to about the
national sin of her country was rather a *triste* welcome;
and as she could not amuse her sisters-in-law she had
better not try further conversation. In a few minutes
the gentlemen came in from their port wine; and as
Lady Blanche moved to the tea-table to make the tea,
Lionel took the seat by the side of his wife and tried
to cheer her by telling her that in the morning he
would conduct her through the house and tell her
something of its history. After they had retired for
the night, Isabel repeated to him most of the conversation about slavery in America. "Blanche," said he,
"has not an idea in her head about anything out of
England that she does not get from the Exeter Hall
people. Don't be vexed, my dear, by anything that she
says."

In the morning,—it was Christmas-day,—after the
inevitable tea, toast, and egg, before they went to
church, Lionel took his wife through the picture-
gallery, where there was a large collection of family
portraits. Lady Clare accompanied them. Isabel
ought to have put on as many wraps as if she were
going out of doors, for the long apartment was not
warmed at all, although the sun shone brightly through
the windows. She wore only a light shawl. There
was but one of the pictures that interested her. They
stood in front of a portrait that hung in a good light,
and Isabel was at once attracted by it. It was the face
of a young lady, painted seemingly at the age of
twenty, and painted with great skill. It was a dreamy,
tender face, and the eyes had a soft gleam that told
strangely of both joy and sorrow. About the mouth
there was an expression of firmness amounting almost
to masculine resolution, but it was relieved by the
general softness and sweetness of the whole countenance. You could see that obstinacy and tenderness
both belonged to her character.

" Who was this lady ?" asked Isabel.

" Her history is very romantic," said Lady Clare.
" It is the strangest piece of romance,—almost the only
one in our family traditions. There has always been
a mystery about her that has never been solved. I
will tell you what is known about her, but perhaps we
had better not stand here longer, for I am afraid it is
rather cold for you."

They walked up and down the long room, and Lady
Clare told all that she knew of

THE STORY OF HENRIETTA GASCOIGNE.

"She was the youngest daughter of my ancestor,
the Lord Gascoigne who rendered great service to
Queen Henrietta Maria, the consort of our King Charles
I., when Her Majesty was obliged to leave England. The
queen condescended to allow my ancestor to give her
name to this daughter, and she sent a silver porringer
to the child, which is still in this house, with Her
Majesty's cipher and the royal arms engraved upon it.
I do not know much about Henrietta's girlhood or
education, but her father was a great deal in London
during the time of the Long Parliament and the subsequent usurpation of Cromwell, engaged in the royal
cause with other Loyalists. These affairs took him
much into the city, although he had a lodging at Westminster, in the neighborhood of the Abbey, in the house
of a former tenant of his who carried on the trade of a
glove-maker. If you have ever read much about those
times you probably know that there was a great deal
of secret correspondence carried on between the Loyalists at home and the little court of our exiled sovereign
at Breda, King Charles II. There were negotiations
with Jew money-lenders; and there were at that time
in the city of London a number of Greek merchants,
who, for some reason, perhaps because of their dislike
of the sects opposed to our true Church, or because
Cromwell had oppressed them in some way, made themselves useful to the loyal English noblemen and gentlemen who sought the restoration of the monarchy.

Henrietta's father transacted a great deal of business with one of these Greek merchants, who had a son a few years older than Henrietta. This young man, who is said to have been an attractive and adroit person, was much at my ancestor's lodging. He fell in love with the girl and she with him. There was a clandestine correspondence, which was discovered. The father of the young man professed to behave very honorably about the affair, and said that he had sent his son to the Mediterranean on business. Henrietta's father sent her to this house, under the care of the steward and his wife, with charge to keep strict watch over her and to allow no letters to reach her. The young man lurked about the neighborhood, and by some means he managed to communicate with the girl, and she eloped with him. They were traced to some Italian port, but beyond that the search was fruitless. It was never ascertained whether they were married. This occurred about the time when General Monk began his movements for the restoration of the king, and in these affairs Henrietta's father was so much occupied that he had to suspend the search for his daughter. Whether the father of the young man was honest in his profession of a purpose to get his son out of England before the peace and honor of our family should become compromised, the accounts that have come down to us do not enable us to judge. But soon after the happy restoration of the king this Greek merchant closed his business in London and left England. Henrietta Gascoigne was never again heard of by her own family. It is the only instance, my dear, in which a daughter of this house ever went astray."

"It is a very singular story," said Isabel; "but what was the name of the Greek family?"

"That," replied Lady Clare, "is what makes one part of the mystery now. The tradition has probably come from members or servants of our family who did not learn the name or who forgot it. There are not known to be any papers that would throw light upon it."

They paused again in front of the portrait, and Isabel studied the face with renewed interest. As they stood there looking at it, Lionel said, "You know, Clare, that I have always considered this story a myth. I believe it was invented by gossiping and romantic people in order to attach a tradition to this portrait, about which nothing certain has been known for two hundred years, although it was probably painted by Van Dyck. There may have been a wild girl in the family who ran away with somebody, but whether she was the girl whose portrait hangs here is, of course, utterly uncertain. If there is any truth in the story at all, it could not have been so difficult to find the fugitives. After the Restoration my ancestor could have had all the official aid that he needed in a search for a runaway daughter. The loss of the name of the supposed Greek adventurer makes the whole thing very suspicious."

Perhaps Lionel spoke with the doubts natural to an official man. His sister, however, did not give up her faith in a story that she had believed since she was a child. Isabel said nothing more, but she told me, long afterwards, that by some fascination for which she could not account she never forgot the portrait or the tradition.

They went to church, where the services were of rather a humdrum order. No tenants crowded around the old lord and offered their Christmas greetings. The farmers and their families were there, but they did not seem to feel a strong attachment to their landlord or his children. They knew that no good cheer was providing for them at the manor house, to make a merry Christmas of the olden time. When the plate went around for the collection, the family dropped into it a few shillings. Isabel took a sovereign out of her purse and laid it modestly on the plate, without a sound. Lionel gave as much as he could afford. The picture of Bracebridge Hall was rapidly fading out of Isabel's imagination as they left the church. Although she was well wrapped in her furs, she felt chilled. In fact, she was taking cold without knowing it.

I pass over the luncheon and the lugubrious afternoon. Isabel tried the piano, but it was not in good tune, and the strings jarred upon her nerves. Lady

Clare asked her to sing, but, after making the attempt, she began to cough, and had to give it up. She went up to her room to dress for the evening. She chose a less elegant dress than the one she had worn the evening before, and, as her diamonds had been remarked upon, she put on only a string of pearls. She even laid aside some of her rings. The dinner that evening was hardly more ample or more lively than the first one. After the ladies had been for half an hour in the drawing-room, Isabel said that she felt unwell, and must be excused for going to her chamber before the gentlemen came in. Lady Clare offered to accompany her, but she said she would not tax her kindness. In truth, she wished to be alone; but, with her usual politeness, she went to Lady Clare and kissed her an affectionate good-night. She went up-stairs, exchanged her dress for a warm wrapper, sat down before the fire, and began to weep. Lionel, as soon as he entered the drawing-room and found that his wife was not there, bounded up the staircase three steps at a time.

In the servants' hall, after the dishes had been removed from the dining-parlor to furnish forth what they might for the supper of

> " The baron's retainers, blithe and gay,
> A-keeping their Christmas holiday,"

as well as they could in such a house, and the gentlemen were left to their port wine, Dinah, who had been found to be a very amusing person, began to tell queer stories. The conversation somehow turned upon the subject of serpents, and Dinah was asked if she had ever seen a rattlesnake.

(I must observe that Dinah did her spelling as she would have done her writing if she could have used a pen.)

" Seen um ?" she exclaimed; " reck'n I hev. I seen wun wunce dat was ten foot long. Massa Julius Pringle killed um in de woods. He was twenty-wun yeer ole ef he was a day."

" 'Ow do you know that ?" asked the cook.

" Know it ? 'coz he hed twenty-wun rattl's.   He grow'd a ratt'l every year. Massa Julius tole me soh."

" 'Ow did he get along with so many bunches on his tail ?"

" He krawl'd on his belly like any udder sarpint wen he wanted ter walk.   Wen he wanted to bite, he kurl'd hisself up in rings, shuck his rattl's, an' giv' a spring, wid his jors op'n an' his teef sot.   He'd hit a rabbet an' swaller 'em rite deown hole.   Don't yer knows dat de old sarpint wot begiled mudder Eve was a ratt'lsnake ? He didn't kurl up a bit wen he talked to dat fool woman ; he jess slid along on de groun', an' tole her abeout dat appuel.   I've seen some of dem same kyind of appuels on a tree in ole Virginny nevar tyre."

" Vere is that ?" inquired the groom.

"Ole Virginny is a grāt big Stāt on de nor' sīd of de ole Nor' Stāt.   De fokes dere eet a powerfu' lot ob dem appuels, an' dey knows a good deel more'n 's good fur 'em."

At this point in the conversation, the house-maid, whose brother was a sailor, and who had heard something about the sea-serpent, asked Dinah if she had ever seen that famous American monster of the deep.

" Yaas," said Dinah, " I seen um wunce off Nerharnt. De fam'ly wuz stayin' wun summer at de Nerharnt Hotel.   I tuk Missus Is'bel out wun day on de rox to ketch tortorg.   I bated de hook fur her an' she fish'd. She was a 'ittl' gurl den.   All ter wunce, a man cum runnin' out an' tole us to look at de see-sarpint.   I look'd out to see, an' dere he was, shure enuf, floatin' on de water jess līk' a long string o' barr'ls.   His hed was out o' water, an' he hed a long mān, like a hoss's, but I reck'n it hedn't ben comb'd fur wun whyle.   His ize was as big as sarsers an' as black as charcole."

" 'Ow long did he stay there ?" was the next inquiry.

" Dey put out in bōtes to kotch 'um, but he mād a big splash an' duv un'er, an' he was'nt kotch'd, an' nebber will be."

Dinah had not been two days in the house without letting her musical gifts be known by an occasional bit of singing. They asked her for a song, whereupon she gave them a ditty, describing some of the miseries of human life in the land of slavery. She said that she had heard it sung by one of the "old aunties" on the cotton plantation.

De skurrel cum deown from de hickery-tree,
An' he brung a hickery-nut to me.
"Crack um !" I sez, "my 'ittl' chap ;"
De skurrel's teef give a rite smart snap :
He bruk de nut an' he stole de meat,
An' he dropp'd de shells deown to my feet.
   "Oh, golly, you sly 'ittl' rŏg, git eout,
   Wot's all your munkey trix abeout ?"

De mockin'-burd sing'd me a song wun day,
An' I tole him to sing dat song alway ;
But he wissled a tchune I nebber hurd,
An' he swore 'twan't him, but anoder burd :
Den he floo aroun' an' stŏl' de berries
An' robb'd de trees ob all de cherries.
   "Oh, golly, you lyin' rŏg, git eout,
   Wot's all your wissling tchunes abeout ?"

De black pig into my gardin brŏk,
An' he gobbl'd up de artychŏk ;
An' de gumbo plants he root'd up,
Dat I kep' for my ole man's Sund'y soop ;
He bit de melluns an' split de squosh,
My gardin was all bruk up, by gosh !
   "Oh, golly, yeou durn'd black rŏg, git eout,
   I'll wĭr a ring in your plaguey sneout."

In the midst of other recitatives of this kind, which Dinah correctly thought suited to the taste of her audience, the door opened and her master called her out of the room.

"Dinah," he said, "your mistress has a bad sore throat, and I am going to send the groom for the apothecary."

"No, Mass' Li'nel, don't dun do dat. Missus Is'bel don' want no pottikery, *I* knows. I'll keure dat sore froat rite quick. Yeou jess go up an' tell her I'll be dere in a jiffy."

Then she went back into the room and procured from the cook some mustard and a jug of hot water. The orthodox Indian meal could not be had, and oatmeal had to be taken as the substitute, to Dinah's great disgust. Armed with what she could get, she ran up to her mistress.

"Deah chile," she exclaimed, "I'll fix it all rite;" and in five minutes she had Isabel undressed and in bed, with her beautiful throat enveloped in an appliance which my American readers will appreciate.

"I nebber see sech a house," said Dinah; "dey ain't got no Injun meel, an' dey ain't got a warmin'-pan."

Isabel was almost inclined to laugh at this picture of destitution, but she was too miserable to be amused. So Dinah sat down by her pillow, and, holding the chilled fingers of her mistress in her warm hand,—her palm was as soft as cut velvet,—she sang over and over, in a low, sweet tone, the following verses, as if she were repeating a nursery song to a child:

> In de Floridy lan' is de dark-green trees,
> Whar de yaller orange hang in de sun;
> Dere blös along de sweet, sof' breez,
> Dat de pin woods giv wen de day is dun.
>
> My darlin' sleep in de hammuck dere,
> Dat swing from de bows in de ebenin' shäd,
> An' de skrecchin' owl shall nebber dare
> To make her 'ittl' h'art afrayd.
>
> We sail a-deown de ribber deep,
> De allygätur draw de böt;
> An' all de way my darlin' sleep,
> Til' on de see's blew wäv she flöt,—
>   Til' on de see's blew wäv,
>   She flöt,—she flöt.

As she repeated the words of the last line, dropping into lower and lower cadences, any prima donna in the world might have given half her fortune to be able to catch the sweetness of her tones.

When Lionel came up for the night, his wife was in a sound sleep, and Dinah surrendered her post. In the morning all danger was over. Lady Clare knocked gently at the door, to inquire about Isabel.

"Oh, Mis' Cleer!" Dinah whispered, "Missus is rite smart better."

Isabel rose about noon, and allowed Dinah to dress her. Lionel had gone out. Isabel wished to have him arrange for their immediate return to Town, feeling that she could not endure another day in that dreary abode. But Dinah did not think that her mistress ought to travel before the following Monday; and, as Isabel was now entirely submissive to that faithful creature, she gave up the plan of getting away at once. In the afternoon it began to snow, and this added to the gloom within. But "time and the hour run through the roughest day," which means that all such miseries come to an end. On the next Monday Lionel brought his wife safely and tenderly back to Town, and she never saw Gascoigne House again for many years, nor wished to see it.

CHAPTER VIII.

AN EARLY WIDOW.

Six months after Lionel and Isabel returned to their modest apartment in Clarence Terrace from their visit to his ancestral home, he received another promotion in the Foreign Office, and his salary became six hundred pounds. He had fairly earned this rise on the ladder of official life by his industry and intelligence; and, if the truth were told, his love for his beautiful wife must be set down as one great stimulus of his ambition. Isabel began to find that she had retained more of what she had learned in her school days than she had until now been aware of; and in some ways, by her knowledge, especially of the institutions and history of her own country, she could help her husband when he had any work to do in which a bit of ready information could aid him. She was quicker, too, than he was, and she could often suggest to him a better form of expression than his own when his writing needed such improvement. These discoveries gave her a new pleasure, and in some degree compensated for

her disappointment in regard to his family and all their
ways and doings. Her father, prompt in the performance of his promise, at once increased her income so as
to keep it equal to her husband's salary. They now
felt able to take a small house in Mayfair, which was
to be let, quite suitably furnished, by a family who
were going upon the Continent for a long absence.
When they were settled in this abode, Isabel began to
make new acquaintances, and she was very much liked
by all who came to know her. Her husband wished
her to be presented at court, but she was unwilling
to ask for a presentation by her sister-in-law, Lady
Blanche. The gentleman who was at that time our
minister at the English court claimed his fair country-
woman, and Isabel was presented by his wife. Sen-
sation would be a very inappropriate word to apply to
the impression which she produced; but I can speak
of the admiration which her graceful manners and her
beauty called forth, as it was described to me afterwards by the lady who heard it on all sides. I was
told that Mrs. Gascoigne's simple dignity was very
striking, and that she appeared to be entirely uncon-
scious of her own charms.

After they had been settled in their new house for
about a year she gave birth to a son, a perfectly healthy
child, apparently destined to inherit the good looks of
both his parents. Although Dinah might have claimed
the office, an English nurse was accepted by Isabel, in
compliance with her husband's wish; but she did not
make this woman or any other the foster-mother of her
child. There was occasionally some bickering between
the black and the white woman about the baby; and
when he was in that state of dentition which makes
mothers somewhat anxious, there was a battle royal
one day between the two servants about the regulation
coral which the English woman had asked Mrs. Gascoigne to order for him.

"Dat red bone ain't no yeouse," said Dinah; "I
nebber seen no good givin' a baby anyt'ing as hard as
dat ter bit."

"Wot do you know about babbies, Miss Dinah?"

asked the nurse, in great scorn. "Mind your *h*'own bizness, and I shall mind mine."

"Bizness!" exclaimed Dinah, "does yeou s'pose I'm gwine to let dis chil's teef be spiled by dat little red creow-bar? Give um de end of a nale-rod an' dun wid it."

"Didn't I," said the irate Mrs. Walker, "nuss the Honorable *Hegerton Hegerton*, sec'nd son o' my Lord *Hegerton*, as is now at *Heaton*, with as fine a set of teeth as ever was, and didn't he 'ave a coral, *h*I'd like to know?"

"Didn't I nuss Missus Thumas Pringle's last baby?" shouted Dinah, "an' does yeou s'pose his mudder ever 'lowed 'im to bīt anyt'ing but a corn-cob? Look at my teef. Wot does yeou s'pose I's rāzed on?" And she showed her white ivory, as regular and firm as ever grew in a negro head.

It was quite too much for Dinah. Marching into her mistress's room from the nursery, she said,—

"Missus Is'bel, don't let de baby's teef be rōoin'd by dat nuss. Jess yeou rite hōm an' git some corn-cobs."

"Some what, Dinah?"

"Corn-cobs," answered Dinah; "dem small wuns dat grōse de pop-corn. Shell orf de corn an' skrāp orf de hulls, an' giv um de 'ittl' end to bīt. It's de bess t'ing in de wurld for a baby's teef."

Isabel laughed and promised to write to one of her sisters, whose maternal experience was quite considerable; but probably in no nursery in Boston· had the question between corals and corn-cobs been considered for many generations.

Not long after this little domestic flurry, Lionel told his wife that he had been asked to go on a short excursion in the Channel, by a friend of his in the Office who had a yacht, and that they had obtained leave of absence for five days. There were to be three other gentlemen of the party, but no ladies.

"Will you mind, Isabel, if I leave you for just this short trip?"

"I beg you will go," she said; "you have been working hard lately on those protocols, and you need some recreation. I shall have the baby and Dinah, and I can ask your aunt, Mrs. Bankside, who is so near, to come in and dine with me every evening."

So Lionel and his friends ran down to Portsmouth, where the yacht awaited them, and were soon out and running under a spanking breeze towards the Channel islands.

On the morning of the next day after their little voyage began, a boy belonging to the crew of the boat fell overboard, while she was making eight knots. The sea was not rough, but the boy was a very poor swimmer. Life-preservers were thrown to him, but none of them came within his reach. The boat was rounded to, to make as short a circuit as possible, but before it reached the lad he went down. Gascoigne was the only gentleman of the party who was on deck at the time, the others being below at breakfast. He was an expert swimmer and an athletic man. It never occurred to him to call upon one of the crew to go overboard and save the drowning boy. He threw off his coat, pulled off his shoes, and was over the side in an instant. He swam with strong strokes to the spot where the boy was last seen, meaning probably to catch him when he came up, or to dive for him. On a sudden he threw up his arms and shouted, "Cramp!" He was distinctly heard, but before any assistance could reach him he sank and never rose again alive.

I have told this melancholy story as simply as I could, and perhaps I ought to have omitted it. But my readers know that I am not at liberty to make my incidents. Poor Lionel! He lost his life in an act of heroism characteristic of his nation, and, let us believe, of his class. The Evolutionists say that the good points of a race will sometimes break out in late generations, while the intermediate ones will be but poor specimens of human nature; and so, conversely, they say it is with the bad qualities or deformities, which may have been suppressed but will reappear. Perhaps the Gascoigne who stood at Runnymede for the equal rights of all free-born Englishmen had something in his blood that reached his remote descendant and made him of a

better mould than any of the intermediate kin. If so,
let us hope that poor Lionel's boy got his share of it.

But how was this dreadful news broken to the young
wife who had so amiably consented to a pleasure-trip
that she was not to share? Many years after this sad
event I met the owner of the yacht, Sir Lucius Bennet,
on the Continent of Europe, at a capital where he held
a high diplomatic post. He told me that the accident
occurred just off the Isle of Wight, where the water
was not very deep. After sailing about and over the
spot for an hour or more, as they had no means for
dragging the water, and had to abandon all hope, they
ran into the nearest port for assistance. He sent two
messages from that place,—one to the Foreign Office
and one to the Admiralty. The former requested the
under-secretary to take such steps as he could to have
Mrs. Gascoigne informed before any afternoon paper
should publish the shocking news. The under-secretary
happened to be in the office when the message came.
He drove immediately to the American legation, and
the lady whom I have already mentioned, wife of our
minister, went with him to the house of Gascoigne's
aunt and communicated to her the death of her nephew.
Mrs. Bankside was the person who told Isabel,—how,
my informant did not know; but he said the whole
society of London was moved as he never knew it to
be by the death of any one who was not a distinguished
person. The sea, he informed me, remained smooth
through the whole of that day, and a small steamer,
sent out by the Admiralty, and guided by his yacht
to the place, found and recovered both bodies before
the sun went down. Lionel's remains were interred
in a few days in the family vault in the church-yard
at Gascoigne Manor, and on the wall of the church a
tablet was placed by his companions of the fatal excursion, on which may still be read, in fitting words, the
grand deed which the poor fellow tried to do. I asked
Sir Lucius why Gascoigne, before he obeyed the noble
impulse, did not think of his wife and child. He
replied that he had asked himself that question a great
many times, and that the only solution he could ever

11*

see was that Gascoigne was so courageous, so much accustomed to the water, and so strong a man, that it probably never occurred to him he was incurring a great peril. One of Sir Lucius's friends informed me that he sold his yacht immediately after Gascoigne's death, and had never since been on the water for any purpose of pleasure. I understood that Sir Lucius and Gascoigne were of about the same age and were intimate friends. The position to which the survivor had risen made me think of what Isabel's life would have been if her husband's had been spared.

This gentleman, Sir Lucius Bennet (it was in 1856 that I met him), made many inquiries of me about Mrs. Gascoigne. He said her husband was not a man of remarkable ability, but that he was sensible and very industrious. They used in the office, he remarked, to think that his bright American wife helped him in his work; the under-secretary often said that Gascoigne's papers showed traces of a finer intellect than his own. He understood that she had been very gay before her marriage, and Mrs. Bankside did not suppose that she was at first much in love with her husband, but that she afterwards became very much attached to him.

"I hear," said Sir Lucius, "that she is now quite wealthy. Why has she never married again? She must have had offers."

"No," I replied, "I do not believe she has had one. If she has, she has remained single from choice."

But I must not anticipate Isabel's history after her husband's death. Painful as it is, I must revert to that time; but I shall pass quickly over the first few months of her widowhood. I am not made of adamant. Old as I am, I have a heart that can feel, even for a grief that is as far back as this one. But why should I dwell upon the shocking suddenness of her husband's death, coming when a prosperous career was just opening to him, the brave young father drowned in twenty-four hours after he had parted in full strength and activity from his lovely wife and child? Why should I speak of her new life, cut short just as she was beginning to accommodate herself to the chances that she told her father she was willing to take, and to find that there was more of happiness than of annoyance in what they were bringing to her? The ways of Providence are past finding out, and therefore let no one presume to interpret what befell her as if it were a retribution.

Isabel had probably given to her husband at first less love than he gave to her, but it came to be a very satisfying return of his affection, and she mourned for him with all the tenderness of her nature. He was more than a true gentleman and a pleasant companion: he was as tender a husband as he knew how to be. For the few years that they were together she was an excellent wife. Her happiness was becoming complete, when the dreadful end of it came so suddenly. It is mercifully provided that where there is good temper, good conduct, and ground for mutual confidence and esteem, love shall grow as life goes on. Isabel learned that the food of general admiration is not a nutriment that will give a woman of sense supreme satisfaction. This change I observed in her when I came to see her again. The influence of a great fault committed in early life, the memory of which cannot be lost, may be very powerful in shaping character to the finest mould. I did not discover in Isabel, for many years, any signs of her remembrance of the one great error of her life; and to me its mystery was never solved. But I saw the change in her; and as I have some confidence in my knowledge of human nature, I am able to describe how it was that her character became developed into one that might not have been anticipated from her life before her marriage. As sorrow does not always crush us, so the memory of any wrong that we have done does not always deprive us of the power to rise above it. Isabel mourned sincerely for her brave husband, and this all could see. If she ever thought with tenderness of Henry Brewster, no one could know it.

But it was not in the nature of things that a woman who was so lovely in person and so sweet in disposition should not continue to be admired. The same American lady, wife of our minister, who did not know Mrs. Gascoigne before she came to London, told me, on her

return home, that it was one of the most interesting
sights in the world to see her in a widow's cap, with
her baby in her arms. This lady was often admitted
into Isabel's own room, while she remained in London.
She said that Mrs. Gascoigne's figure was a little fuller
than it was when she arrived in England, but that it
had retained its perfect symmetry. She described her
dark-brown tresses, falling below her cap and shading
her delicate cheek ; her complexion, which had been a
little heightened by the English climate; and she said
that she never saw a more beautiful or a more interesting woman. Thackeray, in his " Pendennis," has said
that he did not think it was national prejudice which
made him believe that " a high-bred English lady is the
most complete of all heaven's subjects in this world ;"
and he took some pains to let us know that by " high-
bred" he did not mean duchesses and countesses. For my
part, I do not profess to be altogether without national
prejudice ; but, after making due allowance for that kind
of bias, and taking the great novelist's definition of high
breeding just as he meant it, I am disposed to think
that a high-bred American woman, who has had some
experience in life in a different society from that of her
own land, and who has the qualities that I admired in
Isabel Gascoigne, is a lady to be put on a par with any
of her sex in any part of the world. I say this without the least disparagement of our fair English cousins,
many of whom I have found to be most charming
women, and the best of wives and mothers. Neither
am I in the least inclined to portray Isabel as one of
those angelic women in whose natures—as Thackeray
found a few such—there is " something awful as well as
beautiful to contemplate." She never became another
Mrs. Pendennis. I have not concealed her faults and
failings ; and in expecting my readers to hold her in as
high estimation as I did, I do not ask them to overlook
a single trait that they ought to disapprove. The
American lady who saw her in London after her husband's death was no doubt partial to the best American
type of beauty and character ; and I, who knew Isabel
so well, could easily believe all that I heard. One of

the pleasantest things that I heard was that the love
which she manifested for her child—the delight of the
mother in her fine boy—won for her the regard of all
who saw them. I was told that the Americans in England who knew her were very proud of her, and that
the English never spoke of her without strong expressions of respect and the tenderest sympathy. I
repeated these things to my wife, who said that they
confirmed my opinion, that Mrs. Gascoigne had admirable qualities as well as beauty, notwithstanding
her early faults, as I had always maintained.

I trust that, for Isabel's peace of mind, her thoughts
were wholly—as I am sure they were chiefly—occupied
with her child. But after she had been for some time
a widow, was there in her inmost heart a memory that
" would not down?" From the moment when Henry
Brewster left her father's house for the last time,—no
word of farewell spoken between them, no sign of interest manifested by her, not the feeblest expression of
a hope for his welfare,—no tidings of him had reached
her. She did not know if he were living or dead. She
did not know whether he had ever heard of her marriage, or that she was now a widow. If they were to
meet, would it be possible,—I used sometimes to ask
myself,—would it be possible for her, by word or look
or sign, to make him feel that through all these years
of separation there had been in her heart a deep con-
trition? He might be married, and then there could
be no hope of her being able to let him see,—if such
thoughts ever entered her mind, no one could know it.
But I, who knew a great deal of her nature, or thought
I did, often speculated about her possible future. My
wife, for long, long years after the death of Lionel
Gascoigne, looked for something to happen that would
bring Brewster and Isabel together again.

Mr. Bradshaw did not ask his daughter to come home
after her husband's death. He was uncertain whether,
on account of her child and the possible wishes of Lord
Gascoigne, he ought to propose to her to leave England.
He doubled her allowance, so that she might suffer no
inconvenience from the loss of her husband's salary,

i

and left it to herself to determine when she would ask him to receive her. Dinah was with her, and all at home knew that she would be faithfully cared for in everything that such a devoted servant could do for her welfare. She remained in England until her boy was three years old, waiting to learn if the Gascoigne family had any wishes or plans about the child. Neither of her husband's brothers had then married or seemed likely to marry. Her boy was therefore the presumptive heir to the estate and the title, next after both of his uncles. But the old lord and his sons thought that the Boston merchant should do for his grandson what they knew very well they would not or could not do themselves. They did not say so, but they delayed saying anything to Mrs. Gascoigne, because they had nothing to say. The child's education might perhaps be squeezed out of the estate, in a niggardly way; but how about the means of supporting the dignity of the title, if he should ever come to it? The old lord looked for nothing for himself but to be gathered to his fathers in peace. The young lord thought it highly probable that this child of his youngest brother would one day be Earl Gascoigne; but was he to labor all his remaining days for this infant? The clerical brother took much the same view. Lady Blanche and Lady Maud did not see any farther into the millstone. Only Lady Clare wished to have her sister-in-law remain in England, and to have the boy recognized as the presumptive heir.

Isabel, as she told me afterwards, did not think the matter of the child's education was the principal difficulty. She could herself provide for it, without any other appeal to her father's bounty, if she were not required to educate him as a future nobleman. She was fully aware that to be an English earl, one of the peers of the realm, if her boy should ever come to that dignity, would be a grand thing. But she did not believe that her father's money could be, or ought to be, devoted to the rescue of the Gascoigne estate or to a new endowment of the ancient title. Whatever fortune, too, she might reasonably expect from her father, although

it would probably be ample for her and her son in
America, would not be enough to enable him to support
the dignity of an earldom, even if she herself were to
live in a garret. She was slowly but surely reaching a
conclusion, when the question was providentially settled for her. She suddenly received intelligence that
her father had died after a short illness, and that he
had left no will. She was now heiress, therefore, to
one-fourth of her father's estate, subject to her mother's
life-interest in one-third of it. Mr. Bradshaw's property
proved to be a very large one, as wealth was estimated
in those days.

This second bereavement was made specially painful
to her by the recollection of her father's kindness at
the time of her marriage. She reproached herself for
not having gone home immediately after her husband's
death. It seemed to her that the years which she had
lost in fruitless waiting for some action or expression
by the Gascoigne family concerning her child had been
robbed from her father. She must now go immediately
to her mother and sisters. As soon as she could arrange
the little she had to attend to she embarked with Dinah
and her child for America. She determined to bring
no English servant, and the little boy was easily weaned
by Dinah from his English nurse. Lady Clare managed
to come to Bath, where Isabel had lived for some time,
—she gave up her residence in London soon after her
husband's death,—to take leave of her. No other
member of the Gascoigne family came to bid her farewell.

She landed in Boston on her twenty-ninth birthday,
the 20th of June, 1842. On the day before that on
which the packet was expected her mother sent me a
message, asking me, as an old friend, to meet her at the
vessel and bring her "home." She had been gone six
years. If the lady who saw her in London thought
her a·very beautiful woman, I certainly was not less
impressed by her beauty and her charming manners.
She was in deep mourning, but no dress could darken
her winning presence or obscure her smile.

" How good of you to come and meet me," she said,

"and how is your dear wife, whom I shall now know? I received the announcement of your marriage with great joy, and I trust the little present I sent to your wife came safely. But ah! my old friend, to what have I come home? To think that my father should have died and that I was away from him! It is too sad."

Tears filled her eyes, and her voice became choked with grief. For the rest of the drive through the noisy streets neither of us spoke. The carriage stopped at her mother's house, on the very same spot where I saw her depart, as a bride, to cross the great Atlantic, so many years before. She had returned a widow. If the stones before our dwellings could tell of all that has been said or felt by those who have trodden them, what a record there would be at some doors! As I handed her out of the carriage I thought of her last words, spoken to me, as she went away. I parodied them by saying, "Be thankful as I am that you are safe back again." She smiled through her tears, as if she too remembered, and then, offering her hand, she said,—

"Come and see me soon and bring your wife. Give her my love, if I may presume to send it."

I let her go in, followed only by Dinah with the little boy.

My wife and I both felt a strong interest—you can say curiosity, if you like—to learn what had been the effect on Mrs. Gascoigne of her life in England. My wife, indeed, could not compare the present with the former Isabel, as I could, from personal observation. I was anxious, however, to have her know the beautiful widow of whom she had heard so much, and she readily assented to my proposal to call upon her a few days after her arrival. We were shown into the drawing-room, where I had formerly been so often, and had witnessed so many of my fair friend's performances in the days of her girlhood. She came down with her usual grace, and when I presented my wife to her she said,—

"I thank you very much, Mrs. Boylston, for the privilege of knowing you. Your husband is one of my oldest, and has always been one of my best, friends. I hope you will share the friendship and regard for me that he has so long extended to me."

Then, turning to me, she remarked that if she were to take my wife's looks for a measure of time, although she had not met her before, her own absence would seem very short. I thought this a most delicate compliment, and probably my readers will agree with me. At all events, it was not lost upon me. I asked about her mother.

"She is well, but you do not need to be told how this loss afflicts her. I am thankful that I came immediately. You can scarcely imagine what a relief it has been to me to learn about my father's brief illness. They tell me that he was entirely himself to the last, and that he charged them to repeat to me his blessing. He spoke of my boy, and expressed a wish to have him brought up as an American citizen. This was so like my father! You have been, I think, Mr. Boylston, at his country-house, and you may remember that he always kept the stars and stripes floating from a flag-staff where he could see them from a window of his bedroom. He had that flag-staff made from the top-mast of one of his ships."

"Yes," I replied, "he was a noble specimen of an American merchant. His wishes about your son will perhaps conflict with those of your husband's family?" I thought I would hazard this inquiry in a gentle way, but she met it frankly and directly.

"No," she answered, "there is no likelihood of that; and if there were it would not influence me. I am only too glad to be again in my own country, and I look for nothing for my child from his English connections. I tell you of my feelings on these matters because we are old friends, and because I know I shall have your sympathy, Mr. Boylston, and I am sure your wife's will go with yours."

I asked her if she expected to remain in Boston through the summer.

"I think so," she replied; "my mother feels that she can hardly go again to our place in the country, at least for the present, and I shall not leave her. The affairs of my father's estate will make it necessary for us all to be where the lawyers can most easily see us on business. For the same reason, my sisters and their husbands will remain in town. I do not think that my little boy will need to be taken out of Boston."

My wife asked to see the child. Mrs. Gascoigne requested me to ring the bell, and told the servant who answered it to ask Dinah to bring him down. I never saw a finer child. Ruddy and strong, he was a good specimen of the Anglo-Saxon and the American blood united in his little person. He ran instantly to his mother, who lifted him upon her lap.

"Dinah," she said, "took him out upon the Common yesterday, and the little monkey wanted to wade in the frog-pond."

"Yaas, Missus Is'bel," said Dinah, "dat pon's too muddy for dis chile's feet."

"What is his name, Mrs. Gascoigne?" my wife asked.

"James Bradshaw. My husband's family wished to have him baptized by some of the names that had been repeated among them for generations, and, if I had not felt such a strong desire to give him my father's name, I should have chosen my husband's. But he most amiably and generously permitted me to call him for my father, whose kindness to both of us at the time of our marriage, you, Mr. Boylston, cannot have forgotten. The family, I believe, thought that Bradshaw came rather near the old regicide, but I am not aware that my father was descended from the famous president of the regicide court, and my husband did not think it mattered much if he was."

"Not the least in the world," was my answer.

As she had thus alluded to her husband, I ventured to say that her father had frequently spoken of him to me, and had expressed his belief that he would become a distinguished man; "and I think," I added, "that your father was aware of the happiness of your married life."

"Ah! my poor husband," she said, with deep feeling, "he was a noble fellow, and I do not know how it was that I could meet, as I believe I did, his shocking death.

I suppose that I was sustained by the sympathy that surrounded me and by the thought that I must live for this child. From no one of my husband's immediate family, however, did I receive much comfort, excepting from his youngest sister, and she was not a person of strong character. I ought, however, to speak of his aunt, Mrs. Bankside, with the utmost gratitude and respect. She was not a Gascoigne. She was his mother's sister; a gentle person, but one of an uncommon ability to be helpful in such a calamity. She was a religious woman, and I think she did me more good in leading me to something like submission to the will of heaven than any other person I have ever known. But I am talking to you too much about myself and my grief. I have come home,—I have my boy, and I can bring him up as I wish.''

"You must not feel, Mrs. Gascoigne," said my wife, "that we are not interested in your sorrows. This is my first visit to you; it is to a house of mourning, and your lot has been an exceedingly trying one. But it has many alleviations.''

"Yes, my dear Mrs. Boylston," she answered, "and I hope I am not ungrateful for the blessings that remain to me. I shall not feel that your sympathy will be wanting to me. You will both come to see me often, I hope, and I presume you will not at present, Mrs. Boylston, expect any return of your visits.''

My wife assured her that she certainly should not, and then, after we had answered her inquiries about other friends of whom she spoke, we took leave of her.

When we were again at home, in our neat little parlor, I asked my wife what she thought of Mrs. Gascoigne.

"You were right, Peter," she answered, "for once in your life. She has fine qualities. With what genuine feeling she spoke of her father. Did you not notice her emotion? That woman has real tenderness in her nature. Do you think she will ever say anything to you about Brewster? You have known her so intimately, and you were such a friend of his, she may speak of him to you. She seems to be a very frank and open-hearted woman.''

"My dear, it is impossible that she should ever make the smallest allusion to him. There is a mystery about that matter which will always render it impracticable for her even to ask me if he is living."

"I do not feel so sure of that," said my wife. "I judge of her as one woman judges of another. She cannot have lost all interest in him, even if she does not now feel any special tenderness towards him. She can hardly see you without thinking of him. She might, without any deliberation or purpose, make some allusion to him or ask you some question. You had better be on your guard and be prepared with an answer."

"Never fear. That affair is too mysterious and too deeply buried in her heart for her to speak to me on the subject."

"Suppose she were to speak to me about him, and ask me where he lives, or whether he is married. She must be aware that I know the story, and, as she and I are likely to become intimate, she may prefer to ask me rather than you. If she does, what am I to say? Is he married or engaged? I know that he lives at Detroit, but that is all I know."

"The breaking off of that engagement, my dear wife, is a mystery that no one ever understood, and as she alone could explain it, and she did not choose to do so, it must now be a matter to which she could not make any allusion. She may feel interest, or curiosity, or anything else concerning Brewster, but she cannot speak of him."

"I look at this matter now, Peter, somewhat differently from the way I looked at it formerly, when I only knew what you had told me and when I had not seen her. I am now convinced that she has great tenderness of heart, and it cannot well be that a woman of such a heart, who had done what she did, should not wish to atone for it to the man whom she made to suffer, if any atonement is possible. I can believe that she did love Henry Brewster, but that for some reason, sufficient or insufficient, her love suddenly died. That makes what you consider the mystery. But it is a mystery to us, not to her; she could explain it in five

minutes or less. What is to prevent her explaining it
to him, if they should ever meet? If he is married, or
if he loves another woman, of course any explanation
is out of the question; otherwise it is within the range
of possibilities and probabilities, and for that reason I
think it would be well for you to tell me what you
know about him. She will probably have a very considerable fortune, and it would really be poetical justice if Brewster were to have the benefit of it. And
what an excellent guardian he would be to her boy."

"Bless your heart, my dear wife, how nicely you have
arranged it all. But I will tell you all I know, for I
would not keep from you anything that honor did not
require me to keep to myself. I do not know that
Brewster is married, or is engaged to any woman, or is
likely to be. I have not wished to ask him. I only
know that he is becoming very distinguished in his
profession for so young a man, and is leading a very
active life. He is only thirty-two now. But, you see,
whatever it was that made Isabel do as she did, and
whatever the explanation might be, Henry would not
marry her, money or no money. Besides, your dream,
or romantic forecasting of what may possibly happen,
supposes that she would wish to marry him. The one
is as much out of the question as the other. I will
give you the best dress that I can afford to buy if, at
the end of any number of years, you do not have to
say that I have been right twice in my life."

"We shall see, Peter. I wish I could offer you a bet
which you would not have to pay yourself, whether
you won or lost. But as I have no separate purse, my
dear, I will let you off on the dress now, for I feel confident that I shall not win it. You are quite safe. If
they ever meet, and he is not married or in love with
some one else, there will be an explanation."

At this moment our waitress came to call us to our
modest dinner, and in her presence this topic had to be
avoided. But although I did not share my wife's expectation, I was very glad that she had formed such a
favorable opinion of Mrs. Gasgoigne.

I have now to relate briefly Isabel's subsequent his-

tory for a period of seventeen years after her return
to Boston. Her mother died in about six years after
the death of her father. By that time the demand for
commercial buildings had made the Bradshaw residence in Pearl Street untenable by such a family. The
house was sold to great advantage in 1851, and Mrs.
Gascoigne purchased for herself a very fine one in that
part of Boston which began to be known as "the new
land," where the Public Garden, Commonwealth Avenue,
and a world of regular streets have since been created
on what was formerly a marsh. Although she became
a woman of fashion, and entertained a good deal, Isabel's
chief interest in life was now centred in the education
of her son. The boy's paternal grandfather in England
died when he was eight years old; his uncle, the new
Lord Gascoigne, married and had an heir; so that
the probability of a James Bradshaw, Earl Gascoigne,
dwindled to a slender chance, as Isabel's father would
have wished it might, and as she herself was content to
have it. She led an apparently happy life, seeing the
friends that she liked, among whom my wife and I held
a foremost place, doing some good with her money, and
devoting herself to her son. She did not become what
is called a literary woman, but she lived in an intellectual atmosphere, and she read a great deal, that she
might not be behind other ladies in the same society,
and that she might be qualified to direct her son's
earlier studies, so far as to be able to choose good
teachers.

CHAPTER IX.

WILL SHE MARRY AGAIN?

When Mrs. Gascoigne found it necessary to have a
house of her own she had no female relative whom she
could ask to live with her. One of the daughters of
her eldest sister was married, and all her other nieces
had happy homes that none of them could leave. She
needed, too, an elderly person, and it was difficult to

find the right one. Do not imagine, respected reader, that I am going to introduce a shabby companion in a dyed silk, sitting behind in the opera-box or occupying the back seat in the barouche. Such females are useful in novels; they are not a part of my characters. After considerable inquiry, while her new house was slowly getting in order, Isabel learned accidentally that a lady, who was one of her teachers when she was at school, had been for many years retired from that occupation, and was living in the country on the income of a small property which represented the savings of her life. Isabel recollected her as an amiable and intelligent woman, and, having procured her address, she wrote to her a note, which, with her answer, I am able to give.

"TREMONT HOUSE, BOSTON, May 10, 1851.

"DEAR MISS SIMMONS,—When you read the name at the end of this note you may not at once know who I am, but I hope you have not forgotten Isabel Bradshaw, who used to tease you so much about her compositions. My father and mother you surely remember, for you were often at their house in Pearl Street. I lost my father in 1842, and I have recently lost my dear mother. I was married after you left Boston. My husband was an English gentleman. He died in England, and since I returned home I have lived with my mother. Her house has been sold, and is to be taken down. I am about to occupy a new one, in which I shall feel lost if I have no one in it but my little boy and my servants. Will you accept of a home with me, and let me make any addition to your income that you may name? I do not wish for a *dame de compagnie*, or a companion, or a house-keeper, or anything but a friend; and if you will be that friend, you will find one who will be very grateful to you for the sacrifices you may have to make in changing your abode, and who will take care of you to the end of your days, in case you should remain, as I hope you will, for the rest of your life, with

"Your former pupil,
"ISABELLA GASCOIGNE."

!" EAST BRIDGEWATER, May 14, 1851.

"DEAR MRS. GASCOIGNE,—An old lady of sixty, who has been away from Boston for fifteen years, living among her flowers and with a canary-bird for a pet, without either cat or dog,—doing a little worsted work and reading her Bible and her Shakespeare,—will, I fear, scarcely be able to meet your expectations. In my youthful days, before I had to earn my bread, I was a good deal in society. Manners and customs are much changed since then, and I imagine that your house will be one to which many people will be attracted, for I infer that you are well endowed with this world's goods, and I am sure that a daughter of your father, so left, will command any position that she chooses to take. I hope, however, that I have not entirely forgotten how to behave in any company into which I may chance to be thrown. It is not that. I could manage to appear well enough not to make you ashamed of me. But such a connection as you propose ought not to be more lasting than may be mutually agreeable and beneficial. I am not a very fickle person, but I dread the idea of being a burden to any one; and indeed I have enough to be independent when I wish to be. You are too young to tie yourself down to one of your own sex. With the understanding, therefore, that this is not to be 'for better, for worse,' 'until death us do part,' I accept your invitation, and will present myself at your house whenever you are ready to receive me. I must make one little stipulation,—that you allow me to bring my geraniums and my bird.

"Since you have so liberally proposed that I shall name my own terms,—business is business,—and as I have a nephew in Amherst College whom I am helping to get an education, I will say that five hundred dollars will more than satisfy his wants and my expectations.

"I have tried to recall you, but you are aware that a great many girls, of different ages, passed through my hands in the long period of my life as a teacher. I do seem to remember a bewitching child, with beautiful ringlets and a fair complexion, who could not be made to do her composition as neatly as I wished. If

I remember rightly, she was brought to the school and taken home by a colored woman, but I have forgotten the name of the servant. Are you that mischievous little Isabel? If you are, you can count upon the love of

"BARBARA SIMMONS."

This was a most happy arrangement. Miss Simmons was a gentlewoman by birth and education. She was the only child of a highly respectable judge of one of our courts, who served for many years on a small salary. The system of retiring judges on an allowance had not been adopted in his time, and, as his health failed, he was obliged to resign and live on the little that he had saved. On his death he left nothing whatever but a spotless name, and his daughter had to support her mother and herself. Miss Simmons was now a very well-preserved woman for her years, of good temper and pleasant manners, without a particle of jealousy, suspicion, or sensitiveness in her nature, and able to accommodate herself to any kind of life.

She arrived, bag and baggage, bird-cage and geraniums, in about a week after Mrs. Gascoigne was settled in her new house.

"Well, my dear," she said, as Isabel met her in the hall, "I see it all now,—father, mother, and child. It all comes back to me. You must let me give you a kiss."

"Come into the reception-room, Miss Simmons, and rest yourself for a few minutes, while they are taking your trunks up-stairs."

They sat down on a sofa, and talked about the school and Isabel's childhood.

"And so you are a widow, although you have left off weeds. I was right when I said you must not tie yourself down to one of our sex. I should think it would not be long before you will have reason to inform me that some other arrangement will require you to dispense with my company. I shall expect to see the suitors 'come as o'er a brook, to see fair Portia.' I can promise to stay only until your manifest destiny comes to its natural end."

" No, no, Miss Simmons, we will not look forward to anything of that kind. There is no Portia in my house, and there are no caskets to be opened because ' I am locked in one of them.' I am very happy as I am. I have my child to care for, and can bring him up as I choose. Now let me take you up to your room, where you will find Dinah ready to unpack your belongings. Dinah is the name of the colored woman who used to bring me from school. We dine at six o'clock, and you have an hour to get rested before you change your dress. There will be no one else at table but my boy. I shall have him with us always, unless there is company. Dinah will bring you a cup of tea immediately."

Isabel had prepared for the old lady a little surprise. In the rear of her new house there was a small room on the ground floor, with a sunny exposure, which the architect had not designed for any particular use. Isabel gave orders, before she removed from the hotel, to have this room made into a conservatory; and when Miss Simmons arrived it was well stocked with plants, and there was a space reserved for her geraniums. The canary-bird's cage was suspended by a cord run over a small pulley. Miss Simmons was installed as sole mistress of this little green-house, to her great delight. Dinah had it strictly in charge to look after her comforts, and one of the neatest chambers in the spacious house was appropriated to her use. There was no question that the arrangement would prove to be what she considered as the proper one, to last as long as might be mutually agreeable and beneficial.

It lasted, in fact, for eight years. Isabel could go away whenever she liked, and could always be sure of a welcome, when she returned, from this cheerful old friend, who never seemed to be willing to leave her plants and her bird.

Whether her departure was in consequence of the fulfilment of any of her predictions about Isabel's plans, is not to be told now.

I suppose, however, that my readers, of the fair sex especially, will wish to know, apart from Miss Simmons's prognostications, what likelihood there was that this young, beautiful, and wealthy widow would remain unmarried. One knows so little of what people will expect,—there is such a variety of feelings about second marriages in books, while in real life they are almost matters of course,—that one can hardly tell what will please or displease. I am, however, to tell the story of Isabel's life truly, and not as the reader would like to have it told. It is probable that, when this part of her life is reached, there will be a dozen different ways of continuing it to the end, each of which will be discussed at ladies' reading-clubs in town and country, and each will be claimed to be the proper *finale*. It is only necessary for me to go right on with these memoirs.

It would be quite superfluous for me to say that there were plenty of bachelors and widowers, every one of whom would have been ready enough to ask the rich and charming Mrs. Gascoigne to marry him, if he had received encouragement sufficient to warrant a proposal. To be sure, nearly all her admirers who frequented her father's house in the days of her young ladyhood were now married, or gone away from Boston. The Frenchman and the Spaniard, who were such *bêtes noires* to Henry Brewster, had each departed to his native land or to parts unknown. The young Southerner had given himself up to bad ways, and been forgotten. The special friend of Isabel's brothers-in-law was married and had a family. With the exception of the gentleman whom I have described as a person of mathematical tastes and accomplishments, all of her former adorers had dropped out of her life. This gentleman was now fallen a little into the sere and yellow leaf, and he no longer had hopes of more than a place in her friendly regards. When she had a dinner-party, he was not infrequently one of her guests; and she endured good-naturedly his prosaic allusions to old times in Pearl Street. As was to be expected, however, a new set of aspirants for her especial favor succeeded to the old ones, and constituted a numerous circle from which she might have easily selected some man on whom to bestow her hand and fortune. I can mention but a few of the most prominent of them.

For a year before James Gascoigne entered the Latin
School he had a private tutor, who was well qualified
to coach him.   He was quite a presentable man, of
some eight-and-thirty or forty, and very ambitious of
social success.   Whatever other people might think of
his presumption, he himself thought it quite possible
that his tutorship of the son could be made an office
for life.   There is not the least reason to suppose that
the widow was aware of his audacity.   At the end of
the year he received a handsome addition to his stipulated salary, and a flattering recommendation, in which
Mrs. Gascoigne expressed her thanks for his services.
He subsided into another employment of the same kind,
and eventually married the eldest sister of his new
pupil, a plain young lady of an uncertain age.

Lest it may be supposed that there were not others
of more consequence than the private tutor, I must
not omit two somewhat distinguished clergymen, one
with high- and the other with low-church proclivities.
They were frequent visitors at Mrs. Gascoigne's house,
and their ecclesiastical jealousy was not a little tinged
with that other kind which is felt in a greater number
of human breasts, although they treated each other in
her presence with respectful but distant politeness.
The Rev. Mr. Flowerdale, a decided ritualist, had candles on the altar of his church ; he intoned the service
most beautifully, and he preached most learnedly on
the historical claim of the Anglican body to be considered as the true Church of the whole English-speaking race, scoring on the one hand the "Romanists,"
and on the other the "sects," with equal vigor.   If he
had been a successful suitor of the fair widow, early
ritualism would have gained the benefit of one well-
lined purse, and perhaps the Rev. Augustus Flowerdale
would have organized the first surpliced choir in Boston.   I believe that he often said to himself,—

> "I do in birth deserve her, and in fortunes,
>   In graces, and in qualities of breeding ;
>   But more than these, in love I do deserve her."

In manifestation of some of his various deservings, he

sent her his two famous polemical sermons, "published by request," and printed on fine tinted paper. They were accompanied by a note, in which he asked her acceptance and perusal of these discourses, in the hope that she would sympathize in his efforts to disseminate the truth, as he viewed it, although he was aware that *hitherto* she had not looked at these things as he did. "Our Church," he added, "comprehends in her great fold all who agree in *essentials,* and *minor differences* should not keep *congenial spirits apart.*" It was no betrayal of confidence for Mrs. Gascoigne to show to Mrs. Boylston a note that came with a couple of printed sermons. She was not bound to read between the lines of the note and to discover a tender, human, and personal sentiment in the wish of a proselytizing clergyman for Christian unity. Isabel was not prone to that kind of interpretation. She had heard of and had generally followed the rule, that it is best to acknowledge an author's presentation copy of a book before reading it. She therefore wrote to the Rev. Augustus immediately, thanking him very simply for his sermons, and promising to read them. She made no allusion to essentials or minor differences, or to the desirableness of a nearer drawing together of those who had so little to keep them apart. In due time she read both the sermons, and did not like either of them. She thought she had read a good deal of it in England, but when she next saw Mr. Flowerdale she was too polite to tell him that he wore borrowed plumes.

He came one day to dine with Mrs. Gascoigne and Miss Simmons, and he was in his blandest mood. His low-church brother clergyman had not been asked. Isabel avoided having them both at her table at the same time, for she did not quite like their propensity to be a little controversial. In the course of dinner, Mr. Flowerdale, in his most insinuating manner, asked Miss Simmons if he might flatter himself that two sermons of his, which his congregation had printed, had fallen in her way. Every one will appreciate the delicacy of this mode of learning Mrs. Gascoigne's opinion of the sermons.

" Yes," said the old lady, promptly, " Mrs. Gascoigne
gave them to me to read, and I have read them atten-
tively, for I rather like to know what is going on in the
religious world."

Then there was a short pause, the gentleman waiting
for one of the ladies to say something more.

" I am an old-fashioned church-woman, Mr. Flowerdale," Miss Simmons said, " and perhaps my ideas about
the Reformation may differ from yours. I believe Mrs.
Gascoigne thinks as I do on these subjects, but you,
who are such a scholar, can easily show two women a
better way."

" We are two to one," replied the smiling Augustus;
" nevertheless, without going very far into an argument which you will not care to listen to, I will say
that my views of the Reformation have been adopted
after a great deal of study. The apostolic succession——"

" Excuse me, if I interrupt you," Mrs. Gascoigne
said; " we make no question—at least, I never have—
about the ordination and consecration of different
orders of the priesthood in our Church. It is, I
suppose, about practices and observances in public
worship that Miss Simmons and I may feel some hesitation. Most Protestants are inclined to think that
it is well to avoid assimilation to the Roman Catholic
services."

" What would you say, Mrs. Gascoigne," asked the
reverend and learned gentleman, " if we have a better
title to the services which we use than the Romanists
can show? You are aware that the British Church
had an independent existence long before Augustine
came and endeavored to subject it to the jurisdiction of
the Bishop of Rome. The British Church had been
free from Apostolic times. Augustine's mission was in
the seventh century, and although he gained many
converts to Christianity from among the Saxon idol-
aters, he did not succeed in making the ancient Church
in Britain submit to the Roman patriarch. This did
not happen until a much later period. You are also
aware that the English liturgy is substantially the same

with that of the early Christian Church, and that the
Catholic Church of the English-speaking world has preserved in its essential integrity the Catholic worship
and all the other marks of the primitive Church which
show the continuity of the Anglican body, and which
prove conclusively that it has derived nothing whatever
from Rome."

Having delivered himself of this learned statement,
which he considered was in itself all the argument that
could be required, Mr. Flowerdale confidently awaited
the assent which two intelligent ladies must yield to
the inference which he intended they should draw.

"This may all be as you say," said Isabel; "I do not
presume to question it. Still, we all know that at the
Reformation, not only in England, but on the Continent,
there were practices and symbols and doctrines which
the Protestants discarded. We know that at the present day there is, in fact, a difference between the two
great branches of the Christian Church, whether we or
the Romanists have the best right to the designation
of Catholic. All I have to say is, that I do not wish
to see this difference obliterated, because I am a Protestant and not a member of the Romish Communion."

"But you will allow, Mrs. Gascoigne, that we ought
to prevent the sects, as much as we can, from drawing
away our own people, and how can we better do this
than by maintaining our Catholicity, and by asserting
our historic claims? A great while ago something happened in this city which I shall never cease to lament.
That fine old church, King's Chapel, was seized by the
Congregationalists before the apostasy of Unitarianism
occurred. It was a great shame."

"I suppose," said Isabel, "that the pew-owners of
King's Chapel assumed that they could do what they
saw fit with their property, so far as it did not consist
in invested funds bequeathed to special uses; and I
have always understood that there was an amicable
arrangement between Old Trinity and the King's
Chapel people about the Price fund, a great many years
ago. My father, although a young man, was a member
of the Committee of Trinity Parish at the time, and I

know that he considered the settlement a fair and just one."

"Ah, Mrs. Gascoigne, we had no bishop then, and no clergy of sufficient energy to prevent this wrong. There has been a rector of Trinity who could boast that he had driven the last Democrat out of his church by his political sermons; but he did not care where the man went, or whether King's Chapel received him."

At this moment, Mrs. Gascoigne rose, and they went up to the drawing-room, Mr. Flowerdale politely giving his arm to the elder lady and James escorting his mother. In the drawing-room there was a very handsome grand piano.

"This is one of Chickering's instruments, I presume," Mr. Flowerdale remarked, casually.

"Yes," said Isabel, "it is of his make. It is my old instrument repaired. It was tuned only yesterday. Mr. Chickering's people have been very slow in sending it home."

"Will you not give us some music, Mrs. Gascoigne? I never had the pleasure of hearing you, but I have been told that you sing charmingly."

"I should not like to sing now, as I have not tried my voice for some time. But I will play anything you may like to hear. There is a variety of music in the stand. What shall it be?"

"Play Beethoven's 'Moonlight Sonata,'" said Miss Simmons; "I have not heard it in years."

Mr. Flowerdale would be delighted to hear the Sonata. He adjusted the music-stool with polite gallantry, and opened the instrument so that it might give forth its full power. Isabel executed the piece, not as a professional person would have done, but as a lady who could play with far more than common effect. Mr. Flowerdale had some musical taste, and Beethoven's music was then much cultivated.

Miss Simmons softly tapped her left hand with her fan, in token of her applause, when the last note was struck.

"Thank you very much," Mr. Flowerdale said, with a profound bow; "your touch is exquisite. I have just heard, from a friend in New York, that their Trinity Church is likely before long to have a surpliced choir, properly trained."

"You mean a boy choir, I presume, or a choir of boys and men. I have heard them in England, and I must say that I prefer a quartette choir of men's and women's voices," Isabel said, as she rose from the piano and walked to a side table where there was a small silver coffee-urn giving forth a pencil of steam.

Mr. Flowerdale was a little crestfallen. It did not seem that he was making much progress. He made his bow quite soon, after a cup of coffee, pleading some parish work that required to be attended to that evening. When he had gone, Miss Simmons said, with just a little smile in her blue eyes, "Do you not think, dear, that this gentleman's parents made a mistake when they had him baptized by the name of Augustus?"

"Why? Augustus is a very good name."

"Yes, but Augustine would have been much more appropriate."

"He is a scholarly man," Isabel said, gravely, "and I do not doubt his sincerity. He is reputed to be very active in all sorts of good work; but if he is a modern Augustine, I am afraid that his success in bringing over two such women as you and me will not be greater than his prototype met with in ancient Britain. From the very little of ecclesiastical history that I know, I believe that those British prelates told the Roman missionary pretty distinctly that they did not propose to give up any of the practices or doctrines of their ancestors. I have a good deal of the same feeling."

"But it seems to be supposed nowadays," said Miss Simmons; "that our Church anticipates Rome in its liturgy, and that we have the first right to everything that the ritualists wish to revive."

"Very likely," replied Isabel; "but I do not care to go back of the Reformation, and I do not attach much importance to the question that is now made. I think I understand what the Reformation was. But what is that piece of work you are doing?"

"It is only a little piece of embroidery for the fair that is to be held for the blind asylum."

"Oh, to be sure," said Isabel; "Dr. Howe was here this morning, and I asked him to put down my name for a hundred dollars, because I have been so busy with my house that I could not take a table at the fair. If you think I did not give as much as I ought I will increase the subscription. Dr. Howe is a wonderfully energetic man, and his wife is one of the most intellectual women I have ever known."

Some time afterwards, Miss Simmons told me, very confidentially, that she did not think the Rev. Augustus would be the man to captivate our fair friend.

Of the other and low-church clergyman, the Rev. Mr. Cushing, it is not necessary to say much. He was of that branch of the Church of which Isabel and all her family had always been adherents; and, as far as sympathy on religious matters might go, his chances for marrying her were better than Mr. Flowerdale's. But none of us imagined that she would become a clergyman's wife, or that she had either the taste or qualifications for such a position. She was very charitable, liked to do good, and did a great deal. As the wife of a pastor of a parish, high or low church, she would not have been a successful or a happy woman. None of her intimate friends, therefore, felt much concerned about either of her clerical admirers. There was, however, another gentleman, who I might have supposed would have found favor with her. He appeared in her circle after Mr. Flowerdale and the other clergyman had ceased to entertain hopes, so that the field was quite free. Mr. Arnold was of suitable age, excellent character, good family, agreeable manners, and independent fortune. Like Isabel's father, he had made his own way in the world; and he was a man of refinement and cultivation, with more literary taste and knowledge than Mr. Bradshaw ever possessed. I thought he would make a good step-father for James and a good husband for James's mother. I used to wish that she would marry him, but I imparted the wish to my wife alone.

All along, the female relatives and some of the other friends of these several candidates for an alliance with a lady who was worthy of the best of them, whoever he might be, looked to see her make a selection; but none of them could venture to do much to promote the prospects of the one who they hoped would win the prize. All who had known her in the earlier part of her life, or had heard about her, while they felt her undiminished attractions, saw that in some respects she was much changed. She had lost nothing of her former frankness, and her pleasure in being liked and appreciated was as great as ever. Yet in all her demeanor towards any man who now endeavored to gain something more than her friendship there was a decorum, a delicate dignity, which intimated very plainly, when any intimation was needful, that she had nothing more to give. No woman in the same situation ever had such perfect manners towards the other sex. This every one saw. No one smiled significantly when some gentleman's name was connected with hers. People talked of her in respectful whispers when the probability of her marrying again was alluded to, as if the subject were too delicate for common gossip. If I sometimes wished that she would marry, it was because I believed that she could make a new happiness for herself and for the man whom she might accept. Whether she had resolved not to change her condition under any circumstances, or whether it was because she had not met any man who could induce her to break that resolution, if she had made it, she was still unmarried as late as the year 1859. I shall not anticipate here what occurred at that time.

In all these years perhaps she could not bear the thought of giving poor Lionel a successor. I never considered her a romantic woman; yet it is in regard to her feelings about her husband that I have had so much hesitation. The grief of a young woman for a husband lost as Lionel Gascoigne was may be very sacred, and it may last a long time without any great amount of sentiment or romance. I was well aware that Isabel married the young Englishman less for love and more for the sake of being taken from a position in which she was unhappy. Before his shocking death she had given him her whole heart, and it was one in which there was a wealth of affection that she did not herself know of until it was developed in her married life. His death was so piteous, so crushing, that if, through all this length of time, she had a feeling about him like that which Amelia cherished for George Osborne during so many years before she could think of marrying Major Dobbin, I could not blame her. There was nothing for Isabel to learn about Lionel, as Amelia had to learn about George,—that he was not worthy of the devoted love which she gave him while he lived and which she continued to give him long after he was dead.

Mr. Thackeray evidently feared that his lady readers would feel some contempt for Amelia, and he did his best to prevent it. We are all aware what a weak and insignificant little creature most of them consider her. If they did but know it, Amelia is one of the most beautiful characters in English fiction,—a character drawn with consummate art and with an intimate knowledge of the natures of women. Whether she was designed to be the foil to Becky Sharp, or Becky was drawn to be her foil, Amelia is the most finished production of the great artist's pencil. There is far more of nature and far less of the extravagance of fiction in Amelia than there is in Becky. Perhaps it is because Becky is such a smart caricature that readers of her own sex take more interest in her than in Amelia. I would not for a moment intimate that they are attracted by the glimpses of wickedness which they get in the life of the talented adventuress, more than they are by the sweetness and purity of Amelia's character and the pathos of her history. Dear, amiable, lovely soul! No *man* lays down "Vanity Fair" without thanking the author for recompensing her at last for all that she had suffered. Providence often reserves such rewards for the good and faithful, even in this world of sorrow; and the writer of fiction who works out the same result, in a natural course of things,

displays the highest skill of his art. There is another
way of ending the lives of the innocent and virtuous.
When a novelist or a poet terminates in disappointed
love, or in insanity or death, the life of some lovely
woman, he is just as true to nature,—to use the hackneyed phrase,—just as much a master of his art, as
when he makes happiness and joy the end of early
suffering. Yet, when we can have the happiness and
the joy, let us be thankful. Ophelia and Clarissa Har-
lowe and Clara Mowbray and the Jewess Rebecca are
each of them not less according to the truth of this
mysterious world than Portia, or Pamela, or Jeannie
Deans, or Di Vernon. We could not spare any of
them from the gallery of Art, where the immortal portraits are hung. But the realm of fiction is a very
different world from the realm of fact. I am not
drawing a fictitious character; I am describing a life
—the life of a friend—of a woman in society, and
of a period not very long past. I am bound by no
rules of Art; and I am, ladies, no more amenable to
your criticism than Dame Nature herself. If you cannot appreciate my lovely friend as I did, permit me
to say that it will be your misfortune rather than my
fault.

I could know nothing of what was in Isabel's inmost
thoughts when the idea of a second marriage presented
itself to her, if it ever did. My wife repeated to me a
conversation in which she learned something of Mrs.
Gascoigne's feelings about her husband, at a time when
it seemed to us that Mr. Arnold was probably on the
eve of a declaration. It was quite casual, and there
had been no allusion to Mr. Arnold. Mrs. Boylston
was sitting with her one morning in her chamber. On
the dressing-table stood a little upright ebony case, with
elaborately carved folding-doors, which were closed and
locked. Mrs. Boylston had never before observed it,
but Isabel, seeing that her attention was now attracted
to it, said,—

"You never saw my husband, although Mr. Boylston
was at our marriage and was most kind to both of us.
You would not know how good a likeness I have of

him, if I were to show it to you; but perhaps you would like to see it."

She went to the dressing-table, and detaching a diminutive key from her watch-chain, she unlocked the doors of the case. It was lined with black velvet, and in it was hung a miniature set in an oval gold frame. She took it out and placed it in my wife's hands. "This was painted," she said, "about two months before he died. Tell me if you think James resembles him."

"Oh, yes; the resemblance is very strong indeed. I have often heard Mr. Boylston say that James reminds him at times of his father so strongly, that it makes him think it is the father he is talking with. It is very fortunate that this fine miniature was painted: it must be an inestimable treasure to you. I am so glad to have seen it."

"It was a thoughtful gift from his aunt, Mrs. Bankside. She had it painted, and gave it to me on his birthday. The lettering on the back is 'Lionel Gascoigne, Æt. XXXI.' I wore it constantly until he died, and until I came home; but one cannot wear such a thing here, one is so likely to be asked about it. The case in which I keep it I had made after his death, before I left England. My poor husband, Mrs. Boylston, was very different from most Englishmen of his class. I may be prejudiced against them, and of course I have a prejudice in his favor, which I do not wish to get over."

"Do you think that Englishmen are less tender as husbands than Americans of the same cultivation and equally good moral character? I have heard so."

"As a rule, I think they are, in the higher classes of society. I saw very little of those who are called the middle classes. Among the aristocracy and the gentry, the men marry from motives in which love is not always predominant, and the girls too often marry for rank or wealth. Then, you know, the manners and customs are so different from ours. An English husband is not expected to do for his wife what American husbands do,—those little attentions which make so

much of our happiness. Perhaps English women are
more independent than we are,—possibly they are more
self-reliant; but I think they lose something that we
are thankful to have, and that sweetens our married
lives. My father warned me that I should find this
difference, before I married Mr. Gascoigne, but he attached more importance to it than I did. I did not
think it a very great risk. I knew that Mr. Gascoigne
had been for some time in this country and had seen
something of our social life and domestic ways. Before we were engaged, I saw that he understood us very
well, for he thought there might be something good
that was not English. This gave me great confidence
in him, and it all turned out right. He proved to be
an exception to the generality of English husbands; it
was, at any rate, because I believed him to be an exception that I loved him so well. Perhaps I ought to
say that I learned to love him, for marriage, as you
know, is a great school. But I am talking of things
that happened a long time ago. I do not much concern
myself now with these comparisons. I know what you
and Mr. Boylston have always been to each other."

"Yes, we are a comfortable pair, of the old sort.
But did you not at first have to make Mr. Gascoigne
feel that you expected him to be a husband after our
pattern?"

"Not the least in the world. Years ago, soon after
I returned home, I told Mr. Boylston all about the first
and only visit that I made to Gascoigne Manor House.
It was soon after we arrived in England. I might have
been amused by what I saw and heard there,—I tried
to be,—but before the end of a week I became ill, and
my illness was increased by the wretchedness I felt at
finding everything so different from what I expected.
I had Dinah, to be sure, and she, you know, is a treasure.
But my husband watched over me and cared for me
with infinite tenderness and devotion. I shall never
forget what a relief it was to me when he carried me
so tenderly away from that gloomy old house and
stupid family, in which there was not a soul I could
like excepting his youngest sister. I was thankful

enough to get back to our small but cheerful apartment
in London, although London is often a dismal place.
There I began to find the greatest delight in sitting
with my husband in the evenings and helping him in
his work, which I could do very often. I cared little
for any society but his. When I began to go into the
world, I felt that he had a career to make, and that I
could help him to make it; and it was such a joy to
know that he considered me capable of a little service.
The blow that crushed all this came with terrible suddenness, and if I had not been a mother, with a child a
year old, I do not see how I could have been here now
talking to you. If James ever marries, I do hope that
he will marry for love and for nothing else."

"I hope so too, with all my heart," Mrs. Boylston
said; "but one cannot tell what will happen to a young
man situated in life as your James is."

"His situation in life, dear friend," said Isabel, "need
not stand in his way. My fortune, as you know, is
entirely at my own disposal. James need not hesitate
to marry a penniless girl. I want nothing but character, and I hope that if there is beauty, there will be
character along with it. Now let me make a predic-
tion of something that is in my own control. When
James marries, his wife will find a home in which the
proverbial mother-in-law will not be the ruling power."

With a little laugh, in which the two ladies joined,
the conversation here ended. My wife could only infer
from it that Mrs. Gascoigne had not then the remotest
idea of marrying Mr. Arnold, and that her son was, as
ever, the supreme object of all her thoughts and interests. Still, Mr. Arnold was not the only man in the
world. Isabel's present indifference about her own
future, in the matter of a second marriage, might change,
if one should present itself which united all that was
desirable for herself and her son. She was not much
over forty-five at this time, and she was rich enough to
make ample provision for James and herself. I will
just note the period of this conversation. It occurred
a year or so before she made a visit to Saratoga, which,
as it proved, was to have a great deal to do with the

remainder of her life. But I must now go back for a considerable space, and give some account of James from his boyhood down to that eventful summer of 1859.

One thing was, from the first, apparent to us all: that, although a sensible woman, Isabel would err on the side of indulgence from the nature of her affections. The lad, as he grew in years and in fine physical development, did not seem likely to set the river on fire in any way. He was gentle and amiable, but all the teachers in the world could not make him learn easily, or make him overcome difficulties by hard work. I used to think it doubtful if he would have amounted to much if he had been a poor boy and been put to earning his bread; for his mind, while it had all the natural faculties of an intelligent lad, seemed to have them in only about half their proper vigor. Jimmy Gascoigne, as his intimates called him, was just the youth likely to become of no account in the world, by the effect of unlimited indulgence. He got into Harvard by the aid of some looseness and willingness on the part of the examiners; and expensively furnished rooms, unrestricted credit at a fashionable tailor's, horses, theatres, balls and parties in Boston, and similar advantages, did what was needful to supplement the handiwork of nature. I am happy, however, to say that he did not contract any of the gross vices, and that his youth was never stained by anything low, mean, or dishonorable. He was always a gentleman, and a favorite among young ladies who liked good manners, good looks, and a propensity to innocent amusements, and who thought that a young fellow who could spend any amount of money in bouquets a very desirable friend. His male associates generally found him ready to do rather more than his share in the expenses of what was going on in their set, and this is a great cause of popularity. Older people, too, asked why the only son of the rich Mrs. Gascoigne should study a profession, or engage in commerce, or do anything under the sun but take life easily, so long as he lived like a gentleman and did nothing to disgrace himself or to pain his beautiful mother.

So it turned out that Jimmy Gascoigne, after he left college at the age of twenty, became an idle young man; one of those ornaments of society who constitute the *jeunesse dorée* of our American life, for whose existence no particular reason can be given. Whether anything will ever occur to force him to the front, or to develop in him something that cannot now be discovered as a prospect or a promise, is in the future. At present, he must be left with his mother, leading the kind of life appropriate to such a youth, while she enjoys the happiness of his affection, his amiability, and his freedom from any immoral conduct or vulgar tastes.

A rich mother of an only son is, however, pretty sure to have her anxieties about his matrimonial tendencies. Isabel kept her eye upon all the young women among whom her son was a favorite; and she would have rejoiced if he had fallen in love with any one of several whom she knew very well. But she could not discover that he had any preference, and if she had any herself she did not let him perceive it. He became four-and-twenty before anything occurred to attract her special attention to any girl whom they had known, or to any new acquaintance. Parents of the fair daughters of Boston at that time welcomed James Gascoigne to their houses, but neither parents nor daughters laid any plans concerning him. He was universally considered a good fellow; and if he had fallen in love with any girl in the American Athens, there could have been no reasonable objection to his marrying her, provided she liked him well enough. Young men of his stamp are not to be debarred from matrimony because they do not belong to the producing classes, any more than the lilies of the field should be prevented from arraying themselves in a glory greater than Solomon's because they toil not, neither do they spin.

But my readers are not to set down James Gascoigne as a "dude." That character is a production of a later period. To fulfil it requires something of a fool; and James was by no means a fool. He had common sense, and entirely good principles. He lacked an object in life; and while he could not make one for himself of any importance, he was not obliged to find one in ways and things that would make him ridiculous. His mother once tried to induce him to enter politics; and she consulted me about a course of reading that might fit him to take some part in public affairs. I could not, however, give the plan much encouragement. I knew that the public are generally willing to meet rich young men more than half-way, but they require some evidence of industry and capacity. I frankly told his mother that money alone would do little for him, and that some fellow who had not a penny in the world, but who could show ability to work, would distance him in the race. She gave up the idea, but James did read some of the books that I put before him, and perhaps he profited by them afterwards. It is well to sow such seed, even if they are sown among tares. Sometimes the good seed will fructify, and sometimes the tares will spring up and choke them. In this case the result was a good way off. It would depend upon circumstances that could not be foreseen whether James Gascoigne was to become an utter failure, or to make his mark.

CHAPTER X.

BRIEF BUT PERFECT.

AFTER Mr. Charáxes left Boston, he travelled extensively in different parts of the Union, until, finding himself, in the summer of 1837, in the old city of Detroit, he made a longer stay there than he had in most of the places that he visited. Walking one day in the suburbs, he was attracted by the appearance of a large house standing by itself in an enclosure of four or five acres. The building was of stone, and of a peculiar architecture, older than that of any of the neighboring houses. It was unoccupied, and on inquiry he found that it was for sale. When he had examined the interior he determined to buy it; and wishing for the services of a lawyer in the transaction, and knowing no one to whom to apply, he strolled along one of the business streets, until he saw the name "Henry Brewster." He was far too keen a man of affairs to put himself into the hands of a total stranger without any inquiry; but he thought he would venture to take an observation. Ascending one flight of stairs, he found the name repeated on the door of an office. Entering, as he understood was the custom, without knocking, he walked into an inner room, well-lined with books, where a young man, apparently about thirty, was seated at a desk. Rising and greeting the stranger, the occupant of the office placed a chair for him.

"I am in search of a lawyer," said Charáxes, "to assist me in the purchase of a house, but, as I am a stranger here, I hardly know to whom to apply."

"I happen to be a lawyer, sir," replied the young man, "but I have been in practice here for only about a year. Perhaps you could do better."

There was something in the manner of the young lawyer, however, that led Mr. Charáxes to think that he was a gentleman.

"Do you happen to know the Rev. Dr. Pitman, rector of St. Joseph's Church?" he asked.

"Yes, I have the honor to be slightly known to him."

"Well, then, as I brought a letter of introduction to him when I came here, suppose that each of us should consult him as a common acquaintance?"

The result was that Mr. Charáxes learned from Dr. Pitman that Brewster was a young lawyer of New England birth and education; that he had already acquired a good practice in Detroit, and bore a high character. Brewster learned that this foreign gentleman was a person of large wealth and great respectability, but why he proposed to settle in Detroit was not known. Mr. Charáxes placed his business in Henry's hands; the purchase of the house was effected in due time; and from that period they became very intimate. Soon there began to arrive from New York, coming from foreign parts, large quantities of furniture, books, and *objets d'art*, and by the time the house was ready for occupation a number of servants—some foreigners and some natives—made up the domestic establishment. In fitting up his new abode, Charáxes spent money most liberally, but judiciously, and when all the arrangements were completed, it was a very well-appointed gentleman's residence.

. Brewster was then living in a small and modest house, with his sister. She was of great service to Mr. Charáxes in the preparation of his new abode, and he soon appreciated the fine qualities of her mind and character. Scarcely a week passed that she and her brother were not his guests at his dinner of a Saturday evening, sometimes with the addition of a few other persons whom he knew. Among these was the rector—Dr. Pitman—and his niece, Mary Lyndall, a young lady then about twenty-five. She had been left an orphan at an early age, and had been educated by her uncle. Her home was still at his house. The acquaintance thus begun between Brewster and Miss Lyndall ripened into some intimacy, but what would be the result was for a long time uncertain. Brewster's unfortunate love-affair had produced in him a not unusual effect. It had not destroyed his capacity for love, or made him a woman-hater, but it had made him appear cold. Mary Lyndall was a woman as unlike Isabel Bradshaw as any woman ever was unlike another. I never saw her, but I heard a great deal about her in later years, and copies of some of her letters were intrusted to me. I have been told that she was not without beauty of person, but it must have been a beauty very different from Isabel Bradshaw's. In intellect, there was not so great a difference as there was in their early educations. Isabel, although her youthful education was rather superficial, became a very well-informed woman in her middle life, and her experience in the world was much wider than Miss Lyndall's ever became. But Miss Lyndall's education was by far the most thorough and comprehensive; from her earliest years she was more thoughtful, and her feelings were ever under the control of a conscientious rectitude. She had never met a man whom she thought more worthy of esteem and confidence than Henry Brewster, but whether she could love and marry him would depend very much upon himself. It was not until after an intimacy of two years that Brewster asked her to become his wife; and as he did this by letter, while she was absent from her home for a few weeks, it came upon her rather unexpectedly. Her answer will give the reader a better idea of her than any character that I could draw.

"Your letter is full of all that can touch the deepest sympathies of a woman's heart, and it makes me wretched that in answer to it I must utter words which will pain and disappoint you. Until I received your letter, I had supposed that the regard each felt for the other was similar in nature and extent, and that we might continue to meet upon that easy familiar ground which is most agreeable to me in my social relations. I have been deceived,—no, deceived is not the word.—I have been mistaken in regard to your manner towards me. It has seemed to me at times even cold, and I fear that you have also mistaken mine. I am by no means insensible to the value of a strong, pure, and sincere attachment, and I am troubled that you cannot receive from me the return which such an attachment deserves. I would willingly make you happy if I could, but the attempt would be in vain if I could not give you that warm and devoted affection which you would require and which I have always considered essential to the happiness of married life.

"Time has taught me rightly to understand and appreciate the excellence of your character. You have my sincerest esteem and gratitude,—my nearest friends are your friends and would rejoice in my union with you. Yet in the face of this rises the plain and obstinate fact which will oppose itself to any argument of reason. I do not love you. I do not feel for you that deep attachment which I think I ought to feel for one to whom I am to be united by the holiest of ties; an attachment which would give me strength for any duty, and support under any trial that in life might fall to my lot. You have a right to such a love, but I cannot say that you have roused it within me. Mysterious and inexplicable in its nature, it seems almost to defy our control. For this reason I think I could not make you happy, and that I could not give you that true and perfect sympathy which you ask. Heaven knows how unwillingly I pain you, but I must be true to you and to myself, for our future happiness depends upon it.

"Forgive me if I have hurt you, and believe that I have felt keenly every wound that I have inflicted. Let me still continue your sincere friend,

"M. L."

This was evidently not final. It was the letter of a conscientious woman, who doubts but yet may be convinced. Brewster flew to her presence. Their interview was long, but still her scruples were not removed. After his return home, he received another letter from her, which I will not withhold.

"I thank you for your note. It was some consolation to me after our very painful and embarrassing interview; but it was not entirely satisfactory, for I see that you do not yet understand me. I have been in a sea of troubles to-day, because the course of conduct which I ought to pursue at this critical moment of our lives seems dim and undefined to me. One thing alone is clear,—that I ought not to enter into any engagement with you in the present state of my feelings. Neither can I reconcile myself to the idea of encouraging the least hope which I may hereafter be compelled to crush. I cannot trifle with you. It seems to me that the question between us should be settled at once; but if you think otherwise, if you can say that should there be nothing gained there could be nothing lost by deferring my decision for a short time, I am willing to agree to this alternative. At the expiration of a few weeks I must know my own mind upon this subject; there can then be no doubt as to the degree of affection I am capable of feeling for you.

In the interim we could meet, and you could write to me when you pleased. I feel that I cannot commend such half-way measures. I am not satisfied as to their right or their expediency. Every way I turn, however, I must give or receive pain; there is only a choice of evils for us, so that after some reflection this course seems all that is left to me, unless you will consent not to tempt the future, but to rest content with my present judgment in this matter. With the strongest desire to act kindly and justly by you, believe me,

"Your friend,

"M. L."

There was something so confiding and tender in this that the result could not be very far off. When a half consent has been gained from such a woman, he must be a poor lover who cannot win the other half. It was not at the end of weeks, or of many days, that Miss Lyndall found where her heart ought to lead her. It was all settled the very next time they met, and soon she was able to write to him such words as these:

"We shall probably modify each other's feelings and views, and, at any rate, whenever we cannot unite we will agree to disagree. I rely upon you to cut away whatever is morbid or weak in me. I look to you to give strength to my character, rest to my heart, and impulse to my intellectual powers; in return it shall be my earnest endeavor to satisfy you in all things. I will strive to be a kind, affectionate, devoted wife."

Must I write that this perfect union had but three years' duration in this world? Why is it so ordered that in some cases—in which not merely happiness, but the full end of our mortal existence, for the welfare of others, seems to require that two lives shall reach together the threescore and ten—one shall be taken early and the other left? What, in all the twenty, thirty, or forty years, through which the survivor remains and toils and suffers in this world, becomes of that

other one who has gone before? Shall we overtake
those whom we have lost, so that we shall be able to
be as they are, and shall not feel that they are beyond
us and above us? Will those who have gone before
us always be in advance of us, measured by the lapse
of time since they went away? Are there any years
in that state of existence into which departed souls
have gone? Do they take note of time in eternity?
Or are the dead held in undistinguishable and uncon-
scious sleep, until the last trump shall sound, and we
shall all go together to the judgment-seat, as each one
was when this life was ended? For necessary reasons,
doubtless, knowledge of these things has been with-
held from us. We could not bear to know them while
we remain here. Hamlet's madness was not feigned.
Human reason could not endure the "eternal blazon"
of communication with those who are in another world.
If there were such communications, the strongest mind
would be overthrown. This is what Shakespeare meant
to teach, and it is what Nature teaches. "Spiritual-
ism" is a delusion and a sham.

Again Elizabeth Brewster had to become her brother's counsellor, consoler, unfailing friend, in time of
need. A little girl of two years, the Margaret Brewster of these memoirs, was growing into womanhood
under the care of her aunt, during the seventeen or
eighteen years through which I have given some account of the lives of Isabel Gascoigne and her son. As
I am rather careful about my chronology, I mention
that we have now arrived at the year 1859. During
the preceding twenty years, Brewster rose very high
in his profession, and prospered in fortune. His daughter's education was conducted entirely at home, under
her aunt's supervision. Her character will unfold itself
as I go on. It is enough to say that in the life which
she led there was no chance for frivolity. It was rather
too serious a life. She had no intimate friends of her
own age. The young men whom she knew were not
her equals; the young women thought her proud.
But it was not pride. It was superiority, without
affectation, without airs, and without pretension; with

sincere and direct ways, and with no small practical power in whatever is appropriate to a refined and educated woman. Her intellectual qualities led her to understand and to be interested in public affairs; and her father's propensities and conversation developed in her an unusual taste and capacity for such subjects. Although he never was in official public life, his influence was very great when he saw fit to exert himself on any public question. He did far more in shaping public opinion on critical occasions than the noisiest and most active politicians of any of the parties of the time. His marriage took place in 1839, but he did not make it known to me. It is probable that at that part of his life he effaced from his recollection, as much as possible, all his associations with Boston, and that he included me among those whom he then wished to forget. I did not feel hurt by his silence, for I supposed I understood it, and I thought it quite natural. After the time when Isabel married and left Boston, her father never again spoke to me about Brewster. Mr. Dana, too, ceased to speak of him. The story, in the lapse of more than twenty years, faded out of the recollections of almost every one but my wife and myself.

CHAPTER XI.

AN UNEXPECTED MEETING.

ASTROLOGY must have been a fascinating science. I never understood it; and therefore I cannot determine by what "The stars voluminous, or single characters, in their conjunction met, give me to spell" the combinations of the heavenly bodies whereby it was fated that Henry Brewster and Isabel Gascoigne, *née* Bradshaw, should meet in the summer of 1859 at a fashionable resort. I can only tell of things occurring on this mundane sphere in a very natural course of things.

In the latter part of the month of June of that year, Brewster, his sister, and his daughter had been dining

one evening, according to their frequent custom, with
their old friend Charáxes. The weather was exceedingly warm, and all four of them—the two gentlemen
with their cigars—were seated on the veranda. The
moon poured a flood of light upon the waters of Lake
St. Clair, and many a white sail was visible in the distance.

"I have been thinking," said Brewster, "of taking
the ladies to Saratoga. Why should you not join us,
sir?"

"I?" asked the placid old man. "I am too much
wedded to my easy-chair, and it is so long since I have
been in the world that I should be quite out of place."

"Think better of it, dear sir," said Miss Brewster;
and "Do go, Mr. Charáxes," said Margaret. "We cannot be without our mentor. What if we should commit
some solecism in manners, or make some mistake in
threading the mazes of social life at such a gathering
of the fashionable world?"

"I will trust you anywhere, my dear," replied the
old gentleman; "and if you needed a mentor, your aunt
would be a far better one than I."

"But I, sir," said Miss Brewster, "have seen very
little of the gay world, and my brother has been too
much a man of business to be quite at home in such
places. We shall all need you, and I am sure you will
be amused."

"Very likely I may be, for I generally manage to
get amusement out of most things that I see, if they
are not painful. But if you are really going into such
a caravansera of American fashion, I do not know that
I can stay at home, for I should sadly miss our quiet
Saturday dinners, and I suppose you will be absent
nearly all summer. I have seen many motley gatherings,—many menageries of different animals,—and perhaps I may as well see what this continent can bring
together. I will go, if you will promise to let me come
home when I am tired of it."

Both ladies said that he should come away whenever
he liked. With this understanding, the arrangements
were quickly made; and at the end of about a week

after this conversation the four travellers found them-selves at the Grand Hotel, then the most famous one at Saratoga Springs.

Shortly before this, Mrs. Gascoigne, who always left her house in Boston for the hottest months of summer, proposed to her son to take their usual tour. Before they left, Miss Simmons went to reside with her nephew in Mansfield, Ohio. Mrs. Gascoigne and her son arrived at the same hotel in Saratoga before the party from Detroit, and found many acquaintances.

It was not without reason that Charáxes promised himself amusement. There is nothing more striking on the face of the earth than a crowded American watering-place in the height of the season. A showy, stuccoed building, three stories in height, fronts on the principal street, on which it extends a hundred and fifty feet. Lofty, square, wooden columns support the high roof of a veranda, more commonly called in America a "piazza." A broad flight of steps descend to the flags of the sidewalk. At the rear extend back two wings, which, with the main building, enclose three sides of a spacious court, in the centre of which a copi-ous fountain is playing; and the well-shaven lawns are interspersed with gay flowers and flowering shrubs. Gravelled walks, kept hard by the roller, meander through the court. The fourth side is open to the westerly breeze. A great music-stand affords a place for the band, which plays during certain hours. Where else should the sovereign people take their ease but in such an inn as this?

The company is from every quarter of the Union; a mixed and varied representation of the conglomerate nation known as "The American People." Here is the Southern planter, whose cotton or sugar has netted him this year a clear profit of twenty thousand dollars, and he has come North to spend a good part of the money most royally, bringing his wife, two daughters, and a son, and leaving the plantation to the care of his overseer. His ladies are among the best customers at the jewellers' shops in the great cities, and at the dress-makers'; for at Saratoga ladies change their dresses four or five times a day. In the dialect of these good Southern folk you hear the peculiar speech and intonation that come from their negroes, and to which no attempt at written description can do justice. But their voices are musical, their education has been as good as the best, and the women are bright and charming. The planter himself—a large slave-holder—is a sturdy believer in the right of secession, and just now this is beginning to be a matter much thought of in reference to certain contingencies in the political world. The mother of the family is a fine specimen of the Southern matron, toiling night and day, when she is at home, in the care of her numerous dependants, but doing it all with an ease and a conscientious fidelity to a position to which she was born and to the like of which she trains her daughters. The son has just graduated at Yale or Harvard, where he was one of a set of Southern exclusives, and spent a good deal of money. In the event of any sectional trouble, he will be ready to march and to fight, although he does not yet know it.

A staid new England family—the head of which is a merchant on Central Wharf, in Boston, or a manufacturer—have come to "The Springs" for health and recreation; the daughters having won medals at the Girls' High School, and being highly accomplished young women. Their nasal tones and precision of speech leave you in no doubt as to the place of their origin, and if you converse with them you will find that they know a great deal about books, and dress very simply.

Baltimoreans, with their peculiar utterance (I wish I could write "Baltimore" as they speak it), the young women with blooming complexions, fresh and lively, the older ones fading much less rapidly than some others of our countrywomen; Philadelphians, of Quaker parentage, but dressing like "the world's people" and even dancing; New-Yorkers, some with new and some with old riches, and all with a sense of the importance of the Empire State immensely manifested; Western people, with their racy metaphors and a slang that is

never heard on this side of the Alleghanies unless they
bring it (their girls sometimes bring it and fling it
around with something of a graceful crispness that is
a little startling, but not indelicate); the Californian
who was an "old forty-niner," and struck a gold-mine
that made a millionaire out of a common miner, and
one who is fond of heaping diamonds on his women-
kind; stock-brokers and other gamblers, professional
men, politicians, editors, religious persons and persons
of no religion, teetotalers, moderate drinkers, drinkers
of everything that they can pay for, or that others will
pay for; in short, a miscellaneous, motley crowd, such
as Charáxes anticipated. The settled customs of the
watering-place, and a uniform round of amusements,
gave to this multitude of people a certain uniformity
of manners, while they were there, although it was easy
to see how much of good breeding the different individuals had or had not brought from home.

But how am I to describe that part of the life at such
a place which consisted in eating and drinking? Old
Talleyrand is said to have remarked of us, *leur luxe est
affreux;* and well he might. It could not quite be said
that there was to be found at the Grand Hotel

> "A table richly spread, in regal mode,
>   With dishes piled, and meats of noblest sort
>   And savour, beasts of chase, or fowl of game,
>   In pastry built, or from the spit, or boiled,
>   Gris-amber-steamed; all fish from sea or shore,
>   Freshet, or purling brook, of shell or fin,
>   And exquisitest name, for which was drained
>   Pontus, and Lucrine Bay, and Afric coast.
>   Alas! how simple, to these cates compared,
>   Was that crude apple that diverted Eve."

But the purveyor for this *table-d'hôte* did pretty well,
although there was not much to be said for the cooking. The resources of our own land and water were
not mean, and there were not many luxuries that our
commerce could not bring from foreign climes and put
within the reach of money. The orange groves of
Florida had not then produced that delicious fruit
which surpasses all that the Mediterranean sends us;

the grapes of California or Ohio had not then furnished
what they have since. But on the list of wines at this
hotel every vintage in Europe was, or was said to be,
represented; and the prices, high as they were, were no
obstacle to the consumption. The hotels could afford
to take guests who drank nothing but water; for the
guests who drank nothing but wine paid more than
threefold what was needful to make up the difference.
Neither can I borrow more, and say,—

> "And at a stately sideboard by the wine
> That fragrant smell diffused, in order stood
> Tall stripling youths rich clad, of fairer hue
> Than Ganymed or Hylas;"

for, in plain truth, the "waiters" were all black, clad
in linen jackets that were not always as clean as they
might have been. At their head was a portly fellow
who was quite a master of ceremonies, and for a good
round fee he would give a guest his choice of seats,
and see that he was properly served, while others
almost went without their dinners. There was much
rushing about, great clatter, and rather more of a
scramble than was seemly. The popping of champagne corks frequently broke upon the ear.

> "And all the while harmonious airs were heard
> Of chiming strings, or charming pipes;"

for the sovereign people, at such places, must be re-
galed with music at their meals.

The uniformity of manners to which I have referred
begins with some of the persons in such assemblies of
people by imitation. Your free-born American, when
he first comes into the company of those who are supposed to be his betters, and who have ways to which
he has not been accustomed, exhibits a consciousness
that he is as good as anybody, and his manner asserts
it very decidedly, especially if he has money, which is
beyond doubt as good in his pocket as in any one's. By
and by he begins unconsciously to imitate; he catches
the tone and style that surround him; his self-assertion
becomes a little less prominent, but he does not lose his

independence. He learns what good manners are, and ends, in externals at least, in being a gentleman, whom no one, not knowing his origin, would take to have been formerly a vulgar, ill-bred, ill-conditioned fellow. *Mutatis mutandis,* the same is true of our women. I have known factory-girls, born in poverty and dirt, who have become ladies, and if you met them you would suppose that they were born princesses, or duchesses at the very least. But some education is necessary to this result; and somehow or other this is obtained. It is thus not difficult to find the reason why a democracy like ours can develop a refined and elegant society. That some vulgar people who get money remain vulgar people is true enough. It is true enough sometimes of people who inherited their money. But these exceptions do not overcome the general rule. Given the opportunities, and, out of an equal number of people, more Americans, men and women, of humble birth, will rise in the social scale, and come to be gentlemen or ladies, than in any other land with which I am acquainted. What provokes me is to see the airs which people give themselves, who claim to be better than their neighbors because they have money. The claim of being as good as your neighbor, either with or without money, I am always ready to admit, when there is something more than money to back it.

But this disquisition has run off from my pen in a parenthesis. I must return to the Grand Hotel. It was a queer scene for such sober people as the Brewsters and such a philosopher as Charáxes to come to. But the old man was not wrong in supposing that he would be amused. At all events, he found an acquaintance that became very interesting to him.

There was a lively lady at the Grand Hotel, from Detroit; a certain Mrs. Davis. She had preceded the Brewster party about two weeks, and had become acquainted with Mrs. Gascoigne, of whom she knew only that in early life she married an Englishman, that she was a rich widow, and that her residence was in Boston. Mr. Brewster she had long known in Detroit, but she was entirely ignorant of his early history. On the day

following the arrival of the Brewsters, Mrs. Davis was
sitting with Mrs. Gascoigne at the side of a small parlor
which opened from the great drawing-room of the hotel.
She was much given to our American habit of introducing everybody to everybody else; and rarely has
this national custom led to a more extraordinary *contre-
temps* than it did on this occasion. Brewster had never
known anything about Isabel's marriage. He might
have learned a great deal about her from me, but it
was one of the ways in which he disciplined himself
into forgetfulness of that episode in his life, to be without any knowledge concerning her from the time of
their separation. On this morning, he was passing
through the room where Mrs. Gascoigne and Mrs.
Davis were sitting, on his way to the office of the hotel,
to mail some letters. Mrs. Davis called to him, and he
stopped, directly in front of the two ladies.

"Mr. Brewster," said the sprightly little woman,
"let me present you to my friend, Mrs. Gascoigne.
Mrs. Gascoigne, this gentleman is Mr. Brewster, one of
my Detroit friends, and a very distinguished man."

Brewster had not until that moment looked at the
lady who sat by the side of Mrs. Davis, but one look
sufficed. It was?—yes, it was,—the Isabel of his early
love. His surprise may be imagined. But he did not
lose his self-command; he did not speak; he merely
bowed, as any gentleman would bow to a lady to whom
he was unexpectedly presented as a stranger. Isabel,
although shocked by the suddenness of this meeting,
was too much accustomed to control herself to betray
any emotion. She made an inclination of her head,—
as formal a salute as the one she received. She did
not dare to raise her eyes to the face of the man who
stood before her. In an instant there seemed to be a
tacit understanding that they met as strangers heretofore, and that they were to recognize no previous acquaintance. It was a distressing situation for both of
them, but the voluble Mrs. Davis saw nothing in the
manner of either that was at all out of the common
course. She rattled on,—

"I see that you have your daughter with you, Mr.

15*

Brewster. Mrs. Gascoigne's only son is here with her. Young people at these places ought to be acquainted. I hope, Mr. Brewster, you will allow me to present Mr. James Gascoigne to Miss Margaret."

While she ran this off very glibly, Brewster looked at the lady to whom he had been thus suddenly presented, and who sat motionless in the matronly dignity of a still beautiful woman of forty-seven.

Ah, my male reader, did it ever happen to you, without the slightest warning, to see in middle life, or mayhap a little later, a face that you adored in your youth, and that you had not seen for more than a score of years? How you did explore those features, to find the girl who was once enshrined in your heart. She is there,—she is not there,—you find her, you do not find her,—how shall you recall what subdued you in the morning of your days? It is most distressing,—this loss of the young face, this merging of the younger in the older woman, this fruitless effort to see again what was once so glorious and so sweet. When Tom Moore wrote

" Around the dear ruin each wish of my heart," etc.,

what did he mean? Anything but a ridiculous sentimentality? Isabel Gascoigne, however, was no ruin. She was amazingly well preserved, but the girl of three-and-twenty could scarcely be found in her now, even by the keen search of Henry Brewster, which he did for one instant essay to make. Suddenly, he rescued himself, saying that he feared he would be late for the mail, and with a low bow he walked rapidly away. Isabel glanced timidly at his retiring figure, and then, conscious that she could not endure the tumult of her feelings if she remained longer with Mrs. Davis, she excused herself to that lady for leaving her, and went directly up to her apartment.

She had fortunately not brought Dinah to Saratoga. If she had, there would have been one person who would have known but too well who Mr. Brewster was. The maid who was with Mrs. Gascoigne had not been long in her service. Her son was out. As soon as she reached her parlor she sank upon a chair and burst into tears. Her attendant, a good-natured girl, hearing a sob, ran in from the bedroom, and, supposing that her mistress had received some bad news, asked if she should not call Mr. James.

"By no means," Mrs. Gascoigne said. "Leave me, Susan, please, for a while. I have met with something unpleasant, but I shall be over it soon; it is not of much consequence. Give me some *eau-de-cologne*. You can go out to walk if you wish, and need not come back until it is time for me to dress for dinner."

The girl did as she was bid, and then considerately left her lady alone. Isabel rose, locked the door, and then gave way for a few moments to an uncontrolled emotion. It was a needed relief. She then tried to collect her thoughts, and to determine what her demeanor must be. It was evident that Mr. Brewster had instantly resolved to ignore everything in the past, and to have such acquaintance as there must be date from the introduction of that morning. This, therefore, must be her own course. She could never explain to her son that part of her life in which she had known this gentleman before. Her old engagement to him was now so little spoken of, there was so little danger that any one in all that crowd of visitors had ever heard of it, that she soon determined what was best. Fortunately for her, her self-possession, as soon as the first agitation was over, was equal to any trial that she might have to encounter. It was quite apparent to her, from the cold, imperturbable bearing of Mr. Brewster, that no lingering tenderness would be likely to betray him into any allusion to their younger days. Brief as was the moment when he stood before her, and little as she could see, her rapid feminine perceptions told her that a revival of his old love, under any circumstances, would be very improbable. And did she wish for it? Had she ever wished for it, when she thought of the chances of their meeting again? If she ever had, the wish had died away entirely. She did not indulge for a moment in the hope that he would be led to touch upon their past.

They say that the substance of our physical frames undergoes complete change and renovation once in every seven years. Perhaps the substance of our souls, if they have substance, goes through a like process. Isabel was not now what she was at three-and-twenty. She was a woman in middle life, of much experience; she was a mother, and her son was to her all in all. Whatever it was that made her lose the destiny once in store for her, it was now in the far-off past. If it needed any atonement, there could be none. But as she sat there alone, with painful memories crowding upon her, she could not help wishing to know more. Mrs. Davis had mentioned that Mr. Brewster had a daughter with him. Was she to see this girl? Who was her mother? What had been the history of Henry Brewster in all these years? How could she learn more without manifesting an interest that she must not show? But it was in no hope for herself that she wished to know whether the mother of this girl was living. Possibly I disappoint my readers in precluding the probability of a result that they may perhaps expect. I have more than once, however, warned them that I am telling a true story, not shaping a romance to suit myself or any one else.

That evening there was to be dancing in the great drawing-room. A band of musicians, of the highest skill of the time, were preluding for the dancers. Quite recovered from her recent agitation, and in full evening dress, of remarkable elegance, Mrs. Gascoigne entered the drawing-room accompanied by her son. Mrs. Davis immediately joined them, and they took seats on a sofa at one side of the room, about midway between the two ends.

"Mr. James," said Mrs. Davis, with her usual briskness, "I want to present you to a young lady on the other side of the room. I introduced her father to your mother this morning, and I am sure you will both be glad to know the whole Brewster party."

Mrs. Gascoigne looked across the wide space, and saw four persons, two ladies and two gentlemen, near one of the windows. The eldest of the gentlemen was of a very distinguished appearance, and of quite an advanced age. He was seated in an arm-chair, which Mr. Brewster had wheeled up for his accommodation. The two ladies occupied a sofa, at the end of which his chair was placed.

Brewster stood behind him, calmly surveying the company. The eldest of the two ladies was tall, with silvery white hair, tastefully arranged. She appeared to be about fifty-five. She had one of the loveliest countenances ever possessed by a woman of her years. If she had not been a beauty in her youth, she now had the beauty of sweetness, intelligence, and wisdom. Her eyes were very striking,—full, tender, penetrating orbs,—the finest I ever saw in a woman of her age. Her mouth had an expression of as much softness and as much strength as could be combined in that feature of a female face. She seemed to be quietly amused by the scene before her.

The younger lady was not quite so tall as the elder one, but there was a strong resemblance between them in figure and features; not the resemblance that is to be traced between mother and daughter, but that which is transmitted on the paternal side. At first you would not have called Margaret Brewster a beautiful girl, but you would have soon felt that she was charming, and that her character must be an uncommon one. Her hair was a golden brown, abundant and fine; it was worn in ringlets, as was then the fashion. They were brought down from her temples by the sides of her face, but the ends were turned and fastened to the back hair. Her brow and forehead were those of an intellectual woman. Her mouth and eyes were like her aunt's, with the difference only between youth and age. It was a thoughtful face, with an air of *espiègle-rie*, too; she looked as if she could both think and laugh. Refinement and grace and youthful dignity you could see in her whole manner. She must have been bred where the best influences would form a young lady of more than ordinary attractions. You would have said that she was about twenty,—not more than twenty-one.

m

"Mrs. Gascoigne," said the sprightly Mrs. Davis, "suppose we cross over to the other side of the room?"

"I think we are very well here," replied Mrs. Gascoigne; "it is my usual seat. But do not let me keep you here, Mrs. Davis, if you wish to change."

"But I want you to know the Brewster party. That old gentleman over there is a very interesting person, and I think your son would be glad to know the young lady. She is Mr. Brewster's daughter, and the other lady is his sister."

"I will remain here, thank you, Mrs. Davis, but you can take James over and present him to Mr. Brewster, and if the father chooses to present him to the daughter, I presume he will do so."

"Oh, you Boston people are so precise! But come, Mr. James, give me your arm, and let me put you as far into the Brewster circle as your mother will allow me to."

This was said rather tartly, but Mrs. Gascoigne smiled and nodded good-naturedly as Mrs. Davis glided away with James. He was nothing loath to make new acquaintances at any time. He was what the newspapers now call a "society man," and at Saratoga, as elsewhere, he was a general favorite.

"Mr. Brewster," said Mrs. Davis, "this young gentleman is Mr. James Gascoigne, son of the lady to whom I introduced you this morning." She did not say James Bradshaw Gascoigne, as she might have done if she had repeated the name as he commonly had it put on his card. Mr. Brewster extended his hand to James, and then presented him to Mr. Charáxes. The old gentleman did not rise, but with a bland smile he held out his right hand to James, who bowed over it most deferentially. The ladies thought that this young man's manners were very good.

"I presume, young gentleman," said Charáxes, "you are a dancing man. It is singular how fashions change, and how you import them into this country. In my youth, waltzing was not practised everywhere, but now it is universal; in fact, all over the world. You waltz, of course, Mr. Gascoigne?"

"Yes, sir, I do when I can get a partner; but I do not like to ask young ladies to dance round dances, unless I know that they and their friends approve of it."

This was not said with any purpose to recommend himself in the circle into which he had been partially introduced, but it struck Mr. Brewster as evincing rather more modesty than he had seen some young men exhibit. Still, he did not present James to the ladies, and Mrs. Davis began to *fidget*. Standing on tiptoe, she whispered behind her fan, "Mr. Brewster, this young Gascoigne is a very nice fellow, and his mother is one of the first ladies in Boston. Won't you present him to your daughter?"

Brewster had easily divined her object in bringing the young man across the room, but he did not know that it was the tact of his mother that had limited Mrs. Davis's "good offices" to presenting him to the young lady's father. He had been in no haste to comply with the wishes of the officious little woman, but in the short interval that had elapsed he reflected that she would probably accomplish her object in some way, and, seeing that it was getting a little awkward for the young gentleman to be standing there authorized to speak to no one but Mr. Charáxes and himself, he said, politely, "Mr. Gascoigne, let me present you to my sister and daughter." The little ceremony over, James, like any well-bred young man, first addressed himself to the elder of the two ladies,—

"You came only yesterday, I believe, Miss Brewster?"

"Yes; how long have you been here?"

"A little over two weeks. My mother and I always like to get away from the first hot weather in Boston. Are your summers in Detroit very warm?"

"The climate of Detroit is different from yours. I am a native of Massachusetts, but I have lived so long in the West that I cannot now compare the climates of the two cities very closely. We have a good deal of hot weather, but the heat is tempered by the lakes. Is this a gay season for Saratoga?"

"Quite so; the hotels are all very full."

"They seem to be forming quadrilles. Do not let us keep you from the dancing."

"I was about asking your niece to become my partner." Then turning to Margaret, he asked if he might have the honor, etc. She accepted very simply, and they were soon provided with a *vis-à-vis*. The music was most animating, and Margaret enjoyed dancing.

Mrs. Gascoigne watched all that occurred on the opposite side of the room without seeming to do so, and just as James was leading Margaret upon the floor, Mrs. Davis came over, escorted by the old gentleman who had been occupying the arm-chair.

"I have brought my Detroit neighbor, Mr. Charáxes, to pay his respects to you, Mrs. Gascoigne," she said, triumphantly. Charáxes made his bow most gracefully, and took the seat on the sofa to which Mrs. Gascoigne invited him. Mrs. Davis said she would go and speak to Mrs. Harding, her minister's wife; Dr. Harding was at the Springs to drink the waters on account of dyspepsia. By this time the room had become very full, and, as some five hundred people were all talking with their voices raised to the highest pitch, there was a tremendous uproar, in which poor old Charáxes could hardly hear himself think.

"I am afraid, Mrs. Gascoigne," he said, "that I shall not be able to make you hear me in this din, for my voice is not very strong. Is it your climate, or what is it, that makes people talk so loudly in this country, in all large assemblies?"

"It is a national habit, sir, no doubt, but I do not know how to account for it. In some observation that I had in English society, in the early part of my life, I noticed that people did not converse in such loud tones as we do, and consequently it was not so fatiguing to be in the largest assemblies, as it is with us. Perhaps our nervous temperaments make us speak as we do. Our climate is supposed to have something to do with our eagerness; and many of us are more or less under excitement in a large company. A quiet and composed manner is rare among us, in both men and women. You have probably observed this?"

"Yes; but if people would only reflect that it is distinctness of utterance, and not volume of sound, that makes conversation audible by those to whom we are speaking, there would not be this uproar that is so trying to one's nerves."

"But you have probably noticed, sir, that each one is impelled to raise his or her voice, because the other person in the conversation could not otherwise hear, and so the noise goes on *crescendo.* It will probably be a long time before we shall get over this habit and learn to speak in lower tones. Our language ought to be a musical one; and I think you must have observed that many educated English women make it so in conversation."

"Very often, and most agreeably. But how differently their men speak! I do not believe that public men in the time of Burke and Fox had the hesitating, stammering style of speaking that most Englishmen have to-day. It is a modern trick, I fancy. They are by no means so fluent as your public men. But as I have made a criticism upon one peculiarity of your national manners, I can say that I sometimes meet with very good individual manners. Your son, madam, seems to be one of those rare young men who are respectful to elderly people. I think my friends on the other side of the room were quite pleased with him. I am sure that I was."

"I believe that he does know the rules of good behavior; I wish he knew as much about more practical matters."

"Is he not in a profession or in any kind of business?"

"No, he has no steady employment, and although in one sense he is under no necessity to work, I should be happy if he were so situated as to work for some other object. But there is very little chance in our country for young men who are not dependent on their hands or their heads for subsistence. We are getting to have quite a class of educated men who do nothing; and I wish I could take my son out of that category."

"He should come out to the West. There he would

16

find a field for all the energies that he could bring, and
if he brought money too, so much the better."

"I am afraid, sir, that his mother would be an
obstacle to that plan. He is my only child, and I
could not part with him. You can understand how
a mother's fondness may become a stumbling-block in
the path of an only son."

"Well, madam, the gentleman to whom your son
was just now presented—my friend, Mr. Brewster—has
risen to great eminence, and he might be able to suggest to you many things that I cannot, for, although
I have lived for more than twenty years in this country,
I have been a mere looker-on. Will you let me take
you across the room and make you acquainted with
Miss Brewster?"

"The lady with the beautiful white hair? Mr.
Brewster was presented to me this morning, but I
have not met the ladies of his family. Under such
auspices as yours, Mr. Charáxes, I ought to feel quite
safe."

"I have a special motive for wishing my friends
to know you,—quite a selfish one, I admit. I am ar-
ranging a party to go out to the lake and dine *al fresco*
next Tuesday, and I hope you and your son will join us.
I do not know many of the people here, and it is not
always prudent to let the active Mrs. Davis choose
one's acquaintances, although I am bound to say that
for once I am exceedingly obliged to her."

This gallant little speech, made with a bow, quite
captivated Mrs. Gascoigne; and, thinking that it would
be best to let things happen in their usual course, she
rose and took the old gentleman's arm. They threaded
their way through the crowd, and as Mr. Charáxes was
aware that Mr. Brewster had been introduced to Mrs.
Gascoigne that morning, he had only to present her to
Miss Brewster. The lady and gentleman who had been
lovers a long time ago merely bowed to each other, with
a formal "good-evening." Miss Brewster, without the
slightest idea who Mrs. Gascoigne was, excepting that
she was the mother of the young gentleman then
dancing with her niece, rose, greeted the stranger lady

very graciously, and they sat down. Brewster turned and began to converse with Mr. Charáxes. When the quadrille was over the band played a fine march, and the dancers, with others of the company, walked up and down the room in pairs. Margaret and James promenaded in the long procession with a better opportunity for conversation than there had been in the dance.

"I think you said," observed James, "that you have never been in Boston. Shall you not visit it on your way home?"

"I do not know how long we shall be absent. I wish very much to see Boston, but my father is an exceedingly busy man. You, I suppose, will return home soon; gentlemen have so much to do."

"I have nothing to do, and we shall probably remain here until October, unless we go to Lake George for a short time."

"You have nothing to do? How do you manage to exist? Do you not get very much wearied?"

(If Margaret had been a young lady of the present period she would probably have said, "awfully bored.")

"Perhaps I do at times; but then, you see, a fellow who is not in a profession or business of any kind has to have a great deal of occupation in carrying on society. That is my case, fortunately or unfortunately."

"I should say unfortunately, but as we have not much of that where I live, I cannot form an idea about it where it exists. How much time does it take for the social occupations of which you speak?"

"The whole time that one cares to be doing anything. Last winter I was one of the managers of some assemblies that were held at Papanti's hall, and I was kept very busy. I shall not try it again."

"I should think you would prefer travelling?"

"I have never been abroad, and my mother has always been averse to going. I could not leave her at home alone."

"Why not travel in our own country? There is a great deal to be seen. I am sure you would find the West interesting. Scenery, manners, different laws and

customs of different States, the wonderful growth of the
country,—it seems to me that I should like to observe
all this, although we have not the antiquity and noble
buildings and monuments of art that are to be seen in
Europe. If you should come out to the West, my
father could point out to you many things worth
seeing."

"Now that I have had the pleasure of making your
acquaintance there would be a great inducement to come
out there. But then, you see, I should have to come
back to Boston and resume my old life."

They had now returned to the part of the room
where Miss Brewster was conversing with Mrs. Gascoigne, and Margaret was presented to that lady by
her aunt. Mrs. Gascoigne rarely failed to impress people
when she wished to please ; and Miss Brewster had so
much enjoyed her conversation, that when Mr. Charáxes
proposed his plan for the excursion to the lake, and
Mrs. Gascoigne and her son accepted the invitation,
Miss Brewster expressed her gratification very decidedly. Margaret politely joined in her aunt's expression
of pleasure, but she had only just seen Mrs. Gascoigne,
and James had not seemed to her a very interesting
person.

When the evening was over, and James had kissed
his mother a good-night, and her maid had left her, she
sat down to reflect on the strange ordeal that she had
gone through that day. It would last longer,—how
would it end ? Would there be an accidental discovery,
that might make known to Miss Brewster that she was
the woman about whom her brother had probably told
her so many years ago ? How much would it be safe
for her to be in the society of these persons ? What
might that busy Mrs. Davis learn and divulge ? How
would Mr. Brewster continue to comport himself ? She
did not ask herself these questions with reference to
any one's future but her son's. From that moment,
however, one thought suddenly took possession of her
mind and held it for a long time. If James were to
marry this daughter of Henry Brewster,—it might be
a wild hope, but she could not exclude it. The girl

was evidently a very superior person. Isabel's whole
existence was wrapped up in her son. It must not be
assumed, however, that she was about to become a
scheming match-maker. She was a woman of too much
dignity of feeling for that kind of effort. She could
have and could cherish this hope, and watch and wait
for its fruition, without doing anything that ought to
lessen her self-respect. Before the day for the excursion to the lake she heard Mrs. Davis say that Mr.
Brewster had been a widower for many years. This
information, which came to her accidentally and without her asking any question about him, instead of
making the situation more embarassing to her, seemed
to render it less so. She did not in the least fear any
allusion by him to their former relation.

How was it with Brewster himself? The circumstances of his life, the rigorous and severe effort with
which he had torn out from his heart the thought
of Isabel Bradshaw—his marriage, the loss and the
memory of his wife, his absorption in the cares of business and in such public affairs as he took an interest
in, varied only by the education of his daughter and
the society of his sister and of old Charáxes—had made
him appear somewhat cold in temperament, and in any
general company a little formal in manner. A second
marriage in his case had always been improbable, and
a marriage with Isabel, if they should ever meet again,
never entered his thoughts. But now that they had
met, he was a man of so much correctness of feeling
that he was sure to avoid everything that might increase her discomfort. He had never forgotten what
his sister said to him so many years ago,—that Miss
Bradshaw's conduct had better remain a mystery.
Now that they had met, after such a long period, in
which other interests and the great change from youth
to middle life had almost wrought a change of identity
in both of them, he thought, when he thought of their
early days at all, that it was most probable the mystery could never have been explained, because her apparently heartless conduct had been produced by something that she could never have spoken of. At all

events, the secret was her own; if he had ever had a
wish to know it he could not, under any circumstances,
make the least effort to learn it now. Nor was there
any likelihood that he would ever desire to do so, because her son and his daughter had met in one of these
cross accidents of life which bring about encounters
that no calculation could have foreseen. For a long
time he did not think of James in any relation to his
daughter save as a casual acquaintance. He read young
men almost at a glance. He saw that this one was a
well-bred and amiable fellow, but it could not have
occurred to him that Margaret would become interested
in such a person. My readers must not blame me if I
do not shape things to meet their wishes.

CHAPTER XII.

A PICNIC AT SARATOGA LAKE.

CHARÁXES had given *carte-blanche* to a noted "ca-
terer" to provide an entertainment for forty people, in
a pine-grove on the border of Saratoga Lake. The day
was fine; one of those perfect summer days which, in
our climate, seem set apart for storing electricity in the
upper regions of the atmosphere, and holding it in
reserve to be discharged into the earth on the next or
some future day. There was not a cloud in the heavens;
the mercury in the thermometer stood at a high point,
but the heat was not oppressive. The time for the ren-
dezvous was fixed in the invitations at noon. Mrs.
Gascoigne and her son drove out in their own carriage,
and took Mrs. Davis with them. Mr. Charáxes and
the Brewster family went in a hired barouche. The
other guests found their way in different conveyances.
By this time, Mr. Brewster and Mrs. Gascoigne had
frequently met at the hotel, in the company of other
persons, and if either of them felt, neither exhibited
any embarrassing constraint in the presence of the

other. Since the introduction on the morning after
Brewster's arrival, he had not addressed any conversation to Mrs. Gascoigne but the most formal and
casual. His sister, who had become interested in the
Boston lady, and thought her very nice, observed that
he did not pay to her the attentions which gentlemen
commonly pay to ladies; but she was used to his habit-
ual indifference to the society of ladies in general, and
thought little of it in this case. Other persons did not
conclude that Mr. Brewster specially avoided the lady
from Boston. James, without any hint from his mother,
had improved every fair opportunity to converse with
Margaret before the excursion to the lake, but he had
not impressed her as an acquaintance whom she cared
to know more intimately.

The company were all punctually at the place appointed. A sail on the lake was to be the first part of
the programme. They embarked on a small steamer;
over the deck was stretched an awning, which sheltered
them from the sun without obstructing the view on
either side. There was a gentle breeze sweetened by
the odor of the pine woods. All the guests had paid
their respects to Mr. Charáxes before the embarkation.
On the boat, those of them who had not known the
Brewsters before were duly presented. There were
other young men and young ladies in the company who
were acquainted with Margaret, but James managed to
secure a seat by her side, and he kept it through nearly
the whole of the little voyage. Mr. Charáxes had
Mrs. Gascoigne seated on his right and Miss Brewster
on his left. The old man was in his most genial mood,
and talked on a great variety of subjects. Mr. Brewster walked up and down, conversing mostly with gentlemen. He happened for a moment to pause in front
of Mr. Charáxes, when an elderly gentleman from Boston came up and said to him in Isabel's hearing, " I
think, sir,—perhaps I am mistaken,—you will pardon
me,—but I think I have seen you before. Did you
not study law in Boston?"

" No, sir," said Brewster; " I received my professional
education at the Cambridge Law School."

"Ah, it was there perhaps that I may have met you, or have seen you. My son was there at about the same time, probably. Perhaps you knew him?"

"I do not recall you or your son," replied Brewster, "but I am very happy to know you now. I have lived in Detroit for nearly twenty-five years, and have not been in Boston during all that time." The two gentlemen then strolled to the forward part of the boat, where they found seats.

This was one of the little perils to which Isabel was frequently exposed, for there were several Boston people in the company, some of whom were old enough to have known Brewster when she was engaged to him. But, fortunately, nothing occurred to recall that history to the recollections of any of them.

They sailed around the lake several times.

"How does this scenery strike you, Mr. Charáxes?" asked Isabel.

"It is pretty, but diminutive. If the hills were a little bolder, it might remind one of the lakes in Cumberland. But my eye has been long accustomed to grander objects. One who has seen the Nile and the Pyramids, has traversed the deserts of Arabia, has beheld all the scenery of Europe, and has in old age become familiar with most of the great natural sights in America, cannot feel that such scenery as this is notable. By the bye, Mrs. Gascoigne, we shall probably stop at Niagara on our way home. Do you not mean to extend your tour to the Falls? It would give us all pleasure to meet you there."

"Yes," said Miss Brewster, "let us hope that we may meet you at Niagara, Mrs. Gascoigne."

"I was at Niagara," replied Isabel, "when I was very young. They used to ask me in England to describe it, but of course a young girl's recollections could give no one an idea of it."

"Can any one's recollection?" asked Charáxes; "words cannot describe Niagara. I have read most of the prose and the poetry that have been written about it, but they do not give a person who has not seen it any idea of it."

"Yet," said Isabel, "you would not have people refrain from writing about the sublime objects in nature, would you, sir? Coleridge's description of Mont Blanc is something worth having, even to persons who have never seen it. Byron's apostrophe to the ocean, if it had not become so hackneyed by repetition, would move us strongly, although it is certainly no substitute for a sight of the ocean. It seems to me that I have read descriptions of Niagara that were of more value than the service which they perform in the guide-books when they are quoted in those useful publications."

"Coleridge's famous hymn," said Charáxes, "is a very impressive expression of his own emotions, produced by the sight of Mont Blanc. But it will not supply you or me with emotions. Nothing will do that but the awful mountain itself. Come to Niagara, and, whether you comprehended it at all or did not take it in at all when you were young, give yourself, now that your perceptions and your feelings will better enable you to study it, an opportunity to see how it grows and grows upon us the more we see of it."

"My son has never seen Niagara, and perhaps I will think of your suggestion."

"To see it is an education; that part of education which, whenever begun, is never finished."

"My education," said Isabel, "in the appreciation of scenery can hardly be said to have had a beginning, and in art it has been even less. During my married life I seldom went anywhere out of London; and since my return to Boston I have been so situated for many years that I have been obliged to confine my travelling to the nearer summer resorts to which we New-Englanders go for escape from hot weather."

"Why do you not go abroad, and take your son?"

"My residence in England was on some accounts a painful part of my life. I could not go abroad without visiting England, and I could not do that."

"The whole continent of Europe is open to you, as well as the East."

"Yes, sir, but England is closed to me by very sad memories."

The old gentleman saw that this must not be pursued farther; but it interested Miss Brewster still more in the beautiful widow.

They came back to the landing-place shortly before six o'clock. That hour had been fixed for the dinner. The table was laid in an open space in a grove of pines, which shaded it from the rays of the descending sun. The shadows were thrown longer and longer to the east; the twilight extended far on into the evening, mellowing, fading, slowly giving way to the moonlight which came to take its place from the deep vault of an unclouded sky. The night was as perfect as the day had been. They did not leave the table until after nine o'clock. Different groups then strolled among the trees, awaiting the carriages, which had been ordered at ten. James, who had been careful to be with Margaret for the greater part of the day,—she did not avoid him,—walked by her side, with some other young people, and pretty soon they were far enough in advance of the others to admit of a *téte-à-téte.* He was anxious for a little greater intimacy, tentatively experimenting to learn, if he could, how this very composed girl was disposed to feel towards him. Margaret had not thought of his attentions to her as if they were prompted by a tender feeling. She was very willing to talk with him on any subject, but she did not imagine that he was becoming, or had become, in love with her. Love, save for her aunt and her father and old Charáxes, was a feeling that she had never experienced. She did not dream of being asked for it by this young man, whom she had known for four or five days; nor did James think of asking for it now. He wished to learn whether he could probably ever ask for it later on.

"You were speaking the other night," he said to her, "about travelling in America. I felt very much honored by your suggestions, but I hope you see what my difficulties are. I have had no occupation in life, because I did not need one in order to earn my bread. If I were to travel ever so much in our own country, I should come home without being any nearer to a steady and fixed position."

"A girl who has seen so little of the world as I have," said Margaret, "cannot understand such difficulties. I only meant to say that perhaps you would find some opening if you were to go away from Boston and see more of your own country. But it is really absurd in me to talk about such things. My father and Mr. Charáxes could tell you about the West. I hope you will not attach any importance to my opinions."

"I will not, if you forbid it; but one likes to have the sympathy of young friends as well as the advice of older ones."

"My sympathy can do you no good, Mr. Gascoigne, so long as I cannot help you." This was a little severe, but it was not said in an unkindly manner. He thought he would venture to touch upon the probability of their meeting again.

"My mother told me, just now, that Mr. Charáxes said that you thought of stopping at Niagara on your way home, and that he had proposed to her to visit the Falls."

"I believe that there is some plan of that kind, but I do not know whether my father will consent. I shall be very glad to see Niagara, but I really do not know that anything is determined about our movements. Now that Mr. Charáxes has given his party, I think it very likely he will not care to remain here much longer, and I do not myself think there is much to stay for. But I must find my aunt, for I hear the carriages driving up."

James accompanied her until she met Miss Brewster, and saw them into their carriage. He then found his mother. They drove in, almost without a word. Even Mrs. Davis was nearly silent. Isabel was thinking how she could speak to Mr. Charáxes on some other than the chance topics of ordinary conversation. This old man had become somehow strangely connected in her mind with her husband's family. She could not tell how or why. It was a dim and shadowy thought, but it was there. She must learn something of his history, if possible. His notice of her might be only his usual politeness; but it seemed to her that he felt some interest in her. His age rendered it easy for her to ask him about his past life, if she could find any reason for doing so that would not make the inquiry seem to be one of mere curiosity. She could have no reason, beginning and ending in herself, for cultivating an intimacy with him. He was old enough to have been her father, and any regard for her that he might feel could not be anything but the benignant kindness of an aged man towards an acquaintance whom he had found to be an agreeable woman.

They drove into the village past "The Congress Spring." The little park was filled with well-dressed people, sauntering about. On Broadway, ladies without bonnets or hats thronged the sidewalk, going in and out of the shops, which were still open. Moonlight and gas-light made the whole scene very bright. Electric lighting had not then come to cast sharp, weird shadows upon the ground, black and palpably strong. If the man in gray, to whom Peter Schlemihl sold his shadow, had made his bargain at the present day, and had undertaken to detach his acquisition under one of Edison's lights, he would have had a tough job of it. As it was, he succeeded pretty well; for, if I remember rightly, he took the shadow as it was made by the sun at noonday, deftly rolled it up from the feet to the head, put it in his pocket, and walked off with it. I never behold the wild blackness of the shadows cast by an "incandescent" without thinking that Mephistopheles would have found their peculiar properties too much for him. But the moon and the gas did very well for the streets of Saratoga on that beautiful summer's night, and it is quite possible that the gentleman who made the trade with Schlemihl may have been about, picking up here and there, from man or woman, some kind of personal commodity—let us hope that it was not a soul—in exchange for a fatal gift of some sort. He did not venture, however, I undertake to say, into the circle of our friends who grouped themselves in chairs around Charáxes, on the veranda of the hotel. Some one sagely remarked that it was a fine night; whereupon the old man said, "Yes, you Americans are quite right in glorifying the brilliancy of your skies when the air is clear. I once saw a scene on this continent that surpassed, in its way, everything that I have beheld in any other part of the world. It was in New England too. I was staying for a short time in the White Hills, about fifteen years ago. The house in which I was lodged was on a low hill, on one side of a valley, opposite to a range of very respectable mountains. An amphitheatre swept around this spot for forty or fifty miles. The weather had been just as we have had it to-day: a cloudless sky, the atmosphere warm and dry. The sun went down with that lurid redness which foretells another day of the same kind. In that region, when the night is calm, there rises a thick fog from the streams and ponds after the atmosphere becomes cooler than the water, and this mist often overspreads the landscape to the foot of the hills. I rose at three o'clock in the morning, and looked out over the valley. The moon was descending to the western edge of the hills opposite to where I stood, but her light was very strong. Venus blazed near her, with extraordinary power. Over the whole valley lay the hoary mist white and unruffled, as if a lake had suddenly been spread out between the hill where I stood and the opposite mountains. At places where the surface of the mist did not rise above the lower elevations of the ground islands stood distinct and prominent out of the apparent sheet of water, with indented shores, and the trees and banks were reflected in reverse, just as we see them in real water in certain states of light. Far off to the left, at what seemed a distance of twenty miles or more, the mockery of a lake widened out into an ocean, with its horizon blending with the sky. As long as the fog lay motionless, its outer edges were so clearly defined that at a distance of a hundred yards from my windows the line was just as if water had risen to where the rise of the ground had stopped its farther ascent. I watched it until the first rays of the sun struck its surface, and then little ripples began to stir, and then there were waves, and pretty soon the whole was breaking and floating in clouds to the sides of the mountains, up which they crept into the higher atmosphere. I longed for the pencil of an artist to sketch this extraordinary scene, but I have never had a hand of that sort, although I have in my time had an eye that could enjoy such things."

"Well," said Miss Brewster, "I think we may say that you can describe them, if you cannot paint them. Now, do you not think Mrs. Gascoigne rightly said that such descriptions are of some value?"

"My dear lady, you must not put my poor word-painting alongside of Coleridge's description of Mont Blanc. I am no poet, as you know very well. How does it run? If my old memory serves me, these are some of the lines:

> "'Thou first and chief, sole sovran of the Vale!
> O struggling with the darkness all the night,
> And visited all night by troops of stars,
> Or when they climb the sky or when they sink:
> Companion of the morning-star at dawn,
> Thyself Earth's rosy star, and of the dawn
> Co-herald: wake, O wake, and utter praise!
> Who sank thy sunless pillars deep in Earth?
> Who filled thy countenance with rosy light?
> Who made thee parent of perpetual streams?'

"I will allow that there is nothing finer in your language than this sublime hymn. Still, I must repeat that this kind of descriptive poetry, even in its highest flights, cannot stir us as the sight of the objects can and does. If you want emotions, I say, with your Bryant,—

> "'Take the wings
> Of morning; traverse Barca's desert sands,
> Or lose thyself in the continuous woods
> Where rolls the Oregon, and hears no sound
> Save his own dashings.'

"Still I would not go there to remember the poet's admonition,—

> "'Yet, the dead are there.'

"I am rather too fond of the living, and if you will all promise to come to Niagara, I will not try to find how we can there 'lie down with patriarchs of the infant world.' I rather think we shall have enough to do without studying 'the solemn decorations all, of the great tomb of man,' unless another Sam Patch takes it into his head to make the fatal plunge."

And so he rambled on to a late hour, and the streets were still, and the servants came out and turned off the gas, and gave other hints that they had work to do in the early morning, and then the old gentleman arose, saying, "Well, I will go and look for another day;" and with this he bade them all good-night.

CHAPTER XIII.

THE STORY OF JOHN CHARÁXES—A MOTHER'S SOLICITUDE FOR AN ONLY SON.

MARGARET was mistaken in supposing that Mr. Charáxes would be inclined to leave Saratoga very soon after he had had the amusement of his party at the lake. He had found Mrs. Gascoigne more intelligent and conversable than most of the ladies in the company at the hotel excepting the two who were his travelling companions. He and they stayed on for three weeks longer, with Mr. Brewster's tacit and patient assent. In those three weeks James was a great deal with Margaret, but he did not make much progress in her regard. If the topic of their conversation was a light one, he talked pleasantly, and always talked like a young man of refinement and good feelings. If the topic became serious, he soon got beyond his depth, while she was looking for something that did not appear to be in him. In the gayeties of that watering-place life she was not indisposed to share, to be amused, and even merry. I have said that she could laugh as well as think, but she was naturally inclined to be thoughtful. She had lived rather too much with older persons, and not enough with persons of her own age.

She had read a great deal, and much of her reading had been in studies of the severer kind, more so than is common with young women. Of anything approaching to flirtation she was entirely incapable, although she did not lack grace, or animation, or a certain kind of brilliancy.

The weather continued fine through the whole of July, but when the harvest moon of August came in there was a change. One afternoon there was a terrific thunder-storm. The pent-up moisture and electricity that had accumulated in the atmosphere burst forth with great violence. The lightning was incessant and most vivid; it rained torrents; the streets became rivers. When the electrical discharges ceased it "settled down into a rainy night," as the homely old phrase used to have it. It rained all the next day. There was no stirring out of doors. The five or six hundred guests in the hotel were sadly off for occupation. Three and even four meals a day could not fill up the time. Card-tables were set out in the drawing-room and the parlors, and whist afforded some relief. Several of the ladies had light needle-work; a few read; the consumption of cigars was much increased; two men in white linen jackets were kept busy all the forenoon making "mint juleps" and other "mixed drinks," in which their skill was extraordinary. Politics, stocks, and the coming races formed the staple of conversation among the gentlemen who stood or sat around the room where the potations were dispensed, to the enormous profit of the hotel. One of the men behind the counter had a marvellous knack in preparing the beverages. Into a tall tin tumbler he dashed little blocks of ice, clearer than the clearest crystal, which clicked and rattled refreshingly. Then he turned in the liquors with a careless but accurate fling, and sprinkled in bits of the fragrant mint, with a due allowance of sugar and a very thin slice of lemon. Then holding the tumbler aloft in his right hand, he kept up for half a minute an endless pouring into just such another receptacle in his other hand, and so on, back and forth, as if he were a prestidigitator, stretching a foaming ribbon between the two vessels. This done, with a ringing rap he set a glass goblet on the counter, and into this went the mixture, cold, strong, and sparkling with little bubbles, each glass having a long stem of clean white straw standing upright in the blocks of ice; for the true enjoyment was to imbibe the nectar through such a conduit. Waiters glided with these glasses to the card-tables, and brought back empty ones. But you are to understand, if you please, that the fairer half of creation did not indulge in this kind of drinking. If they asked for a cup of tea, it was forthcoming, and the tea and the cream were of the best; and so was the thin slice of bread and butter.

Mrs. Gascoigne remained in her own parlor all the morning. James was down in the billiard-room. At about one o'clock his mother was agreeably surprised by receiving Mr. Charáxes's card, brought by a servant, on which he had pencilled his purpose to call upon her, if she would receive him.

"I have come to bestow my tediousness on you, madame," he said, as he entered, "for my friends are all writing letters. Ah! you have a pretty bit of embroidery in hand. What a blessing to ladies the needle is on a rainy day!" Isabel rose and invited him to take an easy-chair, so placed that the windows would be behind him.

"I am very much honored by your visit, sir," she said.

"Have you made up your mind to honor *us* by meeting us at Niagara?"

"I hardly know; my son wishes to go very much, and I should like it myself, especially as I may not have an opportunity here to speak to you on a subject on which I have been thinking a good deal since I had the pleasure of making your acquaintance."

"Yes? This is as good a time as any. Never put off to the morrow what can be done to-day. How can I serve you?"

"Mr. Charáxes, if you will not think it an inquiry unwarranted by our short acquaintance, may I ask if your name is not of Greek origin?"

"Undoubtedly; the name and the person who bears it are both of Greek origin. But why do you ask?"

"I married many years ago into an English family of rank. My husband was the youngest of three sons of the late Earl Gascoigne. He died early and very suddenly. Perhaps you may have heard of his family?"

"I do not remember that I have. But Gascoigne is Norman, and unless you go back to the Crusades it cannot have had much to do with anything Greek." As he uttered this little sally his keen gray eyes twinkled under the overhanging brow.

"I shall not go back to the Crusades," Isabel said; "I do not know when my husband's ancestors became prominent, or what their earlier exploits or any of their exploits may have been. But in the time of Charles I., Cromwell, and Charles II., there was an Earl Gascoigne who had a daughter, of whom I was told a singular story, that connected her with a Greek name, all trace of which is now supposed to be lost. I never meet with a Greek name without thinking of this story."

"To be sure, the time of Charles II. is later than the Crusades. It is a very respectable antiquity, as they reckon such things in England, but not so far off, one would think, as to have obliterated the particulars of a family story. In what way can my name help you, Mrs. Gascoigne? My family were merchants in the Levant for centuries, six or seven generations of them. I was myself born in Syria. The family name, Charáxes, probably came down from a remote period. It is quite likely (here the gray eyes twinkled again) that there was a Charáxes when Cleopatra came in her yacht to join Marc Antony, and perhaps an ancestor of mine may have negotiated some of the bills which the fascinating Egyptian drew on her treasury at home. If you want antiquity, there is quite enough of it in my family. But tell me, frankly, what is the point of your inquiry, and I will give you all the information I can."

"I said I would not go back to the Crusades, and I will not go back to Cleopatra. But can you tell me whether any of your family were ever established in London as merchants in the time of Charles I.?"

"Seriously, then, I do not know that I can. But it would not be difficult to ascertain. If such was the fact, I did not come of that branch. My baptismal name of John, like my patronymic, Charáxes, is derived from the custom in modern Greece. As to the residence in England of persons of my name at the time to which you refer, I can only say that in old mercantile families in Greece and in most of the maritime towns in the eastern part of the Mediterranean papers and records were often kept a long time. It is quite possible that a distant and younger kinsman of mine, who represents the family more directly than I do, could ascertain a fact which happened only two centuries ago, if it ever did happen. But how can it benefit you to know whether some member of a trading Greek family lived in England in the time of the Stuarts ?"

" Mr. Charáxes, I must relate the story to you, if it will not weary you, and then you must allow me to explain how I came to feel a strong desire to enlist your interest in my search."

Isabel then repeated to him the story of Henrietta Gascoigne as it was told to her by her sister-in-law, Lady Clare, so many years ago. She then added, "You will think me, Mr. Charáxes, a fond and foolish woman, but the thought has taken possession of my mind that Charáxes was or may have been the name of that Greek family."

" Your idea is that Charáxes may have been the name of the adventurer who ran away with your husband's kinswoman about the time of the restoration of Charles II. The chances are equally good that it was some other Greek name. But suppose that it was the same name as mine and that the runaway pair left descendants, whether they ever married or not. Even if I am one of their descendants, or if that young fellow could be traced back to an ancestor of mine, there would still be no kinship between your son and myself, as you are, of course, aware."

" It is not a blood relationship, Mr. Charáxes, that I am trying to make out, great as the honor would. be.

My son is not a Charáxes because one of that family may possibly have married a kinswoman of his father who lived two centuries ago. It is a mere sentiment that leads me to desire to learn whether the young man who induced Henrietta Gascoigne to elope with him was of your name and blood, supposing either that they married or did not marry."

Charáxes was on the point of asking what this sentiment could be. Could it be that this lady had taken up the idea of his atoning in some way for the wrong that had been done so long ago to the Gascoigne family? But although a shrewd, he was a most considerate old man, gentle and kindly. He was much disposed to like Mrs. Gascoigne,—did like her. If the thought entered his mind for an instant that his wealth might have something to do with her desire to make out this connection, he dismissed it at once. She was a lady in every sense, and he in every sense was a gentleman. He accepted the idea of a "sentiment" as a sufficient explanation. He asked for no further explanation, but, after a short pause, in which a calm seriousness overspread his aged face, he said, "I will tell you, madam, more of my own history than I ever before related to any one in this country, and something of what I know of my father's family. You can then judge whether it is worth while for you or me to pursue this matter of the young Greek beyond our present conversation." He then related as follows :

THE STORY OF JOHN CHARÁXES.

"My earliest recollection is of travelling on a camel across the great Syrian desert that stretches from the Euphrates towards the eastern coast of the Mediterranean. I must have been about four years old. An Arab woman rode with and took care of me. The party consisted of a dozen men; their leader was a sheik, mounted on a fine Arabian horse. He and all his male followers were armed to the teeth. Whether they were robbers or traders I never knew; and I was too young at the time to know the difference, if difference there was. I learned afterwards that the whole object of their expedition was to bring me in safety from a stronghold on the eastern border of the desert to Smyrna. I conjectured, as I grew older, that they took me from my mother, and that she was the sheik's daughter. But I can remember nothing but my ride on the camel and one or two of the incidents of the journey. I never learned with certainty who my mother was. I presume that there is some Arabian blood in me, but the strong characteristics of my father's race, and the circumstances of my education and early life, made me more Greek than anything else. We halted one noon at one of those oases where there is always a well of water, a clump of fig-trees, and some coarse grass that affords very good camping-ground. What impressed this encampment on my memory was that I was given some fresh figs and a good draught of water, and that I slept with the Arab woman under a tent. I remember, too, seeing the camels imbibe their stock of water for the further journey. How many days it was before we reached Smyrna I cannot tell; but we rode into the court-yard of a large house; the camel knelt patiently and carefully on the pavement; I was taken down from his back and carried into the women's apartments by my Arab attendant. I do not remember seeing the sheik or any of his followers again. ·In that house I remained until I was seven years old. The master of the house was a Jew merchant, and, as I afterwards learned, a correspondent of my father. I was well cared for, and I suppose I was naturally a healthy child. At all events, I do not remember any serious illness during my childhood. Several Eastern languages were spoken by the different inmates of the house,— modern Greek, Syriac, and Arabic. I was taught to read them, and to read Hebrew also.

"In the year 1775 my father sent for me. I had been told about him, and had learned that I was the son of a Greek merchant who lived on the island of Crete and owned vessels which traded to Italian ports. He had a brother who had been for a long time in the Turkish civil service. This uncle of mine, who held some posi-

tion in the bureau of finance at the Porte, came to
Smyrna on business of the Turkish revenue.   He
brought letters from my father to my Jewish protector,
and the result was that arrangements were made for
my being carried to my father on the island of Crete.
He had never seen me, but he felt a natural desire to
recognize and provide for me.   He had two other
children born in wedlock; for soon after my birth he
married a Greek lady, according to the rites of the
Greek Church and the forms of law.   By the rules of
heraldry the *bar sinister* ran broadly across my es-
cutcheon.   My step-mother, however,—if my father's
wife can be so called,—was a kind and good woman.
She did not object to receiving me; and when I found
myself in my father's house I was treated by her tenderly, and, in fact, no difference was ever made between
me and her own children.   Two, as I have said, were
born before my arrival: they were both daughters;
there was a son born afterwards.   He was ten years
younger than myself.

"I was put to school and learned rapidly.   At an
early age I was taken into my father's counting-house
and bred to mercantile business.   I became expert in
financial affairs; and before I was twenty I knew the
history and present situation of all the important loans
in Europe and what houses had dealt or were dealing
in them.   In the year 1795, Bonaparte was in Egypt,
telling his soldiers that thirty centuries looked down on
them from the pyramids.   What do the centuries or the
pyramids now care for him or his soldiers?   But at the
time he was there the whole Eastern world was much
concerned about the probable doings of the famous
Corsican officer of artillery.   It was feared by many
intelligent people that he might undertake to found an
Eastern empire.   He had some dreams of that kind.
If he had entered upon such a career he would not
have scrupled to make himself a Mohammedan and a
representative of the prophet.   His genius and daring
would have found the way, and his French troops
would have followed him wherever he chose to lead
them.   But the French Revolution was just then in

such a state that, after the siege of Acre, he suddenly
found it for his interest to return to France. It was
while Bonaparte was still in Syria, however, and there
was so much anxiety all through that part of the world,
that my father thought it best to send me upon the
Continent of Europe. He did not intend to give me
the rights of an eldest son or to make me his successor
in business; but he opened the way for me to make a
career for myself. Through some influence of his I
obtained a situation in one of the largest banking-
houses in Vienna. There I remained for several years,
earning a good salary and devoting a part of it to the
completion of my education. Although I spoke and
wrote many languages, Greek, German, French, English, and Italian, my mercantile training had left me no
opportunities to study any of their literatures, and it
was almost wholly for business purposes that I had
hitherto used the languages that I knew so well. In
Vienna I engaged the best teachers and read a great
deal of history and literature with a learned German
professor. The bankers by whom I was employed had
some connection with one of the great monasteries in
Austria, and I used to be occasionally sent there on
business. One of the fathers put me in the way of
studying the ancient classics, and from him I learned
to speak Latin. I mention these things to account for
the fact that, although the active part of my life has
been passed in mercantile and financial business, I have
been something of a scholar; enough, at least, to enjoy
studies of various kinds and to converse passably in the
company of learned persons on most subjects; although
I hope I have been a learner rather than a person who
undertakes to teach people who know more than he
does. When I came to live in this country and brought
over my large library, to which I have been constantly
adding, I became a puzzle to the good people among
whom I established my residence, so that I have passed
for I know not what. But I have never been anything but a commercial man, a traveller, and a citizen
of the world, with a propensity to read, observe, and
reflect.

" To return, however, to my early life: By saving a part of my salary and investing my savings in profitable ways, for which I had good opportunities, I came to be possessed of a little capital, amounting to perhaps ten thousand dollars of your money. With this I transferred myself to Paris, soon after Napoleon had so far mastered the Revolution as to become First Consul. This was in 1799. I did not go there with any liking for him or his new government, and I will tell you presently how I came to have a strong dislike of both. I went there to make money. One of the persons with whom I became intimate was that remarkable man, Count Pozzo di Borgo, who was long Russian ambassador at Paris, and was sometimes sent to England on diplomatic business. I see that you are ready to ask how I can expect you to know anything about such people. But I do not doubt that, like most American ladies, you have a general knowledge of the history of the French Revolution and of the first Napoleon ?"

" Well, Mr. Charáxes," said Isabel, interrupting the old gentleman's narrative, " I am the daughter of a Boston merchant who, in his early life, suffered in his fortune in consequence of some of the doings of the emperor, and I remember to have heard him describe how our commerce was affected by them. I have, too, inherited from him some of those 'French spoliation claims' which I understand ought to be paid by our own government, and have formerly tried to understand these matters, but I have now left them to my lawyer, and ceased to trouble myself about them. I have, as you suppose, a general idea of the events in the life of the first Napoleon, having read the chief histories of that period. But I have no definite idea of the Count Pozzo di Borgo of whom you speak. Tell me, if you please, about him."

" I was not about to explain to you," resumed Charáxes, " the mysteries of the Berlin and Milan decrees and the English Orders in Council, which doubtless caused your father to lose ships and cargoes. As you say, it is best to leave those affairs to the lawyers, who, on the coming in of the Greek Kalends, may get some-

thing out of them and will, perhaps, give you a share.
But of that other Corsican, Di Borgo, who had an hereditary hatred of his compatriot, I can tell you a great
deal that might amuse you and that belongs to this
little narrative of my own life. Some one has said,
that he who writes or relates the small details of his
own life is guilty of a very pretty vanity; and this
vanity he softens into a mode of transmitting to others
the theory of the universe which one carries within
one's self. Is not that very fine?"

Isabel laughed as she answered, "Yes, sir, it is an
excellent description of a certain kind of egotism. But
if we undertake to give any account of ourselves, what
but our theory of the universe is it that we can give?
The egotism does not become vanity unless we put
forward our theory of the universe as the absolute
truth which we alone have discovered."

"You are quite right. Your gloss on the saying
which I repeated is as good as the remark itself. I
thought your woman's wit would find for me an excuse
for mingling my own small adventures with the history
of the great diplomatist, Di Borgo." Here the gray
eyes twinkled again for an instant, and then he went
on soberly with his narrative, in an easy flow, as if he
had secured all the right that he needed to speak of
himself without restraint.

"When I came to Paris I brought letters to the
count from persons in Vienna who thought that my
knowledge of financial affairs would enable me to be
useful to him. He was not a man eager to become rich;
and indeed his ample allowances from the Russian government made it unnecessary for him to seek wealth
for himself. But he was engaged in the negotiation of
treaties that involved great monetary arrangements,
and in these matters he often employed me. He soon
gave me his entire confidence, and I was more than
once sent by him on secret errands to London and St.
Petersburg. On these occasions I had excellent opportunities for investing and reinvesting my own money.
I was in Paris when the great European settlement in
1815 consigned Bonaparte to the island of Elba. I was

there when he landed from Elba and the Bourbons fled. I believed that Napoleon's 'destiny' had concluded to lead him to his final ruin. It was no surprise and no grief to me that the Duke of Wellington beat him at Waterloo, and when he was sent to St. Helena I thought France and Europe had met with a great deliverance. To be sure, this was a proceeding that could only be justified by an overruling international necessity; for undoubtedly when Napoleon went on board the English frigate 'Bellerophon' he did not surrender himself to the arbitrary disposal of the British government. The only excuse that can be made for them is that he had proved to be a person whom no treaties could bind.

"In all these affairs Count Pozzo worked incessantly, and I aided him. But during the Hundred Days, and all through the succeeding perilous times, I was never disturbed by the police, even when it was controlled by that arch-scoundrel, Fouché. I kept steadily on, amassing a fortune by perfectly obvious means; and this brings me to the object for which I desired to be rich; for according to that 'theory of the universe' of which we were speaking just now, every man ought to be able to explain the chief object at which he aims. I had studied a great deal the ancient philosophy of that remarkable people from whom the modern Greeks are descended. Notwithstanding the activity and bustle of the earlier part of my life, I became fascinated with the idea of what Demokritus is traditionally supposed to have taught, the *summum bonum.* This was the acquisition and maintenance of mental serenity and contentment, for which he is said to have advised a life of tranquil contemplation, to be pursued aside from money-making, or ambition, or the excitements of pleasure. This, however, in modern society, is not attainable as Demokritus recommended, or at least it was not in my case. I felt no spur of ambition, and I could abstain from the grosser pleasures, but I could not do without money, for without it I could not attain to the tranquillity of a life of contemplation. I therefore sought for wealth, not as an end but as a means; and at about the time when I came to this country I seemed to myself to be possessed of everything needful for the kind of life which I wished to lead for the remainder of my days. But I have not fully realized my plan, because the attachments which I formed for the friends with whom I have now lived so long since I settled in your great republic, the interest I have taken in their welfare, and the influence on their happiness which the fortunes of their country must have, have somewhat broken in upon my projected serenity. Still, I hope that I have escaped the selfishness that must in a large degree incrust the state of mind that the most subtle of the ancients, as Seneca calls Demokritus, considered as the supreme felicity. But this is an unpardónable amount of the egotism of which we were speaking, even if it escapes the vanity. The only excuse for it is that you, madam, have drawn it out."

The old man here paused, as if this brief outline of his life were all that he supposed would interest his listener. She, however, wished to learn more. "I do not know much," she said, "about Demokritus, but I remember the character of Imlac in Dr. Johnson's 'Rasselas,' which I read in my school-days for the sake of the story. You seem to me to be a sort of Imlac in modern European life, thrown into our Western world. But now, let me ask you, sir, if you never married?" and then she added, with a smile at her own question, "did you consider that marriage would interfere with the *summum bonum?*"

"Ah, celibacy has been perhaps the mistake of my life. I thought so for some time, but then I have always been reluctant to marry, because I really had no country, and a country and a family ought to go together. Until I made my fortune, I was too busy to marry. When I had accomplished this great object, I travelled over the whole of Europe and visited the scenes where my childhood and youth had been passed. But I became tired of this roving life, and went to live for a time in Switzerland, at Lausanne and Geneva. While I was residing at Geneva I conceived a strong desire to see America. The fund of experience and observation that I had ac-

cumulated, my knowledge of various kinds, my habit
of studying institutions and manners, led me to this
country, where I looked, however, for nothing but a
life of tranquil enjoyment. I had no intention of becoming an American citizen,—still less of taking any
part in public affairs. I had been all my life a mere
cosmopolite, a character that is not easily shaken off.
Chance led me to fix my residence in Detroit, and it
was an accident that led me to know Mr. Brewster and
his family. I have lived in close intimacy with them
for more than twenty years. I have found in them all
that I could desire in friendship; so that I do not regret my celibacy, for there are some natures for whom
friendship is better than love. Margaret Brewster is
nearly the same to me as if she were my own child;
yet I have not the responsibility of a parent for her lot
in life."

"She seems," said Isabel, "to be a young lady of a
great deal of character."

"Indeed she is, and her mother was one of the
loveliest women I have ever known."

"Did Mrs. Brewster die young?"

"When Margaret was only two years old. She has
been educated by her aunt, with such teachers as were
needful and could be employed at home. I have had
something to do with the development of her mind,
but her character has been formed by Miss Brewster,
so far as nature and fine inherited qualities needed to
be assisted."

"I am very glad that you have spoken of this young
lady. I wished to say to you—may I, Mr. Charáxes,
confess to you the dearest wish that a mother can
have? My son is four-and-twenty. He has been a
favorite among the young women of our society, but
he has never lost his heart to any of them. I can see
now—although I have never yet spoken to him about
her—that he is in love with your young friend. He
has known her, it is true, for only four weeks, but
they have been thrown together a good deal, and I
suppose he has made or tried to make the most of his
opportunities. Can you be surprised that I should

feel a strong desire for your sympathy in a matter that concerns the happiness and welfare of an only son and only child ?"

"Not in the least; but I fear your son will meet with disappointment in his suit. Margaret Brewster is a girl — I fear I shall wound you — she is a girl whose ideal is very high. The man who is to win her affections must be——"

"Pardon me if I interrupt you, sir. I know what you would say, and I will not ask you to be more explicit. But have you never observed that the influence of such a woman is sometimes very powerful in developing a man who loves her truly, and in raising him to her own level, or even higher? Your experience must have made you acquainted with such cases ?"

"Yes, that has sometimes happened, and sometimes the influence has fallen short of that result, and there has been an ill-assorted union and very little happiness."

"But what if the influence should be allowed to work its way before marriage? No great peril is then incurred by the lady. The man is the one who takes all the risk, and the result may be the formation in him of a character that would come up to the ideal which the woman has cherished, and there may be a happy union."

"I do not feel so sure that in such cases the woman takes no risk. If she be quite young, she may be in doubt about her own demeanor. But, supposing such a case as you seem to have in mind, it might require a long time and extraordinarily favoring circumstances, even supposing that no rival should appear, to reach the result which you have imagined. I sincerely hope that it may turn out as you wish. But I am speaking of another man's child, and of a young woman whom I should never think of trying to influence. That would be out of my province."

"Influence, my dear sir, from any quarter, is not what I would desire. I only meant to ask your opinion about our continuing longer in the society of your friends. My visit to Niagara must be governed entirely by what is best for my son."

"I can see no good reason why you should not extend your tour to the Falls. Your son, since he is, as you think, attached to this young lady, will follow her to her home sooner or later, and it matters not where the *dénouement* may take place. Her father and her aunt will be with her, wherever she is, and it is for them to guard her against any risk, if she needs any guardianship. But now, what are your wishes in regard to the name of the young Greek who is supposed to have run away with that far-off kinswoman of your husband? If we should find that he was of my name and blood, of which there can be but a slender chance, it would add nothing to the interest that I must feel in your son, now that he is so much attached to Margaret that he will probably endeavor to become her accepted lover. I think we had better let that matter of the Greek adventurer drop."

"Certainly, Mr. Charáxes, I will not now ask you to pursue that search, although I have been mysteriously influenced for years by a vague wish to learn the name of that person; and it was this that made me anxious to know something of your own history. May I ask if you expect to remain in this country always?"

"Yes, so far as I can foresee, because I have no country of my own, and because I feel much solicitude about the future of this country and the welfare of the friends who are so dear to me. There is, I fear, trouble in store for the people of the United States. I do not foresee when or how the storm will burst, but I have watched the gathering of the clouds with great anxiety. I have not transferred much of my property to this country, and if what I apprehend shall come about, I shall think my prudence was not ill-judged."

"Do you really think that things are so threatening? Might it not be well for a woman situated as I am to put a part of her fortune where it will not be exposed to the consequences of such a disturbance as you seem to anticipate?"

"No, I would not advise it. Every American, man

or woman, should abide by the fortunes of the country; and, moreover, you could not find any better situation for your wealth, if you have wealth, than it is probably now in."

"All the fortune that I have, Mr. Charáxes, was inherited from a father who was entirely American in spirit and in life. For my English connections I have long ceased to care, in reference to the remainder of my own life, or in reference to my son. It was an episode of my early days, and not altogether a happy one. I am now as thoroughly patriotic as a woman can be. But what is it that you fear for our hitherto happy country? Tell me the worst of your apprehensions."

"The worst that I apprehend is nothing less than civil war. But if that should happen, it will be a war of a territorial character, between the two great sections of the country, and not one in which communities will be divided into hostile and warring factions. So far, therefore, women as well as men will probably suffer only such evils as would attend a foreign war."

"But the very idea of war is so shocking, and civil war, too! Can nothing be done to avert it?"

"Much could be done, but I doubt if anything effectual will be. There is too much passion already enlisted on both sides, and there is too little wisdom. I do not see a single man in public life in this country to-day of sufficient force of character and possessing sufficient influence to control the discordant elements. The great republic seems to be drifting upon the rocks, with no one at the helm to guide her out of danger. But let us talk no more on a painful subject. I have told you of the acquisitions in friendship that I made after I came to this great land. Allow me to say that I have now made another. Will you not join us at Niagara?"

"I will think of it, Mr. Charáxes, and you must now allow me to express my warmest gratitude for your kindness and confidence."

"You know Lord Chatham's saying, 'Confidence is a plant of slow growth in aged bosoms.' In this case it has grown rapidly, but I am sure it is not misplaced."

To say kind things in a kind and sincere way was one of this old man's many attractions. He sat awhile longer, watching Mrs. Gascoigne's needle, which she did not keep entirely still. Then he suddenly looked at the clock on the mantel. Isabel said,—

"Pray do not go, Mr. Charáxes, but permit me to ask you one other question, since you have so kindly taken me into your confidence. Having no family, what made you wish for wealth beyond your personal necessities?"

"You must let me answer that by telling a story. You have heard of my ancient countryman, Xenophon?"

"Why, yes, I think our school-books told us that he was the soldier-historian of ancient Greece. When did he flourish?"

"About 400 B.C. He had at one time high command in the armies of the Lacedæmonians. When he retired from that service he was possessed of a considerable share of the plunder gained in those wars. With a portion of this money he purchased a landed estate at the town of Skillus, near Olympia. He dedicated this property to the goddess Artemis, constituting himself custodian or trustee of it, for the perpetual service of the goddess, and providing for successors in the trust. In humble imitation of this scheme, I dedicated my fortune—you are entitled to smile—to the goddess Philosophy. Was it not a very pretty plan of life?"

Isabel was so much amused by this banter that she thought she would repay the old gentleman in his own coin.

"My dear sir, you are doubtless a very fit person to be the first trustee of such an endowment; but where do you expect to find a successor in the trust?"

"There is some difficulty there. I manage very well so long as I administer, but about a successor I feel at times some misgiving. I have known a great many men who have accumulated wealth, and who, finding that they must go away and leave it behind them, have honestly tried to do some good with it, but have utterly failed. Perhaps I shall add another to

the catalogue. But, really, I am encroaching on your
half-hour before dinner, sacred always to the mysteries
of the toilet."

Whereupon he arose, and with an *au revoir*, uttered
with exquisitely simple urbanity, he bowed himself
out. There is nothing like fine manners in an old
man who has seen much of the world. And what is
there that is so captivating as age, when it is adorned
by wisdom, knowledge, and a sweet temper?

James came in soon after. His mother asked him
how he had spent the forenoon. "Stupidly enough,"
he said. "I have been seeing a lot of New-Yorkers
play a billiard match: that is all. The ladies (he did
not say what ladies) have not been visible. Have you
been here all the morning?"

"Yes, but not alone. I have had a long visit from
Mr. Charáxes. He has quite urged our going to Niagara. What do you say to it?"

"I should like it of all things. You know I have
never seen Niagara. When do the old gentleman and
the Brewsters leave Saratoga?"

"I believe very soon."

For a few moments nothing more was said. Isabel
went on with her needle-work; but presently she laid
it aside, and, going to the couch where James had
thrown "his listless length," she knelt by him, and,
putting her arm around his neck, she whispered, "Tell
me, dearest, are you in love with Margaret Brewster?"

"I do not know, mamma, whether I am or not."
She pressed him to her heart, waiting for him to say
more.

"She seems at times," he at length said, "to like me,
but I cannot quite make her out. I have talked with
her a great deal. She is very interesting, but she has
ideas about life that are so lofty,—I doubt if I should
be successful if I were to try."

"Dear boy, you know the old adage, 'faint heart
never won——' If you love this girl, trust to the influence of a steady and strong affection."

He was again silent for some time. His mother
caressed him with infinite tenderness, smoothing the

hair back from his forehead with her beautiful hand. Soon he turned and clung to her, faltering out, with strong emotion, "My own dear mother, I can keep nothing from you. I do love her, but I have no hope. I seem to be no nearer——"

"Wait, darling, and watch for some sign that will give you courage to speak. We will go to Niagara, for I have every reason to believe that both Mr. Charáxes and Miss Brewster sincerely wish to see more of us."

With this understanding, after they had both become more composed, James left his mother to dress for dinner, and went to his room to make his own toilet. I do not know if my old friend Henry Brewster would have felt flattered if he could have known how little embarrassment Mrs. Gascoigne was likely to feel in his company. Yet he was likely to feel as little in her society, for all his remaining tenderness was now centred in his daughter, as hers was in her son. The difference between them was that she longed to take to her heart the young woman whom she now knew that her son loved; but whether Brewster's could warm towards the young man was somewhat doubtful. There were many obstacles. Will they ever be overcome? Will the fact that he was the son of Isabel Bradshaw be an invincible difficulty? With some men, still capable at fifty of feeling the romance of such a connection, there might have been a charm in it. Whether this will be the case with Brewster I will not predict at the close of this chapter.

CHAPTER XIV.

"THE COURSE OF TRUE LOVE NEVER DID RUN SMOOTH."

MR. BREWSTER had been called home on business before Mrs. Gascoigne and her son arrived at Niagara. Mr. Charáxes, Miss Brewster, and Margaret remained. Mrs. Gascoigne thought it best not to go to the same hotel, but she and James took rooms on the Canada side, the party from Detroit being at one of the principal hotels on the American side. James lost no time in calling upon them, and in the course of an hour Mr. Charáxes came over to see his mother. This visit to Niagara had been deftly planned by the old philosopher for two purposes,—he wished to enjoy more of Mrs. Gascoigne's society, and to afford James an opportunity to see Margaret again. Although Miss Brewster had made no effort to learn Margaret's feelings towards James, she was quite aware how matters stood; but she was too wise to speak to Mrs. Gascoigne on the subject, so that the latter lady had only her own thoughts and hopes to commune with, watching silently and anxiously for the result on which so much depended.

"Well, madam," said Mr. Charáxes, as he greeted Mrs. Gascoigne with all his graceful cordiality, "you are arrived, according to your promise. Now let me lay out a little programme. I find that on the American side the proprietors of every spot where there can be any possible view of the Falls have enclosed the ground and charge money for standing on it. But I have taken the precaution to gratify their greed by buying the right to go where I please with as many friends as I choose to take with me. To be sure, it is most absurd for people to charge a price for standing or sitting on spots that can be used for no profit in any other way; but it is not worth while to quarrel with what you cannot help. At some time or other the governments on both sides of this wonderful cataract must take possession of the land and lay out suitable parks. At present, as the public road on this side skirts the Falls, visitors are not so much annoyed by the demands of private owners of the land. From the veranda of this hotel, too, there is, as you have already found, a fine view.· The ladies will be over in an hour or so, and I propose that we pass the day on this side, dining in the evening at this hotel, and doing the American side hereafter. Perhaps you will prefer to sit still and gaze and think, and may not find conversation desirable ?"

"Why can we not do both, Mr. Charáxes ?" asked Isabel. "We are none of us pressed for time, and, if we wish to say anything, we can say it."

"Very well; but as I have heretofore passed many hours here alone, and as I have rather a propensity to talk when I have any one to talk to, I may not be silent when I ought to be."

"Give yourself no concern, my dear sir, about me. I shall always be happy to listen to you, and will not be more abstracted than I can help."

In a short time Miss Brewster and Margaret, accompanied by James, joined them; and Mr. Charáxes ordered chairs to be placed at the spot which commands the best view of both the Falls and the rapids on the Canadian side. The sun was unclouded and the temperature very warm; but they could shade themselves by umbrellas. At first, they watched the ceaseless plunge of that immense volume of waters into the abyss below in perfect silence. Charáxes was entirely right in saying that no one can adequately describe that spectacle; and probably the reason is, that no one capable of feeling its sublimity ever looked upon it without an awe that can have no expression in words. At length the old gentleman said,—

"I have seen the ocean many times when lashed into a fury in which nothing afloat upon it could apparently escape destruction; but, as I never was wrecked, and this has been the experience of many thousands, it may be that we accustom ourselves to feel that we have a power which the ocean cannot overcome when we exert it rightly. But here all thought of resistance must be given up as soon as we imagine ourselves afloat on those tumbling and foaming rapids. It reminds me of that remorseless Destiny which in our old Greek tragedies was represented as anterior and superior to all human and all divine power; against which struggle was useless, and which swept its victims to sure destruction."

"Why," asked Margaret, "has not public authority interfered to prevent the barbarity of putting live animals upon vessels and letting them drift over the cataract? I have read such accounts with perfect horror. I do not think that if such a thing were to occur here now, before our eyes, that I could possibly look at it."

"I am sure you could not, my dear," said Charáxes. "But public authority has not yet learned, anywhere, to draw the line between things which a true civilization ought to forbid and those which must be left to individual liberty. This may be looked for hereafter, but it is not yet reached. Perhaps a Spanish bull-fight is the most absurd and cruel spectacle that can be seen in any modern country calling itself civilized. But what is an English prize-fight? And what are hundreds of practices that exist in all countries? Some day, in the most advanced nations, there will be a more complete tenderness for the lives of men and animals than there is now."

"But what do you say, sir," asked Miss Brewster, "to the plea that courage and fortitude and skill are cultivated by some of the practices to which you refer?"

"It is a very old plea," answered Charáxes, "and in most cases a very unsound one. I suppose that the future civilization will recognize two truths,—that all animal life exists by the will of the Creator, and that the life of no animal whatever is to be taken except from some necessity or expediency, which arises out of the superior claims and welfare of some higher order of beings; and that human life is never to be taken, excepting in the administration of justice, or in wars conducted by public authority, or in absolute self-defence. But, two of these occasions I presume will be greatly modified. I doubt if the death-penalty for crime will always continue to be inflicted, unless in very rare cases, and I suppose that wars will give place to some other method of settling international disputes."

"But in the present age of the world," said Margaret, "is it not true that war develops very high forms of character? Among all the discussions that I have read, in which the subject has been treated, I do not remember any writer but Dr. Channing who has questioned the tendency of war to form men of the highest qualities."

"I do not question it, either," said Charáxes; "but what I say is that war, while it is a sphere of individual action that may produce very lofty specimens of human character, may and often does produce characters of a much lower grade. At the same time, I do not condemn all wars, in the present state of the world, and if your country, as I fear may happen, should have the affliction of a civil war, I should certainly expect and desire to see your best men put forth all their energies on what they deem the true side."

"Ah, Mr. Charáxes, let us change the subject," said Mrs. Gascoigne. "Do you see how narrow the gorge is through which these waters come rushing down to the rapids compared to the volume of waters perpetually passing between the banks? Have any efforts been made to measure the space that must have been opened by some great convulsion to let through the waters of the lakes?"

"No, it is all at present, so far as I know, a matter of conjecture. Whether there was some great convulsion that tore open this passage, or whether it was worn slowly by the water itself; whether the Falls at one side of which we now sit were in ages past lower down and the cataract has receded westward, geologists have not yet given us satisfactory means for a guess. There are indications that would support either theory. But one thing is palpably plain,—that all the enormous body of water in the lakes that is not evaporated from the surface is poured over this cataract; and, so far as my travels have extended, it is the most impressive exhibition of power in action that nature makes anywhere upon this globe. The power is not only stupendous, but its manifestation never ceases. If we could get outside of our globe and from a stationary point observe its revolution on its axis, or its rapid whirl around the sun, we should see the same kind of manifestation on a larger scale. Moving water, in a vast quantity and ceaseless flow, is perhaps the greatest exhibition of the force of matter. Electric force, whatever it may be, is not in perpetual activity."

"I have sometimes exercised my imagination," said Isabel, "in conjecturing where all this water comes from into the lakes; but I have never been able to form a definite idea on the subject."

"Probably you never will. While such speculations are curious and interesting, they do not, in the present state of our knowledge, afford much of a solution."

They passed many hours at this spot, in alternate periods of conversation and silence, dining at sunset in the hotel. In the evening the moon came forth in its fullest light, and they saw the rare phenomenon of the lunar rainbow from several favorite spots. It was an hour when personal consciousness is almost lost in the overpowering influences of nature. James was not very susceptible of such influences. Margaret walked with him a little apart from the others, and they sat down. She was somewhat abstracted, but not unwilling to converse.

"What is it," he asked her, "that makes you think so much of the probability of war in our country, and its effect on the nation and on individuals?" It was the first time that he had tried to converse with her on such a subject, and there was a little danger that he would not be able to understand her.

"It seems to be almost certain," said Margaret, "from what my wisest friends foresee, that our country is destined to go through a great trial. It is difficult for any woman to comprehend the state of things, but my feelings lead me to think that influences to which none of us have ever yet been subjected will act upon both men and women."

"But why should our domestic and private lives be so much affected by such things? If our happiness is secured by a lot that affords all the advantages of life, why should we not be happy?"

"I think," said Margaret, "that I have heard you speak of the weariness that comes from the want of steady and serious occupation. The employment and development of our energies is certainly necessary to happiness. A life that consisted in nothing but the enjoyment of the good things of life, as they are called, would not be much of a life."

"But have you not left out the happiness of married life? That is not one of the good things that you would exclude, is it?"

James had never before come so near to the point which he wished to reach with Margaret, and it was by an unwonted effort that he made this attempt to understand her. She was silent for a little while. It was new to her to find that he was rather more capable of thinking than she had supposed. At length she said, very gently, "No, but in all that I have seen or known of married life, happiness has been founded on something more than liking; and I cannot understand what love is, unless there is something to be reverenced and leaned upon. But, really, we are talking about something that is out of my experience. You must not suppose that it is anything but a misfortune peculiar to myself if I do not have the common estimate of happiness."

She was almost inclined to say that, since they had known each other, she had been aware of his feelings towards her, and that she was sorry she could not return them. But he had not made a declaration of his love, and she must leave him to infer what she could not say. She rose, and they walked to where her aunt and Mr. Charáxes were waiting for them.

So it went on for several days. All the sights were seen and they had full enjoyment of that education which Charáxes had said was to be obtained in the study of Niagara. But when Mrs. Gascoigne and her son left for their home in Boston, James had not been able to obtain much to sustain his hopes, and his mother felt much discouraged. Margaret's farewell to both of them was very simple; kind, but without the least apparent consciousness of anything but friendly regard. Both Mr. Charáxes and Miss Brewster were very cordial in the expression of a hope that they would meet again.

CHAPTER XV.

POLITICS, LITERATURE, WAR, AND LOVE.

ALTHOUGH Mr. Charáxes, in his conversation with Mrs. Gascoigne at Saratoga, made light of the idea that he may have been remotely related to the young Greek who carried off Henrietta in the time of King Charles II., he felt a good deal of interest in the story. After his return home he wrote to his distant relative in Greece, and requested that a search might be made in the old books and papers of the house, in order to discover if there was any evidence that a member of the family had been settled in business in London during the seventeenth century. The result of the search was that a Charáxes had been in trade in the city of London for thirty years, and that he had a son who was born in England. It was then found, in one of the parish registers of London, that this son was born in the year 1630, and consequently that at the time of the Restoration he was thirty years old. From letters and other papers preserved in the house at Crete, it appeared that the London merchant returned to Greece at about the time assigned by the tradition in the Gascoigne family, but no mention was made of his son's departure from England at or about the same time, either with or without a lady. But there was a Charáxes of the same baptismal name— Stephen—who settled in one of the maritime towns of the Mediterranean, and it was reputed that his wife was an English woman of a noble family. When

all these facts had been collected, Mr. Charáxes communicated them to Mrs. Gascoigne in a very characteristic letter, which is now before me.

"Detroit, November 30, 1860.

"My dear Mrs. Gascoigne,—I will not say that my
pursuit of the *summum bonum* has been seriously interfered with by the prosecution of the researches
which the enclosed papers will show I have had made,
notwithstanding my incredulity. I suppose it was
your superior feminine sagacity which led you to put
more faith in the result of this search than I did; and,
at all events, the interest which the story has always
had for you, ever since you heard it, was reason enough
for my doing everything in my power to gratify your
wishes by finding out all that could be learned. I
accept the probability that the young Greek rascal
who carried off that beautiful Henrietta, whose portrait
so fascinated you, was a member of one branch of
the family to which my father belonged, although I do
not suppose that my father was one of his descendants,
since, whatever the misfortune of my own birth, my
father was of the elder branch of Charáxes, who were
merchants in Greece for at least two centuries, whereas
the London man was one of a collateral branch of the
same name. If Cleopatra's letters are ever discovered
and published, I shall look into them to find her transactions with my ancestors, notwithstanding you seemed
incredulous about our connection with her business
affairs when she came into our part of the world, and
'The barge she sat in, like a burnished throne, burned
on the water; the poop was beaten gold.' What
would not antiquarians now give for a bill of exchange
drawn and signed by the Queen of Egypt, endorsed
by Marc Antony, and discounted for him by the house
of Charáxes!

"But a truce to these old-world stories. Will not
you and your son honor and gratify an old man devoted
to philosophy by making him a visit at the coming
Christmas? You will find a house of which a Western
humorist has said that it is a 'comfortable shelter from

the weather,' and I can promise you some conversible
company. You know what conversation is, and a lady
who can contribute to it as you can deserves the best
that can be offered to her. Miss Brewster, I know, will
be most happy to meet you again, and I am sure that
Mr. James will not be indifferent to the prospect of
seeing once more the young lady whom he so much
admired at Saratoga and Niagara. With all the best
wishes of the coming season,

"I am, dear madam,

"Yours most sincerely,

"JOHN CHARÁXES."

"What is all this, mamma," asked James, when he
had read the letter, "about a young Greek and a
lady?"

"It refers to a story that I was told on a visit that I
made with your father at Gascoigne House soon after
our marriage. I was shown a very striking portrait
of a girl who was said to have eloped with a young
Greek in the time of Charles II. In English families
of rank there are often romantic traditions, and this
one, partly from its wildness and partly from the fascination which the portrait had for me, remained in my
memory a long time. When we met Mr. Charáxes at
Saratoga his Greek name led me to tell him this story,
and to ask if it might not have been possible that this
young man was a kinsman of his. I could hardly give
a reason for this idea, but it had taken possession of
me."

"You never told me this story."

"No, dear. I have never told you a great many
things about my life in England,—much of it was too
painful. Your poor father's death was shockingly sudden, and since you have grown up I have had many
reasons for not telling you about his family. Your
grandfather Bradshaw, my kind and most indulgent
father, who died before I returned home, expressed a
wish that you should be brought up as an American
citizen, and that wish has always been to me a sacred
injunction. Can you not forgive me for having told

you so little of your father's family? The probability
of your succeeding to their property or their honors
came to an end many years ago. Perhaps it was a
weak jealousy that made me so silent about that part
of my life, but my experience with every member of
that family, excepting your father and his youngest
sister, and an aunt of his, was anything but pleasant."

At the time of this conversation James was sitting
with his mother on a sofa in her boudoir. He put his
arm around her neck, and, kissing her cheek tenderly,
he said,—

"Dearest mamma, you have always judged wisely
about everything. I should be most ungrateful if I
were ever to harbor a thought that you have not acted
for the best. But how about this visit? What answer
are you going to make to this letter?"

"I shall be governed, dear, entirely by your wishes.
I should like to meet Mr. Charáxes and Miss Brewster
once more, but if you feel that it is not best for you to
see Miss Margaret Brewster again, I certainly should
not wish to accept the invitation."

"I cannot say, mamma, that I have much hope that
her feelings towards me will change. When we left
Niagara she had, as you know, given me no encouragement, but nothing decisive had occurred. What do you
think yourself?"

"I do not think you should avoid meeting her again,
when it is made so easy for you by this invitation
from Mr. Charáxes; and I do not think, either, that it
would be well for you to feel that you are cherishing a
hopeless attachment. You have staked a great deal
upon it, and perhaps I have done more than I ought
in leading you to be so steadfast and constant. But, as
well as I can judge, the case is not hopeless."

"Then let us go, by all means. I do not know what
I could have to trust to if I were to give up all reli-
ance on your judgment. But what do you suppose it
is that makes her seem so indifferent to an attachment
that she must know is sincere? Do you think that she
may care for some one else?"

"No; from something her aunt said to me, although

it was very slight, I feel quite sure that it was not so. I will tell you what my idea is about her. I think that she is a girl of very fine intellect, most thoroughly and carefully educated. Her father and old Mr. Charáxes, who are both superior men in their different ways, have probably been the only men of whom she has ever seen much. Her standard is thus very high; and from some ideal which she has been led to adopt, she is less susceptible than most girls of her age, and perhaps she thinks that she must find something lofty or uncommon in a man before she can love him. I fancy that until they came to Saratoga she had never been much in the world. Her aunt did not seem to me to be a person who would have aimed to make her very different from other girls, although Miss Brewster is certainly a lady of a great deal of character; but I have never conversed with her much about her niece. I do not see that you ought to consider yourself incapable of winning the love of a girl who has never refused you. She is worth trying for, and it may do you a great deal of good to try. It seems to me that it is best to accept the old man's invitation."

James was never above or below his mother's influence. Her power over him was supreme, from its very gentleness. Her affection for him had not always been wisely manifested, but it had won from him a love for herself that was very beautiful. Fond and over-indulgent mothers do not always get this return from an only son; but Isabel had it in full measure, pressed down, heaped up, and running over. It kept him pure and good, if he was not brilliant. I ceased to care whether he would ever set the river on fire. I knew that his love for his mother had made him proof against the coarser temptations of life, that beset so many young men who have plenty of money and no occupation. To him his mother was always perfection, let other people think what they might.

Mrs. Gascoigne's answer to Mr. Charáxes was both graceful and cordial, and I am sure my readers would not thank me if I did not give it to them, from the copy that I found among her papers.

p

"Boston, December 5, 1860.

"MY DEAR MR. CHARÁXES,—Your most kind and welcome letter deserves a prompt answer. I hope you will not think me ungrateful if I take but little interest in any of the dealings which any of your forebears may have had with 'the Serpent of Old Nile.' I hope she poisoned none of them, and that they made her pay well for all the money that they advanced on her bills. But the later and I suspect more authentic history of your family, which you have investigated for my benefit, and have so kindly communicated to me, I thank you for most sincerely. I now feel that our friendship has quite a romantic origin in a strange past concealed in the web of fate for two hundred years or more, and brought out by the accident of our meeting at Saratoga.

"I accept with very great pleasure, for my son and myself, your kind invitation. We hope to present ourselves at your house early in Christmas week, where we shall doubtless find shelter not only from the weather but from all other annoyances that kindness and considerate hospitality can guard against. You must allow me, however, to be rather a listener than a talker, and to give the *pas* to that wise and interesting lady, Miss Brewster, to whom and to Miss Margaret I beg you to present my kind regards, not forgetting the very useful Mrs. Davis, to whom I owe the honor of your acquaintance. Believe me, dear sir,

"Most gratefully and sincerely yours,
"ISABELLA GASCOIGNE."

Before they left Boston, Mrs. Gascoigne thought it prudent to suggest to her son to change his usual style of putting his full name, James Bradshaw Gascoigne, on his visiting-card. It was a little difficult to assign a reason for this, but on consultation with me, I told her that as James was now five-and-twenty, and as they were going into a part of the country where none of her family were known, I thought that if his visiting-card were to read simply "Mr. Gascoigne," it would be quite appropriate. She proposed this to James, and as usual he acquiesced in her advice, without the least idea that there was any special reason for it. For a similar reason she determined to leave Dinah at home, and to take the same maid who accompanied her to Saratoga.

As I never saw Mr. Charáxes's house at Detroit, I must rely for a description of it and of the incidents of the visit on Mrs. Gascoigne's letters, which I received from time to time.

DETROIT, December 23, 1860.

"MY DEAR OLD FRIEND,—In fulfilment of the promise I made to you and Mrs. Boylston, I write to let you know of the few incidents of our journey, and our reception here. We stayed two days at Niagara, in order to see it in its winter magnificence. The weather had been cold enough to clothe the whole scene in some of the grandeur and beauty of ice and snow, but probably not in the fulness of display that will come later. I remembered a remark that Mr. Charáxes made more than once about the impossibility of describing Niagara in words. It is extremely difficult to give a description of it at this season. You must imagine all the trees but the evergreens stripped of their foliage, and their trunks and branches coated in the morning with the frozen spray, whenever it had been freezing during the night. Soon after the sun struck them this coating fell off, to be renewed on the next cold night. Enormous icicles hung from some of the rocks, but as yet there are no masses of ice coming down the rapids. I think, however, I enjoyed the sights at Niagara more when we were here in the summer. For the two days that we were here last week, the weather was too inclement for me to be out much. In order to take in this wonderful spectacle, one needs to sit still for hours at the same spot, and do nothing but gaze and think.

"After leaving Niagara, we made a *détour* into Ohio, and stopped at Mansfield, in order to see Miss Simmons. I found her most delightfully situated. She lives with her nephew, who is in a prosperous business. The plants which you know I forwarded to her, after she left me, are all in a most flourishing condition. The old lady was disposed to rally me about what she was pleased to consider my neglect of opportunities. As I knew that she did it out of fond partiality and in the most affectionate spirit, I let her run on. If I repeat a little of it to you, you will acquit me of vanity.

"'Well, my dear, I did expect to receive from you an invitation to come to Boston to attend a ceremony, which sooner or later, must occur. How is it that none of them have persuaded you to change your condition?'

"'Dear Miss Simmons,' I said, 'did I not tell you, years ago, that there were no caskets in my house standing ready to be opened? You surely have not forgotten the lottery in which Portia's fate was involved?'

"'Portia,' she exclaimed; 'why! your father contrived no lottery for you. You are perfectly free to choose, and yet you will not choose. There are plenty of caskets, but it is for you to open one of them.'

"'Let me tell you a secret, my dear old friend,' I replied. 'You know that my life is devoted to an only son. James is in love with a young lady whom I am most anxious to have him marry. All my thoughts, all my feelings, are enlisted for him. But it is doubtful what the result will be.'

"'Ah!' she said, 'that alters the case. Forgive my banter, Isabel. I hope I am not a thoughtless old woman. I will join my hopes to yours, and lay aside all expectation of seeing you try to improve your own lot. And after all, I do not really believe that it could be improved, so far as you alone are concerned. But when the felicity that you seek for in your son's happiness does come to you, you will let me share it?'

"'That I will, my friend; you shall know of it immediately.'

"With this understanding, I left her, and both you and Mrs. Boylston now know on what all my hopes are staked.

"We reached Mr. Charáxes's house on the day before yesterday, and were most cordially and gracefully received. You met him once, long before I knew him,

and you know what a charming old man he is. Time
has not taken from him any of the graces of mind or
person that have always distinguished him. He has
but few of the infirmities of age, and his life bids fair
to be a very long one, he has lived so carefully and ra-
tionally. I was most agreeably surprised by his beautiful and well-ordered establishment. You must figure
to yourself a spacious stone house, standing in four or
five acres of well-kept grounds, on a slight elevation,
near the city of Detroit. It was built a hundred years
ago, or more, by descendants of one of the early
French settlers.

"From the front of the house there is a fine view of
Lake St. Clair. On the ground floor there are four
large rooms, two on each side of the spacious hall;
one is a noble drawing-room. The others contain his
very large collection of books, in choice bindings,
works of art and knick-knacks of all sorts, gathered
from many parts of the world, and arranged in some
historical order of illustration of different epochs and
countries. They are mostly, however, European and
Asiatic curios. He does not seem to take much to the
ethnology of our American continent, but there are
enough specimens of this class to make a small department by themselves. He tells me that in the days
of his active life he transacted business with many
persons in remote parts of the world, and was often
able to do kindnesses to men whom he had never
seen, in acknowledgment of which there came to him
quantities of things that it was supposed would please
him. Sometimes the sender, who had met with some
curiosity, would forward it to him and draw upon him
for the price that he had paid. In these cases he
always honored the draft. In the great majority of
cases, however, the things were gifts, sent in acknowledgment of some service, or because the persons sending them thought he would be gratified. There are
people to whom attentions of this kind seem to gravi-
tate by some mysterious law of attraction, although
they are exceptional mortals. Charáxes is one of
them, and his house is full of very remarkable things

that came to him in this way, of which I could not
begin to give you a catalogue, if I were to try.

"But I must tell you of a little thing that occurred
in regard to one of the books in his collection. In a conversation that I had with him at Saratoga, and which
I repeated to you, you remember that I laughingly
told him he reminded me of the philosopher Imlac,
in Johnson's 'Rasselas.' This seemed to amuse him
very much. On the day after our arrival here I was
sitting with him in his principal library, a large room
in the front of the house. He took down from a shelf
two small volumes, printed in a large plain type, which
he placed in my hands. 'This,' said he, 'is a copy of
"Rasselas," that in all probability was handled by the
great doctor himself, for it is the first edition, and on a
fly-leaf of the first volume you will see the autograph
of James Boswell, the second son of "Jemmy." Probably this very copy was given to Jemmy Boswell by
Johnson himself.'

"'How did this copy get into your possession, sir?'
I asked.

"'James Boswell, the son of "Bozzy," was a barris-
ter in the Temple. He died in 1822, a short time before his brother, Sir Alexander, who you recollect was
killed in a duel. They were both intimate friends
of Sir Walter Scott. James Boswell the younger was
a scholar, and edited the last variorum edition of
Shakespeare. His books and other effects were sold in
London, and I bought this copy of "Rasselas" for five
pounds. I showed it to Sir Walter, who verified James
Boswell's signature. He told me many anecdotes about
these two Boswells, who were, he said, very different
men from their father "Jemmy," and that they probably inherited some of their grandfather, old Lord
Anchinleck's, contempt for their father.'

"'Do you think, Mr. Charáxes,' I asked, 'that Bozzy
was such a contemptible person after all?'

"'In some respects he was, and in some he was not.
Both he and Johnson have been a good deal caricatured,
especially by Macaulay. Every one recognizes the
correctness of Macaulay's statement that Boswell, with

all his weaknesses and follies, wrote the most remarkable biography that had been written of any man in the English or perhaps in any other language. Other people have said the same thing long before Macaulay. But, then, to give point to the antithesis, Macaulay exaggerated Boswell's follies, and belittled his intellect. As to Macaulay's characterization of Johnson, it is simply a daub, and not a portrait. An adequate character of Johnson remains to be written.'

"Then he took down Madame de Staël's 'Corinne,' and Byron's 'Childe Harold,' and referring to our conversation at Saratoga about descriptions of great natural objects, he read these two passages,—I translate the French of Madame de Staël,—

"'The Catholic church (at Ancona) stands on a height that overlooks the main, the lash of whose tides frequently blends with the chant of the priests. . . . The soul delights to recall its purest emotions —religion—while gazing at that superb spectacle, the sea, *on which man never left his trace.* He may plough the earth and cut his way through mountains, or contract rivers into canals for the transport of his merchandise, but if his fleets for a moment furrow the ocean, its waves as instantly efface this slight mark of servitude, *and it again appears such as it was on the first day of its creation.'*

> "'Roll on, thou deep and dark blue Ocean,—roll !
> Ten thousand fleets sweep over thee in vain ;
> Man marks the earth with ruin,—his control
> Stops with the shore ;—upon the watery plain
> The wrecks are all thy deed, nor doth remain
> A shadow of man's ravage.

> "'Time writes no wrinkle on thine azure brow,—
> Such as creation's dawn beheld, thou rollest now.'

"'What do you think of this plagiarism?' he asked.

"'Is it a plagiarism?' I asked, in my turn. 'The ideas are what would naturally occur to two persons of vigorous imagination, independently, and I suppose it has often happened that two writers have had the same thoughts, and one has expressed them in prose

and the other in poetry. I was a great reader of Byron when I was young, but I never analyzed his poetry
by looking up the sources of his thoughts or expressions. May not Madame de Staël have had suggested
to her this idea of man's insignificance in the presence
of the ocean by the passage in the book of Job where
the same idea is put in a variety of ways in illustration
of his feelings in the presence of many of the depart-
ments of nature?'

"'There is not much,' he replied, 'in the book of Job
that could have suggested the striking imagery and
expressions of which Madame de Staël made use in that
passage, and I must say that the similarity between
her ideas and language and Byron's is so remarkable
that I should call the poet's a very close imitation. A
critic might find it worth while, however, to look into
sources older than Madame de Staël, although it is
certain that Byron wrote after her. "Corinne" was
first published in 1807; "Childe Harold" in 1812.'

"I asked him if he had ever seen Madame de Staël.

"'Yes,' he replied, 'I knew her a little in Paris, when
Napoleon was first consul, and a common dislike of him
was one bond of sympathy between us. But she never
was a woman to my taste. Her genius was most extraordinary, but in conversation she was exceedingly
theatrical and declamatory, although she often said
grand things, and often wrote them, too. Did you ever
read the letter which she wrote to La Fayette after she
heard that he had been released from Olmutz? It
sounds like the blast of a bugle. It is the voice of
France calling upon her citizen to come back to his
native soil and serve his country as he alone could.
But La Fayette had not the force to contend against
Napoleon. He did well for a time to retire to Lagrange.
There is a little cemetery in an obscure quarter of
Paris, closely surrounded by buildings; it is called the
Cemetery of Picpus. It was there that the remains
of the victims of the guillotine during the Reign of
Terror were huddled in an undistinguishable mass into
a trench. Many of them were aristocrats of the Fau-
bourg de St. Germain; among them Madame de La

Fayette's mother and sister. La Fayette himself was buried in that little cemetery by the side of his wife, and the only inscription over his grave is the grandly simple one,—

"LA FAYETTE

CITIZEN AND GENERAL."

I wish there could be a good and impartial life of La Fayette written. It ought to be done by some American scholar. There has not been an English historian in this century who could have done it fairly. The English never understood him, and never did him justice.'

"These are only specimens of Mr. Charáxes's talk, as he pours it out all day when he has a listener. He does me the honor to say that I am a good one. Just as he ended what he was saying of La Fayette, Miss Brewster's card was brought to me, and Mr. Charáxes directed the servant to show her at once into the library.

"'Ah, my dear lady,' said he, 'I thought you would be glad to see Mrs. Gascoigne.'

"'I am indeed,' said Miss Brewster, pressing my hand warmly; 'I hope you are rested after your long journey. I have just seen your son. I left him with my niece. He seems very well. Remembering the old adage that three are not company, I ordered the carriage and drove out to see you.'

"'And that busy brother of yours,' said the old gentleman, 'has he not returned from Chicago?'

"'No,' she answered, 'but we hope he will come home to a quiet Christmas dinner. I understand that we are not to dine with you, sir?'

"'I reserve that for the following Saturday, when I shall expect you all and some other people, whom I shall ask to meet Mrs. Gascoigne. Now that she has been so good as to come, I shall not let her go away soon.'

"Then he arose, and, excusing himself on account of some business he had to do with a person who had called, he left Miss Brewster with me.

" 'And how has it been with you during the past year?' I asked.

" ' We have all been well, and our domestic life has flowed as usual. But the state of the country lately has given my brother a great deal of anxiety, and I confess that I share it with him. You may not know that he is not a politician, in the ordinary sense, and not a party man at all. But he watches the course of public events very closely. One thing that he has foreseen has just happened,—the secession of South Carolina. It is very startling.'

" 'Yes,' I answered, 'it occurred after we left Boston; we heard of it on the way.'

" 'How do wise people in your part of the country feel about these things?'

" ' It would be difficult to say who our wise people are,' I replied. 'You know that the dominant political feeling in New England has long been against the South. A woman like myself, who does not see many political men, must judge of the state of public feeling by what she hears from her immediate friends. One of my oldest friends is a gentleman of pretty wide observation and cool judgment. He tells me that throughout New England there is a general and unaccountable apathy in regard to what the South may do, which he thinks is a dangerous feeling.'

" 'May it not come from the fact,' asked Miss Brewster, ' that the late election turned on a sectional issue in regard to slavery? It seems to me that this was very unfortunate, and both Mr. Charáxes and my brother regard it in the same way. But what specially troubles me now is the constant intrusion of these political controversies into our domestic lives. We women must, of course, be expected to sympathize in the prevailing political feelings in times of great excitement. Margaret reads almost nothing now but newspapers, and hears nothing talked about but political affairs. All this is telling upon her in a way that I do not quite like. I do not mean that she is becoming less feminine, but I sometimes think that she is getting wrought up to something that I cannot foresee. We come here every Saturday to dine with Mr. Charáxes, and the "coming events casting their shadows before" are constantly obtruding. I am very glad that you came, for I hope it may direct Margaret's thoughts to something else. She sees scarcely any one who is not thinking and talking all the time about public affairs. If there should come a necessity for women's activity, I certainly shall not try to hold her back or be wanting myself in any duty that I can perform. But just now I welcome this episode of your visit.'

"'Mr. Charáxes,' I said, 'expressed to me at Saratoga more than a year ago his apprehensions of a civil war, but I could hardly realize the danger. I remember, however, that he said it would be a territorial war, or one between the two sections of the country, if I understood him rightly.'

"'If it is to come at all, let us hope that this will be the case; but there are parts of some of the Western States where there may be local divisions, and possibly actual conflicts. Mr. Charáxes, wise and foreseeing as he is, long as he has lived among us, and deeply interested as he is in our welfare, is yet a foreigner; he may not see all the dangers. But it is quite unpardonable in me to welcome you with these forebodings. Let us hope for the best. We women can only hope and pray. And now let me have the pleasure of taking you to our church to-morrow. Mr. Charáxes is not a regular attendant at any church; he sometimes goes to one and sometimes to another, and often stays at home. But he contributes liberally to the support of several forms of Christianity, and so I tell him that he is a good Christian. My father was a Congregational clergyman in Massachusetts, and my brother and I were bred in what was called "orthodoxy." But we have been Episcopalians for many years.'

"I accepted this invitation of course, and will write you about the Christmas services in my next."

"December 26.

"Miss Brewster and her niece called for us in their carriage yesterday and took us to church, James and myself. Mr. Brewster had not returned home. We sat in the rector's pew. It seems that the rector, Dr. Pitman, was the uncle of Mrs. Brewster, and, consequently, he is Margaret's granduncle. He is considerably over seventy, and has an assistant. The services were of a rather low-church order, but very well conducted. The rector's sermon was a good one. From something that Mr. Charáxes told me, I understood that Mrs. Brewster was left an orphan at an early age; that she was educated by her uncle, and was married from his house. He has no children, and his domestic affairs are managed by a lady who is a distant relation of Mr. Brewster. Mrs. Pitman died many years ago.

"Our Christmas dinner was a very quiet one, Mr. Charáxes having asked no one to meet us, meaning to give his servants an opportunity to enjoy themselves in their own way. James went to the Brewsters in the evening, but I do not think there is much change in the young lady's feelings towards him. You know the secret hope of my heart, and how much is at stake for him and for me. I can tell better what is likely to happen when I have seen more of her."

"December 28.

"The dinner on Saturday was very elegant. The table, which was a round one, was laid in Mr. Charáxes's larger dining-room, and the silver, porcelain, and glass were superb. Mr. Charáxes put me on his right hand. General Cass was present and he took in Miss Brewster. Mr. Brewster sat next, with Mrs. Davis. James had been assigned to Margaret, and of course he appreciated the old gentleman's thoughtfulness in making this arrangement. Mrs. Davis's husband (he is a wealthy merchant and a man of sense), some of the younger ladies and gentlemen of Detroit, married and single, together with the white-haired old rector, Dr. Pitman, composed the other guests. The party numbered about twenty. You have already heard that General Cass has resigned from the President's cabinet; he came home immediately after his resignation. During dinner Mr. Brewster asked him several questions, which drew from him an explanation of the reasons for this step, but I cannot report political conversations. There was a long and animated discussion of the state of the country, the prospect of a Southern confederacy, and a civil war. All the gentlemen seemed to think that war is inevitable. As I understood General Cass, he differed with the President because he did not think that the President was doing what he ought to do in preparing to encounter the secession of the Southern States. There was a protracted argument about Mr. Buchanan's policy in regard to the Southern forts, in which Mr. Brewster defended the President, maintaining that it was his most urgent duty to prevent as many of the slave-holding States as possible from joining a Southern confederacy, and that arming forts in the South would only make matters worse. Miss Brewster led the way for us to the drawing-room, leaving the gentlemen to their political talk; but it was all, so far as I heard it, in good temper, and most interesting and instructive. After we had returned to the drawing-room, and I had taken a seat on one of the sofas, I was agreeably surprised that Margaret came and sat by me, as if she wished to show me some attention. I do not think, however, that it was because I am James's mother. I presume it was because I am Mr. Charáxes's guest. It was the first time that I had ever had an opportunity to converse with her in a *tête-à-tête*. The other ladies were gathered around a table, looking at some prints. I can repeat a little of our conversation.

" 'I suppose, Mrs. Gascoigne,' she began, 'you were a little wearied by so much politics as we had at dinner?'

" 'No,' I replied, 'I was very much interested in the conversation. Our country is in a situation to make all of us, especially women, very anxious.'

" 'But do you not think, Mrs. Gascoigne, that if we are to have a war, the energies that it will call forth will elevate the general and individual characters of the whole people?'

" 'War, my dear young lady, is always a calamity, and civil war is the greatest of all calamities. I am not old enough to remember anything of the war with England, but the misfortunes which it entailed upon our commerce followed my father for years, and his children have not wholly escaped their consequences. But it is not so much because of the effect on the business and pursuits of our people that I deprecate a war, as it is that lives must be sacrificed, that the land must be filled with widows and orphans, and that personal sufferings must be incalculably increased and intensified.'

" ' But in the alleviation of that suffering, in diminishing it as much as possible, there will be a great call for individual energies, in women as well as in men; and for men, who must do the work on fields of battle, will there not be demands that will test the character of the nation and its sons ?'

" I thought these were very singular sentiments to be professed by a young woman of one or two and twenty, and they explained to me her aunt's feeling that she was getting wrought up to something that could not be foreseen. Very likely Margaret had heard some of these ideas expressed by other and older people, but she had evidently carried them farther in her mind than one would have imagined any woman of her age would be likely to do. I made an effort to change the conversation. I tried books, society, music, various topics on which intelligent young women like to talk; but, although she is manifestly an accomplished girl, none of these subjects seemed to interest her now. Yet she is so intellectual, and at the same time she has so much feminine grace and such gentle manners, that I could not have helped being attracted by and interested in her, even if I had not had such a strong reason as I have for observing her. It is very doubtful, however, whether she will ever feel towards James any differently than she has since they have known each other. I should say that she has a kind of enthusiasm that is not likely to take the form of love.

" We shall remain here only three days longer, and in that time I do not look for any further developments. I say nothing to James now on this tender subject, for I fear that I have already said too much. In regard to what the future has in store for our country, my feeling is one of unspeakable dread. I hope I am not without patriotism. I could cheerfully give half of my fortune to the country if it were needed; but, as you, my dear friends, know very well, I was not made to be a Roman mother. My only child would be a gift to my country that I do not believe I could make. It is my daily prayer that I may be spared that trial. But it may come. May God give me strength to meet it, as he has to meet other sorrows."

Already there were in the far-off Southern regions mothers who were ready to devote their sons to what they considered a holy cause; wives who could give up their husbands; maidens who could see their lovers depart, at the call of that country which they all hoped to make. Already there was spreading through those regions a conviction that the time had come for the people of the South to establish for themselves an independent government. It were idle to impute the great sectional revolt to the work of politicians. It were useless to inquire whether our Southern friends had real grievances. They believed that they had, and they believed that it was best for them to separate themselves from us. When this has become the conviction of a people the bonds of such a political system as ours will be broken. The theory of the Constitution which prevailed throughout the North was, I have always thought, the most logical, and the most in accordance with the facts which attended its establishment. But it was encountered by another theory, and a very different one, in which the people of the South believed; and as there could be but one final arbitrament, after every form of discussion had been exhausted,—as that arbitrament must be a resort to force if the secession of the South should not be acquiesced in by the North,—the people of the Southern States resolved to take the step which resulted in the formation of a separate government, and to pre-

pare to make good their independence. Troops were
raised. Fort Sumter, in the harbor of Charleston,
was beleaguered; the first gun was fired; the fortress
was surrendered, after a gallant resistance, and the
dreadful note of war resounded throughout the North.
While these events were rapidly transpiring, the executive authority of the Federal government passed
from the hands of President Buchanan to President
Lincoln. The fall of Fort Sumter took place on the
21st of April, 1862. An executive proclamation was
issued, calling for seventy-five thousand volunteers
from the States that remained loyal to the Washington
government. Every one knows what followed. It is
for me to tell how the happiness of the persons in this
little history was affected by the public occurrences.
Will the softness and tenderness of Isabel Gascoigne's
nature be equal to the trial which she feared might
come upon her? Will she have less fortitude than the
Southern matrons were to show? Will her son be developed into greater vigor, and become of a loftier
moral and intellectual stature? How will the enthusiasm of Margaret Brewster find a sphere fit for the
exertions of a refined and delicate girl?

My readers must have observed that in Mrs. Gascoigne's letters to me she had said nothing of Mr.
Brewster's demeanor towards herself while she was at
Detroit. After she had returned home I thought it
would not be indelicate, considering our long intimacy,
to ask her about it. I had a reason for doing so, which
was not the gratification of mere curiosity. I made
some allusion to the subject, and she immediately said,
with her usual frankness,—

"My dear friend, there is no reason in the world why
you should not ask me anything on that subject that
you wish to. I think it best that both you and your
wife should know how matters stand. I, of course,
never think of Mr. Brewster but as Margaret's father,
and it is quite plain that, if he thinks of me at all, it is
only as James's mother." She then told me that she
returned Miss Brewster's visits and accepted freely all
her attentions. Sometimes she saw Mr. Brewster at

his own house, and they met at other houses; there was no embarrassment for either of them. He conversed with her as he did with the other ladies, and to all outward appearance their acquaintance began in the summer of 1859, at Saratoga. Miss Brewster, she was sure, knew nothing of any earlier acquaintance. When Mrs. Gascoigne told me this I felt some inclination to ask her to give me an idea of the cause which, so long ago, produced the sudden change in her destiny. Perhaps it was my wife's desire to fathom that mystery which almost led me to touch upon it with our friend. But I checked myself, recollecting how long it had remained an unexplained and apparently inexplicable secret, and satisfied that Brewster and Isabel would never be drawn nearer together than the union of his daughter and her son, if that union was ever to take place, would make them, I left the subject just where she chose it should remain. I asked my wife, however, if she were now prepared to receive the dress which I had contingently promised her nearly twenty years before; and as she replied that she was, I went to a shop and bought for her the handsomest silk I could afford. This, I considered, closed all expectation of seeing Mrs. Gascoigne become Mrs. Brewster. On what might happen to the young people I should not have offered or taken a wager. I had plenty of hopes and some fears. James, I fancy, had about an equal amount of both. His mother was rather despondent after their visit to Detroit. I asked her to give me her impressions. She said that James had a long interview with Margaret on the day before they came away, but she could only infer that Margaret, although gentle and kind, had given him no encouragement. Mrs. Gascoigne thought that the only solution of his failure in his suit was that Margaret was a girl who looked for something more in a man than an amiable disposition, good character, and purity of life. She did not profess to see what would be the effect on him, or what might happen to change the young lady's feelings. All that she now felt confident of was that James could not give up every hope.

CHAPTER XVI.

A PERFECTLY RATIONAL FEMALE QUIXOTE.

WHEN Mrs. Gascoigne told her son, before their Christmas visit to Mr. Charáxes, that it would do him a great deal of good to try and win the heart of Margaret Brewster, she gave a hint that she did not fully explain. If she was entirely sensible of the reason why he had not been successful, she could not tell him that it was because his life had been too insignificant for the indulgence of such a hope. She could let him know what she thought of Margaret, and that she did not believe there was any rival to be feared. But this was all she could say. Something, however, may have been said by Margaret to James when he last parted from her which made him feel keenly that he was not the kind of man to gain her love. If anything of this nature was said, it was doubtless said kindly, for Margaret, although very frank and direct, was a most gentle girl, and she had nothing to reproach herself with in her intercourse with James. The succeeding winter was a dreary one for him. He lost all interest in amusements and went but seldom into any of his old haunts. As the months wore away he began to perceive that his mother may have meant more than she could explain. His difficulty thus far had been that he could not understand why a sincere affection was not returned. He now made a discovery that aroused in him a far greater energy than he had ever before exhibited in his life or had ever been conscious that he could put forth. It came upon him about as suddenly as the call for volunteers broke upon the country, and at the very time when the note of war resounded through the land.

Did Margaret foresee the effect that she might produce, or had she any conscious purpose to bring it about? Probably not. I should almost say certainly not; for she had hitherto regarded James as nothing but a pleasant young man of society, of good temper, good principles, and an affectionate disposition. She had never discovered in him any force of character, and she probably did not think highly of his abilities. James, however, under the impulse of a hope that he could not abandon, went at his first opportunity into a life that was a new one to him and to all who entered it as he did.

There had been in Boston, from early colonial times, a military organization known as the "Independent Cadets." It had a kind of regimental organization, and its commander always held the rank and commission of a colonel. It was rather an ornamental corps, —at least for one or two generations back,—its chief function being to act as the governor's escort on public days. It was somewhat pompously styled, "The Governor's Body-Guard." It was composed of young men of the best families in the State, and the colonel was always a person of good social standing. It had never seen a day of actual military service since the War of 1812, but it was a well-drilled and soldierly body, for a holiday function; and a very good school, in fact, for the formation of officers, who would be fit for real service when occasion might call for them. The most notable occurrence in its history, during my time, was when a rather stately gentleman, who held high the dignity of the office, was governor of the State for nine years; an unexampled endurance of popularity in a State where the elections were annual. It was the custom, on the assembling of the Legislature early in January, after the newly-elected dignitaries had taken the oath of office, for the governor and council and the two houses of the Legislature to go in procession from the State-House to the Old South Church, escorted by the Cadets, to hear what was called "the election sermon," in which the preacher generally treated any political subject that he chose to touch upon. It happened on one of these anniversaries, an extremely cold day, the colonel of the Cadets, instead of marching his corps into the church after the procession had passed in, conducted it to a place of entertainment not far away,—as he afterwards said,—for shelter from the inclemency of the weather; but perhaps to obtain some refreshments also. When the services in the church were over and the governor and his staff and the other magnates came out, the Cadets were not on the ground to take up the escort back to the State-House. The civic part of the procession walked on, the governor in dignified indignation, and when His Excellency had reached " Park Street Corner" the Cadets came up at double-quick, and the colonel tendered the escort, with an apology. Neither escort nor apology was received; the governor strode on and entered the council chamber without any of the customary formalities which had always been observed, time out of mind. In a few days the colonel was cited before a court-martial, to answer charges of neglect of duty and disrespect towards His Excellency, the commander-in-chief. The trial was conducted *de riguer*, according to all the forms; it lasted six months, cost a good deal of money, and I totally forget the result.

In this military body James Gascoigne had been a private for some two or three years prior to the time when there was a call for volunteers to defend the Federal capital and the Federal authority. He had learned a little, but not much, of military affairs. It was more of a pastime with him and a good many of the other members than anything else: one of the pleasant forms of Boston social life; a matter of course, for Boston men of good family to belong to the Cadets. The President's call for volunteers was instantly followed by the organization of regiments throughout the loyal States. An older friend of James's undertook to raise a regiment, and was promised by the governor the command of it. While they were enlisting men I was a little surprised one day by the receipt of a note from James, informing me that he was engaged in raising one of the companies for this regiment, and asking me to apply to the governor and obtain for him a captain's commission. My first thought was of his mother. How would she take it? Before doing anything I determined to see her. She told me that she had observed for some weeks that James was beginning to manifest an energy that she had never seen in him before. It might be the influence of his associates and their example that was operating on him. But she thought that there was perhaps another stimulus. When I told her that he was about to take an irrevocable step from which he could not withdraw with honor, and therefore that if she were to interpose any objection she must do it before the commisson was asked for, she turned very pale. She inquired whether any sum of money that she could give to the expenses of raising and equipping the regiment would not be considered as her quota of contribution to the public interests, without giving up her son to this dreadful war. She was both able and willing to give a large amount. "No," I said, "money is not needed, although you can give whatever you think fit, and you had better do so. It is men that are wanted ; and James should not be behind his equals."

"An only son," she said,—"an only child,—must I give him up? Oh, my old friend, you have been the friend of nearly my whole life, help me to avert this trial."

"I will help you, my dear Mrs. Gascoigne, in the only way I can ; I firmly advise you to make the sacrifice, trusting that God will bring out of it, in some way, blessing and remuneration for all that you suffer. We cannot tell how Providence will reward you, but James must be allowed to obey the influence which impels him, whatever it may be, and wherever it may lead."

I spoke with some energy, for I knew that there was no one else who would so speak to her, and I had great confidence that she would act as became her. She dried the tears that flowed freely while we were speaking, and then, with entire composure, after a little while, she said, "I believe it must be as you say ; write to the governor, or see him. I consent."

From that day Isabel was calm and firm, but I will not say that she did not suffer. The imaginations of women are apt to exaggerate the personal dangers of war; but we men can know but little of what such a woman as Isabel must undergo when called upon to give up to all the hazards of war an only son who had been reared as James had been and from whom she had never been separated for a day since he was born. She busied herself at once with energy and judgment in the affairs of the regiment, spent money freely in the purchase of materials, threw open her house to an association of ladies who worked in making clothing for the soldiers, and superintended the work herself. Dinah undertook James's personal outfit, by her mistress's permission. It was very diverting to witness that good creature's perplexity about the war. She had a vague idea that it was something that concerned her own race in some way, because she heard people say so; but she did not understand it. She wondered whether Mass' Julius Pringle and Mass' James would meet and fight. Mass' Julius was her paragon of a young gentleman when she was in the land where she was born, as he was with most people in his neighborhood, white or colored. He must, when the war began, have been between forty and fifty, and very likely he would be an officer in the Confederate army. Dinah, however, always continued to think of him as he was at two-and-twenty, when he killed the rattlesnake which she described at Gascoigne House. Mass' James had been all his life her other idol, since she brought him from England as his nurse when he was three years old. Now that he was going to the war, she rather aggravated his mother's anxieties, but she worked for him in preparing every possible comfort, and a good part of it consisted in things with which he could not encumber himself and for which he could have no use. But the love and devotion shown were all the same.

The regiment went into camp for a short time, two or three miles out of Boston, for drill and instruction. James studied the military art most diligently, and he very soon became the most useful and efficient captain in the regiment. His influence over his men was remarkable, and under him they learned a great deal. Pretty soon this infantry regiment was transferred to

Washington and mustered into the service of the United States. It formed part of the troops that, along with other immense bodies, were organized into the Army of the Potomac in the summer and autumn of 1861.

In the month of November, the young general, McClellan, who had achieved in the West almost the only success that had hitherto attended the Federal arms in any part of the country, was called to Washington and invested with the command of all the forces there. He had some distant relatives in Boston, who offered Mrs. Gascoigne a letter introducing to him her son. The ideas then entertained by people in general of military affairs were pretty indefinite, but Mrs. Gascoigne accepted the friendly offer as a great kindness, and forwarded the letter to James. It spoke of him as an energetic and intelligent young officer in one of the Massachusetts regiments. I backed it by other testimonials. James left the letter at the general's head-quarters, not expecting that any particular notice would be taken of it. It happened, however, that the general, at about that time, was making up his staff, and was inquiring about the best officers among the volunteers. He sent for James, was pleased with him, and, having learned more about him in a day or two, he caused him to be detailed from his regiment, and appointed him junior aide. In that capacity James went with the general when he led the Army of the Potomac upon the Peninsula. Captain Gascoigne soon became noted for his gallantry, intelligence, and activity. All through the siege of Yorktown, the pursuit of the Confederates towards Richmond, and wherever the general had to be, Gascoigne was constantly with him and constantly rising in the estimation of the commander and the army. Before the army reached and was detained at the Chickahominy by floods and other obstructions he was more than once commended in the general's despatches to the War Department, and recommended for a command. But the general's recommendations were not always attended to. Just here I must leave my young friend, for I have to tell of one

whose silent influence was the real cause of his entering upon the life into which he had thrown himself
and which was developing in him something that no
one had anticipated.

About a month before the Army of the Potomac
was transferred from Washington to the Peninsula,
Margaret Brewster disclosed to her father a plan that
she had formed for doing some service to the Federal
cause. She had been quite active, along with her aunt,
in the work which the ladies of her native city, as
elsewhere, did for the volunteers. But this kind of
work did not satisfy her; she wanted another sphere,
in which she could find direct activity in the exercise
of her energies. She thought of a plan for joining the
army in some capacity of a lady-nurse for the sick and
wounded. Such a scheme must have been very crude
in her first thoughts, for a young woman of her age
and position. After she had matured it as well as she
could by her unassisted reflections and inquiries she
broached it to her father. He was rather surprised,
but he listened to her, as he always did. When she
had given him a general idea of it, he said,—

" Well, my dear, what does Aunt Elizabeth say to
this ?"

" I have not mentioned it to her," Margaret replied.
" I thought it my duty to consult you first."

" But how is such a thing possible ?" her father asked ;
" how could it be worked out by a young lady like you ?"

" I must have suitable attendants, of course, women
and men and all proper appliances. I know of a very
good woman, of mature age, whom I could take as my
principal assistant. Why could I not have a vehicle built
that would be both a travelling-carriage and an ambulance, and fill it with everything needful ?"

" What is an ambulance ?" Mr. Brewster inquired.

" I have understood that it is a vehicle for the trans-
portation of the sick and wounded. They are preparing some of them in Washington now. The whole plan
would cost a considerable sum, but the establishment
would be my own and under my control, if the military
authorities should accept my offer."

"I do not mind about the expense. I must give money in some way to the expenses of this war, and I may as well contribute it in one way as in another. But to give an only daughter to such a service is another matter. What is it that has led you to think of this?"

"It is only the belief that I can do good and give a good example, and because I feel that I have the power to carry it out."

"Well, my dear, I will think of it and will make some inquiries. The first thing to be done is to ascertain if the government will accept such a volunteer. But I think Aunt Elizabeth's judgment on the whole plan, in regard to the feasibility of such an undertaking by a young lady, is of the utmost importance. She can determine better than I can, after she learns all the details. I have never known her judgment to be at fault."

After some correspondence with the military authorities in Washington it was found that the offer would be accepted, and that Margaret and her people could have all the protection in the field that could be afforded to any non-combatants. Miss Brewster, when she understood the plan and found that Margaret could be provided with the proper attendants, gave her consent. Mr. Brewster at once set about the necessary preparations. The carriage was built under Margaret's directions, and equipped with everything that could be useful for such a purpose. Her father accompanied her into Virginia until she had reached General McDowell's corps, then marching under orders to effect a junction with McClellan's right wing. He then left her and her attendants in communication with one of McDowell's lieutenants, to whom the plan was explained. Before she left home Mr. Charáxes presented her with a considerable sum of money in gold and personally attended to the selection and instruction of two men who were to go with her, as a kind of body-guard. One of them was an Arab, who, about a year before, had brought over some horses which Mr. Charáxes had taken a fancy to import from Syria. He was a tall, muscular man, of great gravity and taciturnity. When he understood that this young lady and her female attendant were to be under his special charge he became graver than ever. He seemed never to need sleep, and wherever they rested he mounted guard all night, with a drawn sabre in his hand and pistols in his belt, standing bolt upright at the door of the house or before the tent where they slept. When Margaret was moving about or anywhere visible, this man's eye, although he did not seem to be watching her, was never turned from her. The other man was a half-breed Indian, whom Mr. Charáxes obtained from Canada,—one of those persons who are so useful as guides. He had extraordinary skill in purveying and cooking.

Mr. Charáxes paid these men enormously high wages, and whether they served for anything but gold or because they became interested in the welfare of the young lady, they were both eminently trustworthy. I have understood that the old gentleman, after Margaret had done with them, sent the Arab back to Syria with money that would have bought a moderate caravan, and pensioned the Canadian boatman for life.

My readers will, perhaps, be curious to learn whether Margaret had been influenced by the idea that she might be helpful in some way to the young man who had so long sought her love. It may be supposed that, if she had much tenderness in her nature, she could not help thinking of him with some interest. As what I have related of her conversation with her father and what I am to tell in addition I received from herself at my house in Boston, after her campaigning was over, I can enlighten the reader's curiosity. Just before James and his mother returned home from their visit to Mr. Charáxes in December, 1860, he asked Margaret if he might write to her. She said it would not be best for either of them, and he could only acquiesce in her decision. She did not know that he had entered the army until after she had reached that part of Virginia where operations were going on. She then heard of him accidentally. When General McDowell's forward movement was arrested, by orders from Washington, Margaret, who was at liberty to go within the

Federal lines wherever she thought proper, came with her establishment and servants into the neighborhood of General Fitz-John Porter's command, which constituted the extreme right of McClellan's army. One day she heard an officer speak of Captain Gascoigne as a member of General McClellan's staff; she inquired if he was from Boston, and was told who he was and that he was reputed to be a very distinguished young officer in much favor at the head-quarters of the army. She concluded that he would be exposed to hazards in the discharge of his duties as an aide in such engagements as were now taking place every day and almost every night, and she therefore moved on as fast as was practicable towards the point which the columns were aiming to reach by the flank movement to the James; and during the Seven Days, after each engagement, she did what she could in the care of the wounded, and often did for the Confederates who were taken prisoners just as she did for the Federalists who had been wounded and had not fallen into the hands of the enemy. Thus she happened to be near Harrison's Landing on the first day of July, which witnessed the end of the toilsome and perilous march of the army of the Potomac to a new base on the James. What occurred there the reader will learn from a subsequent chapter. It will appear that James, from his position on General McClellan's staff, must have heard of the lady who was known at head-quarters to be somewhere with the right wing, with a novel but very useful kind of establishment. In a short time her name became known among the officers surrounding General McClellan, and James heard it. But while the effect on him was naturally a new and stronger impulse to exertion, his duties rendered it impossible for him to make any special effort to meet with her.

CHAPTER XVII.

THE ROMANCE MAY OR MAY NOT COME.

THE flank movement of the Army of the Potomac from its position in front of Richmond to the James River in the summer of 1862 is historical. No more difficult or more brilliant achievement of the same kind is recorded in military annals. The Federal commander had been baffled by his own government, which had by its orders prevented the junction with his right wing of the troops on which he relied to enable him to confront the superior forces of the Confederates. This junction had been expressly promised to him; the promise was broken, and he had to save his army by marching it to a new base of supply on his left or see it cut to pieces. All the world has heard of the Seven Days of marching and fighting through which that new base was found. The persons in whom I hope the readers of these memoirs are interested were but a little fraction of that vast host; and it is only on account of what befell my friends on the last day of that struggle that I am to speak of these events.

The final engagement took place at or near an elevation called Malvern Hill. There the Federal commander made in person the disposition of his troops to await and repel the last attack of the enemy. The hill covered an area of three and a half miles. It was well cleared of trees and was crossed by several converging roads. In front there were defensible ravines; the ground sloping gradually towards the north-east, giving clear ranges for artillery in that direction. Towards the north the descent was sharper, into a ravine that extended to the river. The attack was to be expected on the left wing of the Federal army, which rested on the hill. It was here that the troops were massed. Having made these dispositions, the commanding general returned to his right wing, which curved backward

towards a point on the James. The battle lasted from
nine o'clock in the morning until nine at night. If the
enemy could be repulsed, the Army of the Potomac
would be saved. It was the last engagement in which
McClellan personally commanded during his campaign
in Virginia.

At about seven o'clock in the evening it became necessary for the general to direct the movement of certain
brigades from the right to reinforce the left of the line,
where fresh troops of the enemy were accumulating
and where the ammunition had become exhausted during the day. The situation was so critical that if the
reinforcements did not reach the left wing in time it
would, in all probability, be crushed. To carry the
general's verbal message was a dangerous duty, for the
regiments that were to be sent to the left had to be
withdrawn from corps that were still fighting. At the
moment when it became necessary to send this order,
Captain Gascoigne was the only aide at the general's
side. In terse and brief words the general explained
the movement to the young officer, and then said,
"Captain, this may be a dangerous duty, but I know
that you will perform it gallantly. Take an orderly,
and may God protect you! We are all in his hands!"
Gascoigne touched his cap, and, followed by the orderly,
rode rapidly away. His route lay directly to the front,
where the officer in command of the troops that were
to be withdrawn was stationed, and a galling fire of
musketry swept over the space which Gascoigne had
to cross. He was seen, and before he could reach the
officer to whom the order was to be given he was struck
by a bullet in his side, which curved round into his back.
Driving the spurs into the flanks of his horse, he rushed
on, met the commander of the division, delivered the
order clearly and precisely, and then sank to the ground.
The wound bled freely. The orderly, who was unhurt,
placed the poor fellow on a bank, and in a few minutes
a surgeon appeared. There was but a desperate chance
of saving him, and that chance depended upon his
being at once removed. He was carried, as soon as
means could be procured, to a large house near Harri-

son's Landing, which was already filled with wounded men, brought in as the day was closing.

And now, is that young life to end, cut off by one of many thousand bullets hissing through the air, some of which strike down their victims, while others fall in remote places, innoxious, to the earth? Oh, God! what is the dire necessity that compels these sacrifices of precious lives, while at home anxious hearts are trembling and praying for the loved ones who may and may not return?

At nine o'clock on that last of the Seven Days, when the fighting was over, the commanding general did one of those acts which made him so dear to his soldiers. He rode to the house where so many of his wounded men lay writhing in agony, and passed from one to another, soothing and cheering them, telling them that the army was saved by what they had done. At length he stood by a cot where his young aide was stretched, on whose gallantry the whole of the last movement turned. With a heart almost breaking he said a few words to the surgeon. He did not venture to speak to James, but he thought of the lines,—

" A soldier of the Legion lay dying in Algiers,
　There was lack of woman's nursing, there was dearth of
　　woman's tears."

He could not remain. As he was leaving the house an ambulance, drawn by two strong horses driven at full speed, dashed up to the door. A young lady in a plain blue dress, with a small tricolored cord around her hat, descended from the vehicle, followed by a middle-aged woman similarly attired, and two men in livery. The general had never seen the young lady before, but he had often heard of her, and now had no difficulty in knowing who she was. Lifting his hat, he said, "You are Miss Brewster, I presume. Will you take my arm?"

"Can you conduct me to Captain Gascoigne, general?"

He took her directly to the cot where the young officer lay. His eyes were closed, his senses dazed. The surgeon was making his preliminary preparations to

probe the wound. The lady drew nearer, bent over
the sufferer, and his hand was closed in hers.

"Do you know me?" she asked.

He opened his eyes, tried in the dim light to read her
face, thought that he knew the voice,—but no, it could
not be. His eyes closed again,—his mind wandered.
She whispered for a moment to the surgeon, who nodded
an assent. She then again touched his hand, saying,
"James, it is Margaret Brewster." Then she bent
down to his ear and said, "You must be very quiet. I
have everything ready here. I shall not leave you;
my people are bringing in what you need, but you
must be very still."

"Oh, Margaret, is it you? or is it an angel? Tell
me, am I to die?"

"I hope not, but you must lie very still."

"But tell me, if you are Margaret, how did you
know—how did you come?"

"I came through the Confederate lines; they did not
molest me. I had done something for their wounded.
As soon as I got among our own troops an officer told
me that you were wounded and had been brought
here. But now do not try to talk. I shall not leave
you; let that be enough."

The general, who stood a little back, did not hear
what was said, but he saw that these two persons were
not strangers to each other, and he surmised a great
deal. He spoke to Margaret in a low tone, pressing
her hand. "I leave him in good care; send to head-
quarters if you need anything. The enemy are with-
drawing; you are entirely safe here."

He then went out, mounted his horse, and, after he
had spoken to an officer who commanded the guard
stationed at the house, he galloped swiftly away, followed by two orderlies. Far off, along the road which
he took, the cheers of the troops broke wildly on the
night as they cried, "God bless you, little Mac!" The
crews of the gunboats that lay in the river caught
and echoed the cheers.

The long night wore away. The distant boom of
cannon broke occasionally upon the ear, but ere long

the Confederates retired. The surgeon did not venture to probe the wound. James appeared for some
hours to be sinking. Margaret sat by him all night,
administering anodynes and stimulants. The tall Arab
stood just within the door, where he could see her, and
through the whole night he never changed his position
or looked away from her. The other man brought her
what she needed. As the day began to break, nature
asserted the force of a strong constitution. James
rallied sufficiently to be carried on a stretcher on
board of a steamer that lay in the river. Margaret and
her retinue came with him to New York. There his
mother and Dinah met them. Margaret had informed
Mrs. Gascoigne by telegraph that James was wounded,
and had given the name of the vessel by which he
was to be taken to New York. I offered to accompany the distressed mother, but she thought I could
be more serviceable by remaining at home and assist-
ing to receive James. She was wonderfully calm, but
none of us then knew how bad the case was. Bullet-
wounds are very uncertain things; "unco rash, un-
canny things," as Edie Ochiltree said of the "fugie-
warrants." Sometimes the treatment of such wounds
is very simple, and sometimes the case baffles the
highest surgical skill.

Margaret also telegraphed to her father to come to
New York. When he arrived there he found her and
her servants at another hotel than the one where she
had placed James in his mother's care. When Brewster
and his daughter were alone together she said to him,
in all the frankness and directness of her nature, " My
dear father, you have long known that James Gascoigne loves me, and that I have not returned his love.
But it is now different. He has gained a high reputation in the army, and he has done a great and heroic
action. I can now respect him as well as love him. I
suppose that I may have saved his life by my accidental presence with the army. I shall marry him if he
lives, and if he should die I shall still wish that we may
be united, if it is possible."

" My child," said her father, " you have made him

worthy of your love, and I am rejoiced that you can
give it to him. But now come home with me, and let
us wait to learn the result of the examination which
the surgeons here are to make. Probably it will not
be best for me to see him in his very weak state. But
you can tell him when you take leave of him—I suppose your purpose is or will be known to him—that he
has my blessing and my consent. Such a love as his
has been, when he learns that it is returned, ought to
give him a new life."

Margaret did not see James again in New York.
She went to the hotel and asked to see Mrs. Gascoigne.
Isabel said that two of the most eminent surgeons of
that city had found it impossible at present to trace the
course of the ball; they had recommended that James
be taken home to Boston, and that after he had recovered a little strength the final effort should be made to
reach and extract the bullet. This gave a new turn to
Margaret's determination, for it made it necessary for
her to see James either before or immediately after the
operation. But she told his mother that when it would
be safe for her to see him he would know what she
meant when she said, "I shall not leave you."

How shall I describe Isabel's joy? The hope of
years had come to gladden her. She pressed Margaret
to her bosom; she poured out her heart to the girl:
"My child, my child, you are my daughter now; if he
lives you will be his wife,—if he dies you will be united
in heaven." It was arranged between them that Margaret should follow them to Boston, and that James
should know of her intention to do so, but that Margaret should not see him now.

Brewster hesitated whether he should accompany his
daughter. She might go under the protection of her
own servants, and might come to my house. Finally,
however, he decided to go with her, for the marriage
might take place very soon, and he ought certainly to
be there and give her away. James was brought by
his mother and Dinah and two male attendants on a
special train. The journey was made with several stops,
and he bore it well, until he was safely deposited in his

own room in his mother's house. Brewster and his daughter came directly to my modest little establishment, and my wife, by good management, provided comfortably for them and placed their servants in lodgings near by.

And now the anxious day approached. The surgeons had great difficulty in fixing with certainty the spot where the bullet had lodged, but there was some indication that it lay close to the spine. They were told by Mrs. Gascoigne of the tender secret that must be communicated to James before or after the final operation. One of them was a man of great experience and wisdom. To him his younger colleagues deferred. He said that he felt entire confidence in the operation, and that even if James should not recover from the effects of the wound, he would not die suddenly. It was here, therefore, that Margaret's firmness was put to its greatest trial. Softening and penetrating her remarkable self-control had come the tenderness that she had not before been conscious was an undeveloped part of her nature, and that now longed to be spoken in the holy name of wife. But she was patient and composed. She was with Mrs. Gascoigne, in an adjoining room, when the surgeons did their final work. The two women held each other's hands, they sat still, they whispered little prayers. The surgeons came out, after a long suspense, leaving their patient with the nurse. Everything was well, they said; the sufferer had sufficient strength. He would live, but there must be many days yet before he could bear any excitement. Margaret stole down-stairs and joined her father and me in the parlor. Mrs. Gascoigne did not come down. Dinah followed us to the front door, her honest face beaming with joy. "Miss Margrit," she said, "yeou hev saved him."

James's recovery was more rapid than any of us had expected. At the end of three weeks his mother, one day, prepared him for a visit from Margaret. He had been dressed and was able to sit up. "Do you remember, dear," she said, "that Margaret told you on that dreadful night at Harrison's Landing that she should

not leave you? What did you suppose she meant?
Did you think that she meant only that she would see
to your welfare as she would care for any of the wounded
men whom she was accustomed to provide for?"

"I do not know, mamma, what I thought. It was
so long since I had given up all hope that Margaret
would change."

"Take a new hope, dearest. Margaret's words meant
a great deal. When she comes to see you you will find
it so."

"Dear mother, are you sure you have not dreamed
this?"

"You can dream it, too, my darling. It is a dream
worth having. It will come true, and some dreams do
not."

During these weeks Brewster found it very difficult
to dispose of his time, even with my assistance and my
wife's. He went out very little, made no new acquaintances, and avoided old ones, or those who might possibly
have recognized him. He did not see Mrs. Gascoigne.
We both concluded that it would be best for him to
meet her only at the marriage ceremony. He said to
me, as I knew before, that their acquaintance now
dated from the time of their meeting at Saratoga as
strangers, in 1859; and he and I both thought that it
would be best for Mrs. Gascoigne to have that tacit
understanding continue.

The marriage took place very quietly at Mrs. Gascoigne's house. Her nearest relatives, a few of her
most intimate friends, including myself and wife, along
with Mr. Brewster and the officiating clergyman, were
the only persons present who were not inmates of the
house. All that was known to society in general was
that these two young people met at Harrison's Landing; that the wounded officer fell in love with the lady
of the ambulance, and she with him; that they became
engaged before she came to Boston, and that her father
brought her here to await her lover's recovery. This
was a very pretty little romance, and it was as good a
one as the case needed. No one but James and his
mother, Margaret and her father, my wife and I, knew

anything more, excepting her aunt and Mr. Charáxes, who were far away at Detroit. The old gentleman sent his blessing and a magnificent set of diamonds to the bride, which, however, were not displayed or reported in the newspapers. As I stood there in Mrs. Gascoigne's drawing-room, at the marriage, and saw Brewster give his daughter to the son of Isabella Bradshaw, and then, after the clergyman had said, "Whom God hath joined together," and the father had kissed his daughter,—I saw him approach Mrs. Gascoigne, and I thought what a strange web is this, our human life. Brewster was almost cold, studiously polite, imperturbable, somewhat formal. He offered his hand, Isabel extended hers; their eyes met for an instant. I did not hear what was said. Her heart was full, but I am sure that she did not think of their youth. She might have said, exultingly, as she remembered, "The Lord is my shepherd. . . . Thou anointest my head with oil, my cup runneth over."

Brewster and Isabel never met again in this world.

But I must not omit Miss Brewster's letter to Mrs. Gascoigne, which came two days before the marriage.

"DETROIT, September 16, 1862.

"At this time, dear Mrs. Gascoigne, a journey to Boston would be more than I can undertake; for, as Margaret and her father are both away, I cannot leave Mr. Charáxes. He is now, I suppose, nearly ninety, and although he is remarkably well preserved for so old a man and entirely cheerful, he is very dependent upon me for company. I pass many hours every day with him, leaving him at night to the care of his excellent valet, the Swiss who has been with him so long. Your son's heroic conduct at Harrison's Landing was a matter of public news, and there was a nice little romance invented by the newspapers, about a young lady who suddenly appeared after he was wounded and took him to New York. But it was not until I received Margaret's letters that I knew the whole, and knew that your hopes were to be realized. I have followed all three of you with my prayers through this painful suspense, and now that you are so blessed by the kind mercy of a merciful God, the word 'congratulation' is too tame and feeble to express what I feel. You know that I have watched Margaret since she lost her mother when she was only two years old. Her character is one for which I have some responsibility. You know how closely I followed the course of that true love which did not for a long time run smoothly for your son, and you are not wholly unaware why it was so. But I, who was so near to Margaret, and who knew so much more, can perhaps explain her to you better than you can explain her to yourself.

"Margaret's ideal of life was certainly very high, but I did not especially try to make it so. I did endeavor to make her superior to the common race of girls, but nature did far more for her than I could have done. It was not through my influence that she looked for the grand, the heroic, or the uncommon in the characters of men; or that she seemed to have less of that susceptibility and tenderness which in most women responds so easily to the true and steadfast attachment of a pure and good man, and which often responds but too well to the love of one who is not pure or good. This trait in her character, this apparent lack of feminine readiness to receive and return affection, this seeming coldness and indifference, were, I think, inherited from both her parents. It was a long and a slow process that brought her father and her mother together; but when the final discovery had been made, when their hearts had found what each was seeking, their union, for the short period of its earthly duration, was the most perfect that I have ever known. It has never been in the least strange to me that my brother has not married again, and, as I believe, has never wished to.

"Margaret's peculiar patriotism, or rather the direction which her patriotism took, was partly the effect of circumstances and partly the natural result of her practical and energetic temperament. She had a kind of exalted but regulated enthusiasm, which could only

work itself out in a feminine way and under the conditions imposed upon women. When her plan of following the army as a volunteer lady-nurse to the sick
and wounded was first mentioned to me, I was very
reluctant to have her undertake it. But we learned
that, with the proper means, appliances, and attendants, and with the sanction of the government, her
plan could be carried out without any sacrifice of the
dignity of a lady. A most excellent and suitable
woman was procured to be her attendant and chief executive officer,—her father and Mr. Charáxes supplied
all the needful funds,—and she took the field with an
admirably appointed establishment. The general result you know. But you may not know one part of
her course that was very characteristic. Although she
was intensely anxious for the success of the Army of
the Potomac and the Federal cause, and really belonged
to the Federal army, she was often within the Confederate lines, in the rapidly-shifting scenes of different
engagements, and did not hesitate to do what she
could for their wounded men. General McClellan, she
was told, did not disapprove of this ; and the Confederates, recognizing the breadth of her humanity, not
only did not interfere with her movements, but they
reverenced her and were grateful to her, as if she had
been an angel descended from the skies. 'When this
cruel war is over' the memory of this example will do
something to soften the bitterness that such a conflict
will leave behind it. Our country is supposed to be
typified by a personage of our sex whom we call
Columbia. I thought that Margaret might be taken
for at least her representative, so catholic and so wide
was her sympathy for all engaged in this fraternal
strife. When will its dreadful scenes be ended ? Mr.
Charáxes says it must be fought out, and that, although
the end is far off, the Federal cause must and will
prevail.

"And now, my dear friend, that Margaret's *military
life* is ended, and her heart has found its greatest need,
and she is about to become your son's wife, let me once
more tell you how poor and inadequate are all the

ordinary forms of felicitation on such an event. You will know all and will feel all that I would say if I could be with you. Give them my tenderest love, and reserve in your heart—it is a very large one—a place for   "Your affectionate

"ELIZABETH BREWSTER."

CHAPTER XVIII.

"GATHERED, NOT HARSHLY PLUCKED."

MISS BREWSTER's letter to Mrs. Gascoigne, written at the time of Margaret's marriage, spoke of Mr. Cha-ráxes as then at about the age of ninety. He lived nearly three years longer, dying in 1865, just at the close of the Civil War. Miss Brewster gave to Mrs. Gascoigne some account of his last days, when the funeral ceremonies were over.

"DETROIT, May 10, 1865.

"MY DEAR MRS. GASCOIGNE,—Our aged friend, whom we have watched so carefully and loved so much, passed quietly away less than a week ago. His remarkable powers of mind and stores of knowledge, which have for so many years delighted us, remained undisturbed and undiminished to the last. His death was like that which the Archangel Michael foretold of Adam:

"'Gathered, not harshly plucked, for death mature;
    This is old age.'

"I had long felt a strong interest to know his religious sentiments. Although he was neither a Roman Catholic nor a Protestant, I have always considered him a Christian. In the whole of his residence here he never regularly attended any of our churches, but he was most liberal in his donations to all of them; and since his death it has appeared that his charities were munificent and wise. During his last ten days of life I conversed with him a good deal on religious topics. I said to him, one morning, that it would interest all of us, including yourself, to know his religious views with some accuracy.

"'I have never intended,' he said, 'to go out of the world leaving you in ignorance of my belief in the Christian religion, and as to dear Mrs. Gascoigne, you know how highly I value her regard. I am rather afraid that she considers me as having no religious belief, because I have formerly told her so much of my love of philosophy. But when I am gone you will all know where to place me. There will be found, in the same package that contains my will, a paper which I wrote some time ago, in which I have expressed my religious opinions. It was not written for publication, but for the private information of my friends. Send a copy of it to Mrs. Gascoigne, and inform her that she is entirely at liberty to show it to that faithful friend of hers, Mr. Peter Boylston, to whom I am under some obligation, and whose good opinion I value very much.'

"I said that I had never been entirely satisfied with any definition or theory of inspiration that I had met with.

"'You have had no good reason to be,' he replied. 'I cannot now do more than refer you to the paper of which I have spoken. In that you will find a full explanation of my own view of what is called inspiration, when the sacred writers are mentioned.'

"On the day after this conversation James and Margaret arrived, and he saw them as soon as he had been dressed and placed upon the couch where he usually lay for some hours.

"'Well, my dear,' he said to Margaret, 'you have not brought the little boy to whom you have given my name. When he is grown up he will have to satisfy the curiosity of curious people in regard to the combination of Puritan, Greek, and Anglo-Norman names by which he will be known. John Charáxes Bradshaw Gascoigne has not a bad sound, and I don't believe it ever will have. But you will find, my dear, that there will be something to aid in the development of any of the strains that there are in his blood, although he derives from me, and perhaps from my race, nothing but one of his names. It is a great comfort to me to have you here. You have travelled far to see an old man die, and I cannot continue much longer. I have lived already much beyond the usual term of human life, and I am not unwilling to go. But, as you see, I suffer no pain, and I am entirely at peace with my Maker. I do not say on what I rely for that forgiveness of which every human being stands in need. I say only, that to have lived an innocent life, to have done some good in the world, cannot, in any sensible view of what is called salvation, be considered as of no moment in the great accounting of the hereafter. When that time comes, we shall know with a certainty that we cannot have now what is that process of atonement by which our sins are to be wiped away. Our belief in it during this life, our conception of it, our efforts to comprehend it, may more or less conduce to good living; but the great thing to understand is what is meant by the eternal life recorded in the Gospel of Christ. My conception of this, differing widely from that which is common, you will find explained in what I have written.'

"After this he conversed but little. Day succeeded to day with a progressive diminution of strength, and the end came without a struggle or a pang.

"It was found that he had left directions to have his funeral conducted with entire simplicity; but this did not prevent a great concourse of people from following his remains to their last resting-place. After the funeral his will was read. He made most liberal provision for all his servants, and for little John, your grandson, there is a handsome legacy. A considerable part of his property comes to Margaret. I think that the paper on his religious belief will be to you, as it is to me, most satisfactory. He was buried in a tomb which he had himself prepared. My brother will place upon the monument the following inscription :

'JOHN CHARÁXES.

A citizen of the world,
A believer in the Christian Religion,
And a friend of mankind.
Born in Syria, May 1, 1772,
Died at Detroit, May 5, 1865.'

"The funeral ceremonies were conducted so as to conform as nearly as possible to what we believed to have been his religious sentiments. James and Margaret will return to Boston immediately. From them you will learn more particularly the provisions of the will, and they will bring you a copy of the paper which was found with it. It was written entirely by his own hand and signed with his name. We may say of him, in Milton's words,—

> " 'Nothing is here for tears, nothing to wail
> Or knock the breast, no weakness, no contempt,
> Dispraise or blame, nothing but well and fair,
> And what may quiet us in a death so noble.'

"And now, my dear friend, I know not if we shall ever meet again in this world; my own age admonishes me that I cannot have many more years, and the little that remains to me must be devoted to my brother. If I can feel any assurance of anything, I can, in all humility, believe that I shall know and love you hereafter as I have here. But as long as I continue to live, those who are nearest and dearest to you will ever be so to

"Your affectionate,

"ELIZABETH BREWSTER."

THE RELIGIOUS BELIEF OF JOHN CHARÁXES.

"The most important thing for any one to know is what is meant by the inspiration of the Scriptures, in which are recorded the life and teachings of Christ. The next thing that we need to know is, what is meant by the eternal life that Christ came to reveal.

"The idea that the Holy Spirit dictated every word that was penned by an Apostle—that the human writer merely held a pen that was guided by the Holy Ghost—is one extreme. That the Apostolic writers were not instructed by the divine wisdom in any way is another extreme. There is an intermediate view, which seems to me the better one. It does not shut up all inspiration within the limits of Scripture. There may have been other appointed ministers of divine wisdom besides the writers of the Old or the New Testament. We must include among the 'inspired' all who, in any age, have taught truth or have served God. We have express warrant for this in the text which declares that 'every good and every perfect gift is from above, and cometh down from the Father of lights, with whom is no variableness nor shadow of turning.' The objection that by a broad interpretation of this text we degrade the inspiration of the sacred writers to a rank below that in which it should be accepted—that we deprive it of its special authority—is untenable. If we understand the meaning of the text in a sense that leads to this result, we do not understand it correctly. It does not say that every good and perfect gift is of the same value as every other gift. It says that the source of all truth and wisdom is the Father of lights, who does not vary his teachings of what truth and wisdom are. All, therefore, that the heathen writers have inculcated, and that accords with the teachings of Christ, must be regarded as coming from the fountain of divine wisdom. It may not be the whole truth; it may be mixed with error; it may fall short of that full and perfect supply which came from the fountain when it was opened by the Son of God. But it is none the less derived from that fountain when it coincides with the teachings of the one great Revelation.

"In the early days of Christianity there was a doctrine of inspiration which may be called the primitive doctrine, and which included the testimony of what truth is that was borne by any one on whom there had been bestowed any 'good and perfect gift,' any gift that was good in itself and perfect as far as it went. It is, I suppose, quite certain that the Christian school of Alexandria held this doctrine of inspiration, and the Greek Christians of a later age held that the poets and philosophers of the heathen world often uttered the voice of God, although they may not have been conscious that he breathed into their minds what they wrote or said. This doctrine of inspiration does not militate against that other doctrine which assigns to the Apostolic writers a more direct, special, immediate, and, therefore, a more full, communication from the 'Father of Lights.'

"This full and, as I suppose, final communication has come down to us in writings that need interpretation. How are we to know that we understand them rightly? How, in the multitude of glosses and explanations, are we to select those which we ought to accept? The doctrine of literal and verbal inspiration leaves much that must be explained. I do not believe in the present existence of any authoritative and final interpreter of the Scriptures.

"The primitive churches and the earliest age of Christianity had this advantage,—that they were instructed by the Apostles, and, therefore, there is a certain value, and a great value, in what they accepted, so far as we can learn it with certainty. But we are to consider the situation and composition of the first churches. Look into the Apocalypse of St. John, for example. The book that is called the Revelation of St. John, and is supposed by some scholars to have been erroneously placed at the end of the New Testament because it is there out of the chronological order of its production, was sent, we are told, by the divine command to the seven churches which were in Asia: Ephesus, Smyrna, Pergamos, Thyatira, Sardis, Philadelphia, and Laodicea. It was written on the island of Patmos, and probably in A.D. 68. The internal evidence and the contemporaneous condition of the Roman Empire are supposed, by the symbols employed in the book, to point almost with certainty, at least with a high degree of probability, to this date. There is a theory that the extraordinary symbols made use of were employed by the Apostle to disguise his meaning from the enemies of Christianity, but that the churches to which it was sent would readily understand them to mean events and persons that had then lately transpired or lived, or that were to come immediately. But those seven churches were most variously composed. Some consisted of Jews, and some of Gentiles. Accordingly, the Apostle was commanded to address each of them

by special encouragement and praise and special rebuke
and threatening, adapted to the condition and tendencies
of each. But to each of the seven churches went the
same Book, with the tremendous vision which the
Apostle saw, crowded with symbols of what was hap-
pening in the world, of what had come through Christ
and was yet to come. The whole closes with a rapt
and vivid prophecy of the coming of Christ's kingdom,
under the symbols of the water of life, the tree of life,
and that realm where there shall be no more curse, but
the throne of God and his Lamb shall be in it, and his
servants shall serve him, and they shall see his face, and
his name shall be in their foreheads, and there shall be
no night there, and they shall need no candle, neither
light of the sun, for the Lord God giveth them light,
and they shall reign for ever and ever. Now, whether
the seven churches, or any of them, understood the
symbolic representations as the Apostle meant them,
they would be likely to interpret variously the doctrines of Christianity, unless they were more specially
instructed in those doctrines than they were in this
one Book of the Revelation. For this reason, it has
been supposed that we ought to place this Book in
its chronological precedence of the other and later
writings of the same Apostle. Those later writings
express his conception of the Christian doctrines far
more directly and distinctly than the Apocalypse. He
was the last survivor of those who had seen the Lord ;
he was the Apostle whom Jesus specially loved ; he
was at the crucifixion ; on him was devolved the care
of the Virgin Mary, and he took her to his own home ;
his mother was the Virgin's sister ; on the morning of
the resurrection, after he had heard that Christ had
risen from the dead, he ran to the tomb and found that
the body was not there, and that nothing remained but
the linen clothes in which it was enwrapped at the
burial ; he was present on at least two occasions after
the resurrection, when Jesus appeared among his Apostles, and manifested his identity by proofs that removed
all doubt from the minds of any who had doubted. I
am but repeating things that have always been known.

But perhaps it may not have occurred to those who will read what I now write, that St. John, when he wrote his Gospel and his short Epistles, had lived to a time when the Gospel had not only been presented to and accepted by Jews and Gentiles, but when he had accumulated in his own experience, studies, and reflections an amount of knowledge that far exceeded that of all other living men. There is a tradition that the elders and bishops of the different churches specially requested him to write those productions which may now be considered as the grand supplement to the Apocalypse. This tradition, however interesting, is only so far important as it marks the estimation in which he was held and his supreme authority as the best living expositor of the life and teachings of Christ. I am not aware that the tradition goes so far as to signify that those who made this request expected that a special inspiration would be vouchsafed to him. Their expectation in regard to this is not material. We are to consider what he said in his Gospel and Epistles concerning himself. In his Gospel he does not write in the first person. He speaks of himself as the disciple whom Jesus loved, for the purpose of identification, referring to a fact known to every Christian believer; and at the close he announces himself as the writer in this wise: 'This is the disciple which testifies of those things, and wrote these things; and we know that his testimony is true;' or, as it should be understood, 'I who have testified of those things know that my testimony is true.' The sources of his knowledge were twofold: first, the things which he had previously witnessed, or of which he had heard by tradition; secondly, the things which had been taught him by the Holy Spirit. In the latter we are to look for the inspiration of which he was conscious, or of which he believed himself to be conscious. It is expressed in the assertion that he 'knows' these things to be true; and in reference to the doctrines which he explains and to his exposition of the essential truths of Christianity we must understand this knowledge to have been imparted to him by something more than his own studies and reflections. In the Apocalypse he states the circumstances under which the Revelation which God gave unto Jesus Christ came to *him*, John. He says that God sent and signified it to him by an angel; and that he, John, bare record of the Word of God, and of the testimony of Jesus Christ, and of all things that he saw. Then, when he comes to speak of his own situation at the time he received the command to write this Book, he says that he was in the Spirit on the Lord's day, in the island of Patmos, and that he heard behind him a great voice, as of a trumpet, commanding him to write what he was to see in a book and send it to the seven churches in Asia. It is quite plain, therefore, that St. John meant to assert that in writing this Book he received direct instruction and command and prophetic vision from God himself, through a messenger, described as an angel and as a voice. What *he* meant by inspiration, although he does not use the word, is clear enough. It is equally clear that, in writing his first Epistle, he considered himself as speaking under the influence of that same inspiration; for he says, 'That which we have seen and *heard* declare we unto you;' and by what he had *heard* he did not mean mere tradition, for he says, ' This then is the message which we have heard of *him*.' So far as his Gospel comprehends more than narrative, more than historic details of the life of Jesus, the *knowledge* which he asserts must be taken to have been derived from the same source to which he refers in his first Epistle. Here, then, we reach that idea of inspiration of which this great Apostle believed himself conscious, and which must have been believed in by those for whom he wrote. The whole of his manifold exposition of the truths of Christianity has been again and again analyzed; and after the most elaborate and apparently consistent system of doctrine has been framed, or the last and simplest analysis has reduced everything to the one idea of ETERNAL LIFE, men dispute, always have disputed, and to the end of time will probably continue to dispute, about the conditions on which that life is to be obtained, or even what it is to

be. Is there, then, any authorized interpreter now on
earth, whose readings must be accepted?

"I presume that what I am about to say would not
be accepted by any Church at the present day with
which I am acquainted. But I am giving my own
views for the information of my friends. The idea
that St. John, who was accepted by the churches to
which he wrote as the authorized interpreter of Christian doctrine, was succeeded by some other person or
persons authorized to make certain those things in
respect to which his exposition was supposed to require
further elucidation, presupposes that this office was
after his death laid on such person or persons, to be discharged with the same kind of authority with which
he wrote or preached. Whether this was effected by
what is called 'Apostolic succession,' or whether this
authority was assumed by single churches or by the
churches collectively, or was assumed by their 'Pres-
byters,' it necessarily proceeds upon the idea that there
was perpetuated a function of making and continuing
to make authorized and final interpretations of the
word of God, supplemental to those which had been
given by St. John, or by the other Apostolic writers, or
by him *and* the others. Hence has come about, as I
understand, the claim of authority which is asserted in
different ways and degrees by the different churches
into which the Christian world is now divided. Each
of them defends its own authority upon principles
which to some extent are common to them all, but
which in many respects differ fundamentally in the
reasoning and in the facts that are assumed as the basis
of the reasoning. But in whatever sense we understand the infallibility of the Church of Rome, or the
authority of the Greek Church, or that of the churches
now called Protestant, one thing is true of each of them,
—that each addresses itself to individual belief in the
authority that is asserted. The very diversity in the
principles on which the authority is claimed, and in the
facts which are supposed to establish it, is, to my mind,
the strongest proof that there is now on earth no authoritative and final interpreter of Christian doctrine to

which all must bow or remain in doubt respecting their inclusion in the kingdom of Christ. Believing, as I do, that God reigns, and that the Gospel of Christ is a revelation of his word, I cannot conceive that all this diversity of interpretation and the different bases on which the authority of different Christian bodies is rested was not permitted for a special purpose. That purpose, as I conceive, was to leave the whole body of Christian truth to be adapted to human nature as the diversities of intelligence and individual wants demanded, in order to make the religion effectual to the welfare of mankind to the greatest possible extent. Does this view take away the value of those expositions of what the eternal life promised by the Gospel consists in, as variously interpreted by the different churches, because it denies that any one of them can claim special and exclusive authority? By no means. It places the value of their interpretations upon their power to reach the convictions and to govern the lives of mankind.

"What I have now written will explain why, although I believe in the divine origin of Christianity, I have never been able to accept any existing church as the authorized and final interpreter between me and my Maker. There must always be some persons who cannot stand within the pale of any church, but who are yet not to be regarded as unbelievers, whatever any church may say.

"Still, it will be said that the tendency of such views as mine is to do away with church organizations, with the preaching of Christianity, and even with the public worship of God. If a philosophic and scholarly person, like myself, is to be his own sole judge of Christian truth,—a class that must comprehend only a very small minority,—it will be asked whether the multitude of persons who are unqualified to expound the Scriptures for themselves will not be led to neglect all study of them or to reject all aid, and finally to become unbelievers?

"The idea that it will not do to leave private and individual judgment to its own unassisted means of discov-

8

ering truth, and to have no special inculcation of motives to right conduct, does not become necessarily sound, because there are numerous persons who, if so left, would go astray. There will always be a great amount of ignorance, intellectual incapacity, and indifference, as there will always be a great amount of temptation to sin. But it is, after all, to the individual acceptance of truth that every form of teaching is to be addressed, as it is to the individual capacity to feel the motives to virtuous conduct that the appeal must be made. Because there are some who can teach themselves by a study of the Scriptures, searching in them to find eternal life, it does not follow that there are not others who stand in need of other aid. So great is the variety of human beings, in respect to the capacity to understand the Christian religion, that I look upon all the different religious organizations and systems as providentially ordered. This is not merely the statesman's or the political view. It is a view which rises higher than all the kingdoms of this world, higher than all the objects of making human government easier and more successful, because it recognizes the kingdom of Christ.

"I have sometimes been asked if I look for what is called Christian unity, or the fusion of all the churches into one. My answer to this is that I do not look for a union of all the churches in this age or in any age, so long as the world continues, in any sense but this: I look for the second and final coming of Christ; for his kingdom; when there shall prevail universally a correct conception and a realization of the eternal life of the Gospel; when, in this respect, the churches on earth shall be one with the church in heaven.

"' Part of the host have crossed the flood,
And part are crossing now.'

"Those who have crossed already and those who are crossing now may have attained here the eternal life that was typified by St. John under so many symbols at the close of the Apocalypse. When all have attained a true idea of eternal life, and are living that life, there will be but one church. The vulgar idea that eternal life is a

life of endless duration supposes that Christ came to
reveal something in which the heathen were to have
no part. Every human being who has ever lived or
ever will live will have an endless existence, if any one
of them has been endowed with that privilege. If one
human soul is incapable of annihilation, all others are
so; and it cannot depend upon my belief whether I am
to live forever or not. The eternal life which Christ
came to reveal was not an indefinite existence; it was
not a duration, to be measured by any idea of time, ter-
minable or interminable. It was a state of the individual soul—a life—a living—a conduct—a holiness as
contrasted with sin. The epithet *eternal* should have
a broader meaning than the idea of endless duration.
There may be an endless duration of a state that is not
the eternal life of the Gospel, just as surely as there
may be an endless duration of that life which Christ
came to teach. The resurrection of the dead cannot
be supposed to comprehend only the saints. There is
to be a judgment after the resurrection. Those who
have led the eternal life of the Gospel will be separated
from those who have not led it, and in both classes may
be comprehended those who have not heard of the
Gospel on earth.

"Perhaps it will be asked whether I believe in universal salvation. In the salvation that consists in the
state which is described as eternal life I certainly do
believe. There may be means provided for the attainment of this state in the cases of those who have not
had such means in this world, or, having them, have
neglected them.

" I will touch upon only one other point in this brief
account of my religious opinions. Since the revelation
that came through Christ there have been, as it was
foretold there would be, other supposed or pretended
revelations. Some of them have been very gross fictions; others have been plausible; all have been more
or less accepted, according to the character of the age
and the state of society in which they have appeared.
But no matter what may have been their claims, their
merits or demerits, there is one answer to be made to

them all, whether they have claimed to supersede or to
be supplemental to the revelation of the New Testament. That answer is, that the argument and proofs
which sustain the finality of the Christian revelation—
making it the last communication of God's word that
will be made while the human race continues on earth—
are so strong that they overthrow the probabiliy of
any subsequent communication of the same kind. I
have heard it argued that God is constantly revealing
himself in different ways ; that new proofs of his power,
beneficence, and care for the human race are constantly
accumulating ; that Christ and his Apostles were men
of very humble birth and limited or no education ;
that in the course of ages, as the wants of mankind
seem to the divine wisdom to require farther revelations of truth, it would not be strange if persons of
equally humble origin were to be selected as the agents
through which they were to be made, and that there
is *a priori* no reason why a succession of such revelations should not occur to the end of time. But this
kind of reasoning overlooks two very important circumstances, and bases itself upon an *a priori* assumption.
It overlooks, first, the great fact that the miracles which
attest the divine origin of Christianity,—the miraculous
birth of Christ, the miracles wrought by him during his
life, and his death and resurrection,—if believed on satisfactory evidence, constitute a body of proof that he
was truly the Son of God and a messenger sent from
heaven, to which no subsequent prophet, or teacher,
or supposed instrument of a new revelation can lay
claim.

" Secondly, the Christian revelation, taken as a whole,
with all that it comprehends, bears internal evidence that
it was intended as a finality, because it is so complete
and consistent ; because it satisfies every conceivable
want of the human race while the race shall continue
on the earth ; because it affords and must continue to
afford the means of attaining eternal life ; and when
that has been attained by the whole human race there
can be no conceivable state remaining beyond it. While,
therefore, it may be true in the physical world that

God reveals himself in different ways as different necessities arise for enlarging the bounds of human knowledge, if we find that in the spiritual world he has made a revelation that is marked by no imaginable deficiency as a means of influencing the human race, and that has never yet been found to need addition, and that will accomplish for our race all that such a being can be supposed to intend, there is no necessity for resorting to *a priori* speculation about the claims of subsequent supposed communications of the same nature.

"At the end of this world there will be an infinite variety of human characters formed under the influences of the different systems of religion. There will be those who died without any character at all,—the idiots and the infants who perished before character could begin to be formed. The system of morality taught by some of the heathen religions is as pure and beneficial in some respects as the Christian morality. But the Christian morality surpasses them all by the doctrine of eternal life as that life should be interpreted. Belief in the doctrine is not the only thing that is needful. The state of character must result from the belief. But the attainment of that state depends upon a true conception of what the eternal life of the Gospel is. If we make the revelation to consist in nothing but an assurance that we are to live forever, we shall fall short of a true conception of what was inculcated. I am aware that this is not in accordance with the teaching of some Christian theologians, and that it rejects the efficacy commonly imputed to rites and ceremonious observances, which are, after all, only helps to the formation of that condition of the soul that is meant by eternal life. Perhaps I am too broad for the broadest churchman, and perhaps my peculiar studies have led me to the adoption of views so different from those of the current theology. But my religious opinions have been formed with much study and reflection, and in the exercise of the right and performance of the duty of interpreting the Scriptures for myself.

"It will be seen, from what I have written, in what

sense and why I believe in universal salvation. If we narrow the vast scheme of the Almighty, as some theologians are disposed to narrow it, we must remember that, before the mission of Christ, millions of human beings were allowed to be born who never heard of the Gospel, and many of whom could not have received it if they had heard of it, because they were born and died without sufficient sense to know anything, or died in infancy. And since Christ came upon earth, millions have been born and have died to whom the light of the Gospel never came. Is it conceivable that in the scheme of salvation there is no provision for those who could not attain here that state of the soul which is described as eternal. life? That conception would leave a great blank in the scheme of the Almighty, which we have no warrant for imputing to him. On the contrary, we have a warrant for believing that what is really meant by eternal life is attainable hereafter. There may be those who will persistently refuse to avail themselves of the means of grace, but it is not in accordance with my conception of God's purposes to suppose that the door will be forever closed against them. Whether they can enter it will depend upon their repentance and upon their striving after and attaining eternal life.

"JOHN CHARÁXES."

CHAPTER XIX.

GOING HOME AT THE END OF FORTY YEARS.

THE reader has probably not forgotten how strongly Lady Blanche Gascoigne disapproved of Mr. Bradshaw's purchase of Dinah when it was related to her by Isabel at the time of her only visit at Gascoigne House. To be sure, the purchase made Dinah a free woman, but then, in Lady Blanche's view, it gave a certain sanction to the idea of property in human beings. I presume if her ladyship had been living at the time of which I am about to speak she would have as strongly

disapproved of what Dinah herself did, for it certainly
did not show that she cherished the hatred of her
former owners which Lady Blanche would have considered natural, if not right. In the long period of her
freedom Dinah had accumulated a considerable sum of
money. Mr. Bradshaw, while he lived, saw that her
money was duly deposited in a savings bank; and after
she became Mrs. Gascoigne's servant that lady took
care that her wages, so far as she did not need to spend
them,—she was very prudent and needed to spend extremely little on herself,—were put into a position to
have interest regularly added to principal. In the
early days of the anti-slavery societies some of the
excellent ladies in Boston and the neighborhood, who
were concerned in those associations, made efforts to
get Dinah to contribute to the cause; but she was quite
aware how they used their money, and did not loosen
her purse-strings at their solicitation. She had a vague
idea that she might at some time wish to buy the freedom of some man or woman,—a thing that her abolition friends never did.

When the Civil War had been going on for some time,
Dinah became very anxious to learn about Colonel
Julius Pringle, of the Confederate army, the son of her
old master and mistress. Mrs. Gascoigne helped her to
follow the accounts of the different battles in which the
colonel's regiment was engaged. He was killed in one
of the last engagements in the Wilderness, just before
General Lee's surrender to General Grant at Appomat-
tox; and some time after the peace came, and intercourse between the North and South was reopened,
Dinah learned that the colonel's wife and children were
left in an almost destitute condition. From that moment Boston, Mrs. Gascoigne, James, Margaret, everything that was not connected with her old Southern
home, occupied a second place in Dinah's feelings and
thoughts. A love that was older dominated every other
and later affection.

"Missus Is'bel," she said one day, "I'm gwine by de
nex' steamer to Charlst'n, to see my fokes. I want all
my munny to take along."

"Certainly, Dinah, you shall have your money, and more if you need it. But will it not do as well to have a letter written, and get Mr. James to attend to what you wish to have done?"

"No, Missus Is'bel, it won't. I dunno ef dey hev eny ob de lan' lef', nor whar de niggers air. How's dem chill'n to be rāsed? Dat lady deown dere is rite bad orf, an' heer's ole Dinah livin' comfurt'ble an' doin' nuffin."

"But, Dinah, I hope you love me still. You will come back to us, will you not?"

"I dunno, missus; I will ef I can. I lub yeou deerly, —didn' I rāse yeou from a leetl' gurl? Didn' I nuss Massa James eber sence he wus tree yeer ole? De Lor' 'll tāk keer o' yeou, ma'am. Bress'd air de peure in hart, for dey s'all see God."

"Well, Dinah, you shall go; but get some one to write to me. Promise me that."

Dinah promised. No time was lost. Her money was withdrawn from the savings bank, and arrangements were made to enable her to use it as she wished. Mrs. Gascoigne charged her to call for more if she needed it. But her own accumulations had made her, in the course of so many years, the mistress of a few thousand dollars. It was a painful parting when she went away; but it was a mission from the great and triumphant North to the fallen South, and the missionary, although an humble, was a suitable one. In a few weeks Mrs. Gascoigne received from a gentleman in Charleston, son of a former correspondent of her father, the following letter:

"CHARLESTON, S. C., June 1, 1867.

"DEAR MADAM,—I remember hearing, as a boy, of the purchase by your father of a negro girl who was sold in this city among other servants of the late Mr. Thomas Pringle. It made some talk among us at the time, but it was forgotten in the greater and more distressing events that followed. I received a few weeks since a call from a very respectable old colored woman, who made herself known to me as the girl your father bought and carried to Boston. She said that her name was Dinah, and that she had never had any other name; that she had been your servant for many years, and that she had come to Charleston to see the family of the late Colonel Pringle, who was the son of her old master. I put her in the way of finding them. Colonel Pringle inherited from his father a very good sea-island cotton-plantation; but the negroes on it were all dispersed after President Lincoln's proclamation, and the colonel's widow and children have been living in the city for some time in very straitened circumstances. The eldest boy has not been able to find any employment, and the other children are quite young. Dinah seems to have the command of money. She has already put the family into a condition of comfort and has placed the young gentleman at school. She is now, with my assistance, making arrangements to get possession of the land from some intruders who have been on it for a good while, and to collect a few hands to plant a crop of cotton. If she succeeds, the family will go back there to live. I must tell you that the widow does not hesitate to receive this providential aid, for she knows, as all of us do who are acquainted with the case, that it comes from a love that was created by a system never well understood at the North while it lasted, and that has now passed away. Whenever there is anything further that it would interest you to know I shall not fail to communicate it. Believe me, madam, with very great respect,

" Your obedient servant,
" JOHN ELLIOT.

" MRS. ISABELLA GASCOIGNE,
" BOSTON, MASS."

Success attended all Dinah's plans; for, known only to her, the money needful to obtain the land and restore it to a productive condition was supplied by Mrs. Gascoigne. Dinah never returned to Boston. Her young master, as she now called the son of Colonel Pringle, came in due time to manage the property. There Dinah spent her remaining years, in the scenes where she was born, tended by loving hearts. Two or three times a year a letter was written for her to Mrs. Gascoigne. She lived to a great age. On the day she died she interrupted the clergyman who prayed at her bedside: "Ycou hevn't praid for Missus Is'bel—Missus Is'bel Gaskwine,—dat's her name,—pray fur *her.* Bress'd air de peure in hart, fur dey s'all see God." And so the old woman died, remembering the Sermon on the Mount which her mistress read to her when she was a child. She lies buried on the plantation, and on her grave-stone is this inscription:

DINAH

Born in slavery
Freed by a Citizen of Massachusetts
Purchasing her from her owners
She came home after an absence of
Forty years to help and succor
A family who had sheltered her
Childhood and youth
" Blessed are the merciful, for
they shall obtain mercy"

CHAPTER XX.

THE LAST SCENE OF ALL.

PEACE came at last. The land that had been "drenched in fraternal blood" found repose from the further conflict of arms. The resources of the Southern Confederacy reached an end; and as the Northern government sent column after column into the field to be cut down until the Southern forces could fight no more,—and still the Northern power was not exhausted,—the war was at length over. Magnanimity and forbearance marked the conduct of the victors, so far as the military authorities could settle the terms of peace. Worn, weary, and destitute, the brave men of the South wended their way to their homes, to rebuild their shattered society and to turn their swords into plough-shares. But long years of civil contention had yet to be passed before it could be certain that the political institutions of the country had come out of the conflicts of civil war in their substantially normal condition, so that "Liberty and Union" could be truly said to be "one and inseparable." It is not here that an account of public affairs during the years that immediately followed the war needs to be given. It is for me to tell how my friends, the persons of this narrative, like all others in the land, were affected directly or indirectly by the public events. It was not until the year 1870 that things appeared to be so settled that Mrs. Gascoigne, James, and Margaret could think of going abroad. He had never been able to return to the army after his wound; and while the war lasted all the public service he could render consisted in acting sometimes as a military adviser of the Governor of Massachusetts. But now his physicians recommended travelling in Europe, and his mother decided to accompany them. I saw them embark, little thinking that I should never see Isabel Gascoigne again. But at the end of two years I received from James the following letter, and as I read it I thought of Longfellow's lines,—

> " Art is long, and time is fleeting,
>   And our hearts, though strong and brave,
> Still like muffled drums are beating
>   Funeral marches to the grave."

" CANNES, July 2, 1872.

" PETER BOYLSTON, ESQ.,
    " BOSTON :

" MY DEAR SIR,—To you, my mother's oldest friend, who knew her longest, and for whom she ever had a very warm regard, I have the distressing duty of communicating her death, which occurred here yesterday, after an illness of only ten days. She had written to you from time to time since we have been in Europe, but I believe not later than six weeks ago. We came here a fortnight since, and soon after our arrival she became ill. At first, we were not alarmed about her, but, notwithstanding the most skilful medical attendance and our utmost devotion, the disorder made such progress that we were obliged to give up all hope about five days since. There was, however, but little suffering, and her death was most tranquil and serene. Her naturally strong constitution and usual good health had preserved her great beauty, and although she had considerably passed the age of sixty, she retained to the last her personal loveliness. Her sweet disposition and rare intelligence were unimpaired to the last moment. She spoke of you and Mrs. Boylston on the day before she died, and bade me send to both of you her most affectionate remembrances. You are both mentioned in her will, which she executed before we left home, and which is deposited in the probate office. It was very fortunate that a clergyman of the Church of England was here and administered to her the holy communion, according to the rite to which she had always been accustomed. Margaret has been to her and to me, in these last sad days of my poor mother's life, all that you would have anticipated, as she has been every moment since our marriage. We are making arrangements to embark with the remains as soon as possible. The interment will be at Mount Auburn immediately after we arrive.

"I do not think that my mother wrote to you any account of our visit to Gascoigne Manor while we were in England. Probably it was too painful; and, now that I look back upon it, I wonder that she had the fortitude to go there. She did it entirely on my account, proposing it herself. We heard that my uncle, Lord Gascoigne, and all his family were in London, and my mother was glad to have me see the place without meeting them. We stayed at a neighboring inn, and thence we walked to the church-yard and visited my father's grave. Then we went into the church and read the inscription on the tablet erected to his· memory. It is in these words :

'In Memoriam

LIONEL GASCOIGNE
Late Clerk in Her Majesty's Foreign Office
Third and Youngest son of
Marmaduke
Fourteenth Earl Gascoigne
Born at Gascoigne House
August 15 1818
Married Oct 1 1836 to Miss Isabella Bradshaw
Of Boston U S
Drowned near the Isle of Wight
September 16 1839
In an heroic but unsuccessful effort to save the life
of a fellow-creature
Daniel Hodgkins
A Boy belonging to the Crew of the Yacht
Calypso

His sorrowing companions of that fatal pleasure trip have placed here this memorial tablet to perpetuate the memory of him whose manly virtues came through a long line of ancestors from one of the

Barons of Runnymede

"Where were ye, nymphs, when the remorseless deep
Closed o'er the head of your loved Lycidas?
For neither were ye playing on the steep,
Where your old bards, the famous Druids, lie;
Nor on the shaggy top of Mona high,
Nor yet where Deva spreads her wizard stream:
Ay me! I fondly dream
Had ye been there, for what could that have done?"'

"While I was copying this inscription my mother's tears were falling fast, but after we left the church she became entirely composed. As we walked towards the manor-house, along the avenue, under the great lime-trees, she leaned on my arm and told the story of my father's death, which I had never before heard. 'I think, dear,' she said, 'that you had an inheritance of some qualities which it only needed Margaret to bring out from their dormant condition in your nature. The gentlemen who put up that tablet might have added more of Milton's lines:

> "Fame is no plant that grows on mortal soil,
>   Nor in the glittering foil
>   Set off to the world, nor in broad rumor lies,
>   But lives and spreads aloft by those pure eyes
>   And perfect witness of all-judging Jove;
>   As he pronounces lastly on each deed,
>   Of so much fame in Heaven expect thy meed."'

"You, my dear sir, can excuse the repetition of what my dear mother meant to imply for me in this fond and too partial thought.

"When we reached the manor-house we sent our cards in to the housekeeper. She soon made her appearance, but she was not a person whom my mother had ever seen, nor did she know exactly who we were. When told that we were connections of the family, and that we came from America, she offered to show us the house. My mother said that there were only two rooms that she wished to see. We went first to a chamber and dressing-room near the head of the great staircase, which I concluded was the apartment that my mother occupied with my father at the time of her only visit there, soon after their marriage. She turned very pale when she entered this room, but did not utter a word. Then she asked to be taken to the picture-gallery. I supposed, at first, that she expected to find there a portrait of my father, but this she did not seem to have anticipated. She walked directly to a part of the room where the portrait of a young lady, in the kind of dress that is seen in Van Dyck's pictures, hung in a strong light. This face she studied for a long time, and I presume that it was the portrait of Henrietta Gascoigne, whose story I believe you know. The only inquiry my mother made of the housekeeper was whether there was any portrait of 'Lady Clare.' The answer was, 'No, ma'am, Lady Clare was never painted. She died ten years ago.'

"We were not long in the house. As we walked back to the inn my mother told me that Lady Clare was my father's youngest sister. Of the other members of the family she did not speak.

"You remember the portrait of my mother that was

painted by Rembrandt Peel when she was a young lady, and that has long been in the possession of her sister, Mrs. Perkins. I wished to have a portrait of her as she has been in late years, and when we were in Paris last winter I had one painted by a capital artist. She charged him at every sitting not to flatter her and not to forget her age. He produced an admirable likeness, and one that gives all her matronly beauty and sweet intelligence. But of course the artist could not do what Nature had never done,—make her look all the years that she had lived. . To the day of her death there was never a line of gray in her dark hair or a wrinkle upon her brow. It is an unspeakable comfort to me that she was willing to sit for this picture and that she was entirely well when it was painted. After it was finished, an English gentleman, who saw it at the artist's studio, asked if it was not a portrait of Mrs. Gascoigne, of Boston. He said that he knew her in London during my father's life, and that she had changed so little that he recollected the face at once. This picture was sent from Paris about three weeks since, and it will perhaps reach my agent before we arrive. I beg you will have it sent to your house and unpacked, so that you and Mrs. Boylston can have it before your eyes until we want it.

"I thought that you would be interested to know what I have written, and that I should neglect a sacred duty if I did not inform you when we may be expected, although I have cabled to my agent in Boston to have everything needful in readiness when the remains are landed. With our kindest love to Mrs. Boylston and yourself, believe me, as ever, dear sir,

"Your affectionate

"JAMES BRADSHAW GASCOIGNE."

How strange are the concatenations of our lives! Here am I, an old man of seventy-eight, about to follow to their last resting-place the remains of an early friend, which I must by my presence, at least, assist in receiving at the self-same landing where I met her as a blooming young widow more than thirty years ago, returning to her mother's house after her brief married life was over. Well, my old wife and I cannot long survive her. We shall soon be "each in the narrow cell forever laid," in that beautiful and renowned city of the dead. "I have lived my life," and, although it has not been like King Arthur's, it has been a pure and useful one. I have no fears about the future for myself or for the dear companion of my pilgrimage——

POSTSCRIPT.

Mr. Boylston's MS. here ends abruptly, and his literary executor must close the record. He did not die so soon as he anticipated when he received news of the death of Mrs. Gascoigne. His death occurred in 1878, and his wife did not long survive him. James and Margaret remained in his mother's house until they had rendered the last duties of friendship to those two old people, who never had any children, and who had been the friends of his mother for so many years. They then left Boston and went to reside in Detroit, in the house that had belonged to Mr. Charáxes, which came to Margaret by provisions in his will, that continued in her father, in trust for her, the title to the property which had stood in Mr. Brewster's name ever since Mr. Charáxes bought it. It was for the sake of being near to her father and her aunt that Margaret chose to reside in Detroit. Miss Brewster never knew that Mrs. Gascoigne was the lady who was engaged to her brother in his younger days, and he never made known to his daughter or her husband that he had been acquainted with Mrs. Gascoigne before they met at Saratoga in the summer of 1859. Miss Brewster died at a very advanced age in 1879. After her death Mr. Brewster took up his abode with Margaret, in the house where the library of old Charáxes and all his collections remained just as he left them. Margaret's life was a supremely happy one. The lofty ideal of patriotism which she formed in her youth had found its sufficient realization in her husband's capacity for heroic deeds and heroic suffering. In his love she had the reward which her nature needed for what she had done in developing his character. Their union was blessed by children, in whom were blended the qualities that came from the English and the American blood that flowed united in their veins. James was never a strong or an active man after what he had suffered, but with great care and prudence he enjoyed a reasonable share of health, and so long as this was his lot Margaret was happy. It was at their house in Detroit that the editor made their acquaintance, so that he is able to verify so much of these memoirs as relates to the two youngest persons of whom they give an account. Mr. Brewster died before the editor knew them.

Of Mr. Charáxes's great fortune not quite a third had ever been transferred to this country. This portion came to Margaret by his will. The residue was divided between his relatives in Greece and one of the principal monasteries in Austria. The will was never a subject of litigation. The testator had taken every precaution against such a scandal.

The publication of this tale of the Civil War has been delayed until the year of the imprint for reasons that would not interest the reader.

THE END.

www.ingramcontent.com/pod-product-compliance
Lightning Source LLC
Chambersburg PA
CBHW031952060726
47497CB00016B/1456